Robert Altman

Critical Essays

EDITED BY RICK ARMSTRONG

McFarland & Company, Inc., Publishers
Jefferson, North Carolina, and London

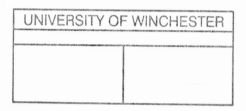

LIBRARY OF CONGRESS CATALOGUING-IN-PUBLICATION DATA

Robert Altman : critical essays / edited by Rick Armstrong.
     p.   cm.
   Includes bibliographical references and index.

   ISBN 978-0-7864-4414-4
   softcover : 50# alkaline paper ∞

   1. Altman, Robert, 1925–2006 — Criticism and interpretation.
I. Armstrong, Rick, 1966–
PN1998.3.A48R625   2011
791.4302'33092 — dc22
[B]   2011001871

BRITISH LIBRARY CATALOGUING DATA ARE AVAILABLE

Front cover: Robert Altman on the set of *Beyond Therapy*, 1987

Manufactured in the United States of America

McFarland & Company, Inc., Publishers
  Box 611, Jefferson, North Carolina 28640
  www.mcfarlandpub.com

Preface and Acknowledgments

Robert Altman's position as both an innovative and popular filmmaker makes him a unique figure to study. He is responsible for some of the most iconic films in mainstream American filmmaking: *M*A*S*H* (1970), *McCabe and Mrs. Miller* (1971), *Nashville* (1975), *The Player* (1992), *Short Cuts* (1993), and *Gosford Park* (2001). He has been nominated for five Academy Awards in addition to winning other honors and a Lifetime Achievement Award in 2006 before his death at age 81 in November 2006. Since then, interest in Altman's work has risen as some of his older films have been released on DVD.

I became interested in creating an edited collection on Altman not long after he died. The Independent Film Center in New York had an exhaustive retrospective of his work in January 2007, which led me to think that there might be interest in a work of essays on Altman. To confirm this, I contacted Robert T. Self who teaches at Northern Illinois University and has authored two books on Altman's work: *Robert Altman's Subliminal Reality* and *Robert Altman's* McCabe and Mrs. Miller: *Reframing the American West*. Self agreed that the time was right and agreed to contribute an essay. Also, Elliot Gould and Michael Murphy, actors who worked with Altman numerous times, offered to help. All of this indicated to me that the time was indeed right; I especially wanted to understand the direction Altman scholarship is headed.

Altman scholars are interested in music, cinema and history, genre (Altman was known for his revision of classic movie genres, such as the war film, the western, the detective story, and the murder mystery, among others), and performance, and this work focuses on those topics. I believe it is valuable because it presents a range of different viewpoints in one volume which can be accessed for years to come.

An edited collection requires work from a variety of people, and I have many people to thank for their support and help. I would first like to thank my colleagues at Kingsborough Community College (CUNY) for their advice and support. My colleagues Frank Percaccio and Patrick Hickey were indispensable in getting still photographs. My office mate Kevin Kolkmeyer was always supportive in discussing Altman's films and accompanying me to see them. Conversations with him and my colleague Eben Wood helped to circulate ideas in my head. Robert Singer generously shared his expertise in film analysis along with sound advice when I was figuring out how to put this together. Chloe Graef has offered both her love and her insight while I have been completing this project. I sincerely appreciate her patience, support and intelligence. I would like to thank Mitchell Zuckoff, who I have not met personally, but whose *Robert Altman: An Oral Biography*, published recently, is a necessary resource for future Altman scholars.

I would like to thank all of the contributors for their patience and consistent engagement. I would like to cite two specifically who were engaged in this project early on, helping to guide me through some challenging moments. Krin Gabbard generously offered advice on the publishing process. The dean of Altman scholars, Robert T. Self, provided enthusiasm and expertise that were necessary for this project to exist. If he had not consented to participate, I would never have done it. The same could be said of Altman collaborator Michael Murphy, who contributed a very personal essay. Actor Elliott Gould, too, was also there to assist when asked. Their participation has greatly enhanced this work. Despite their busy shooting schedules, they have been responsive to any questions I have had. I would also like to acknowledge the City University of New York's faculty union, the Professional Staff Congress, for giving me a generous grant for the fall term 2009 to help me complete this project. Above all, I would like to thank my parents, Dorothy and Steve Armstrong, for instilling a passion for film in me from a young age and for being supportive in this and all endeavors of mine.

And of course, I would like to thank the one person without whose hard work this collection would not have been possible: Robert Altman. I never met him personally; however, his vision has meant a lot to me as it has to the many who have seen his films. He lived his gambler's life and struggled to get money so he could bequeath his unique films to us. Thank you, Mr. Altman.

Table of Contents

Introduction:
"Diving Off the Deep End"

Rick Armstrong

When I picked up *The New York Times* on November 22, 2006, and discovered that Robert Altman had died, it had a surprisingly powerful effect on me. In the past I had not really thought much of celebrity deaths because I never personally knew any celebrities. Thus, their lives and deaths were purely conceptual to me. I could never understand the way people saw the famous as related to their own existences and then grieved publicly when celebrities died. However, I felt some sincere sadness at Robert Altman's death because (as the cliché goes) the world would be a less interesting place without him making films. I was not aware that he had finished *A Prairie Home Companion* while battling cancer and thus was aware of his own mortality. A major part of my sense of connection to Altman derives from being a pre-adolescent in the '70s, old enough to be aware of the adult world, but young enough to be totally ignorant of what really went on there.

Getting glimpses of Altman's films in my early teens gave me a sense of the way adults behaved and despite the alienation depicted in *M*A*S*H*, *Nashville*, *The Long Goodbye*, and *California Split*, I was fascinated and elated that adult human interaction could be so amusing and compelling. His characters' lives somewhat paralleled my suburban California upbringing because many of them also felt disaffected in the supposed paradise of the alleged Golden State. These people were heroes to me despite (or because of) their weaknesses and compulsions. There is a whole aesthetic tradition devoted to the idea of teenagers (many of them male) recoiling at the idea of growing up, resisting the onset of adulthood whose paradoxes supposedly differ from the purities of childhood innocence, J.D. Salinger's novel *The Catcher in the Rye* being perhaps the most famous example. However, after seeing Altman's films (most of which I didn't understand completely), I couldn't wait to become an adult and experience the mercurial and cluttered existence similar to those that Altman's characters live in his films.

In January 2007, the Independent Film Center, a rich cinematic resource in New York City, programmed the most thorough retrospective of Altman's work in some time. In the spring of 2006, perhaps sensing something, the Museum of the Moving Image in Queens offered a twenty-two film retrospective that included Altman making two appearances. Even so, the IFC's festival was more comprehensive than the MMI's though it was not quite complete. Surprisingly, for a director of Altman's stature, many of his films are either not available or have only recently become available on DVD and thus have not been seen by the much of the public, including *That Cold Day in the Park*, his first comeback after an unpleasant experience at Warner Bros., which features an initial supporting role for Altman stalwart Michael Murphy (a contributor to this collection), and *Brewster McCloud*, which Altman proclaimed his favorite among his works[1] and which is the subject of two essays in this volume. Sensing a rare opportunity that could not be missed, I attended several of the screenings during the retrospective. Sadly, some of the prints were scratchy and a bit washed out, and some of the films do not represent the man at his peak form. However, seeing those films on the big screen and in their entirety reminded me of why as a preteen and teenager I anticipated the coming adult world with such excitement. When I was an adolescent, Robert Altman had given me a map of adult existence and that map still proved accurate thirty years later.

This project grew out of Altman's death and the subsequent retrospective at the IFC. After attending several films at the retrospective, I figured that there might be an interest in examining the unwieldy career of a filmmaking innovator. Wanting to get some corroboration, I contacted Robert T. Self, who had published the influential *Robert Altman's Subliminal Reality* in 2002. He agreed with me that the time was right for a collection of essays surveying Altman's work, agreeing to contribute an essay. Since I have been working on this project, Mitchell Zuckoff published his indispensible *Robert Altman: The Oral Biography* in 2009 and Self published his study of *McCabe and Mrs. Miller* in 2007. All of this work indicates the continuing fascination Altman holds for scholars and the film-going public. Robert Altman influenced film in many ways, including manipulating the sound in a film either by toning it down, something which irked Warren Beatty after he had first seen *McCabe and Mrs. Miller*,[2] or by using overlapping dialogue as he does in *The Long Goodbye, California Split* and other films.

He also famously refined the ensemble film which, as Maria del Mar Azcona points out in her essay, had existed in Hollywood at least since *Grand Hotel*. The ensemble film involves a large cast of characters interacting together. However, Altman loosened and expanded the ensemble genre where the plot often gets lost and the film becomes a documentary-like depiction of people's lives in flux. In her review of *Nashville*, Pauline Kael says, "Altman uses a *Grand Hotel* mingling of characters without giving false importance to their unions and collisions."[3] Altman's influence continues to be seen in the work of filmmakers such as Alejandro Gonzales Inarritu, whose *Amores Perros* is an Altmanesque ensemble film set in Mexico City; Altman's protégé Alan Rudolph, who was the assistant director on *Nashville* along with other films; Paul Haggis, whose *Crash* somewhat inexplicably managed to accomplish something that Altman's films never did: win the Academy Award for best picture; and Paul Thomas Anderson, who was the backup director for *A Prairie Home Companion* because of Altman's illness at the time and whose *Magnolia* is an overt homage to Altman complete with regular Altman actors Michael Murphy and Henry Gibson. *Magnolia* and *Crash* are examples of a large ensemble film like *Nashville* though the latter has more of a contrived purpose than Kael sees with *Nashville*.

Altman's well-known belief was that making a film is like making a sand castle with one's friends. When he accepted the Academy Award for Lifetime Achievement in 2006, Altman stated, "You build this beautiful structure, several of you, and then you sit back and you watch the tide come in, have a drink, watch the tide come in, and the ocean just takes it away. And that sand castle remains in your mind."[4] He was aware that filmmaking was a transient experience. For most of his career, Altman was moving from project to project, building his sand castles only to have the water take them away. However, films are not as temporary as sand castles because they endure to be seen repeatedly by many. Such repetitive viewing can lessen the power of a film. However, as Altman notes in his speech, the quality films counteract the commodification and remain in the viewer's mind to be referenced when they are relevant to human existence, which Altman's typically are.

Altman is associated with "the easy riders, raging bulls" generation of late-'60s and '70s Hollywood directors as coined by Peter Biskind in his book of the same name. In his comment later in this Introduction, Elliot Gould states that Altman was the last in the line of the '40s generation of Hollywood, tracing his career back to the likes of Howard Hawks and Preston Sturges. However, those filmmakers worked within a very rigid studio system, churning out studio-defined products. Those filmmakers are admired for their ability to add artistic flourishes within an industrial system.[5] However, Biskind argues that the '60s generation differed from the directors of the classical Hollywood system. The studios were in flux and thus the directors had more creative freedom than John Ford had in his day. Biskind puts Altman in what he calls the "first wave" of the directors of this period "born in the mid- to late-thirties,"[6] except that Altman was born in 1925 and thus is much older than any members of the first or second wave of that generation.

Also many of the baby boomers of that generation were known to have gone to film school, learning the history of film in addition to the craft of filmmaking, sometimes referencing earlier studio directors in their work much as Martin Scorsese references John Ford's *The Searchers* in *Mean Streets*. However, Altman learned filmmaking through making industrial films in the '50s and by directing television in the late '50s and early '60s. He was already twenty years old when Martin Scorsese and Francis Coppola were born. Altman was born in Kansas City to an upper middle class family. His great-grandfather built what became known as the Altman Building in 1888, where *Birth of a Nation* was shown, Altman's father Bernard Clement (B.C.) being the projectionist presenting that film and who grew up to sell insurance.[7] Lotus Corelli Altman Monroe, Altman's second wife, calls Altman's father "a con man" who "made his living off the people he knew at the country club." She concludes that "Bob did take after B.C. in that he could sell anybody anything."[8]

Unlike his film school-educated colleagues, Altman jumped from job to job, improvising his career path much as he improvised his films. He was a bombardier, flying risky missions in the Pacific theatre during World War II. After the war, Altman did not envision himself a filmmaker. He participated in a venture with two other men using money that his dad provided to start a dog tattooing business in which the company tattooed dogs inside of the right hind leg as a form of identification in case the dogs became lost. People would pay them money for the tattooing and they would pay the counties to keep files on the tattooed dogs. This was not his long-term plan; he and his partners were hoping to sell the business to Purina for "a few hundred thousand dollars and then walk away." They managed to tattoo President Truman's dog; however, the business failed when one of the other partners absconded to Ireland with most of the company's money.[9]

The failure of the dog tattooing venture would prove somewhat fortuitous. Perhaps he would have proceeded to make films anyway. However, ever the improviser, Altman then decided he was a writer. Today if someone wanted to be a writer, she would apply to a creative writing program and attempt to get both the training and credential that would label her as a writer. However, in 1948 Altman lived in a house his father owned in Malibu and met George W. George, who was the son of Rube Goldberg. Altman styled himself a writer and George fancied himself a director. They managed to sell two screenplays to RKO because George had a connection there. This would prove his first experience in creating a film. However, his small success was ephemeral. He sold nothing more and then headed back to Kansas City. He recalls, "Film schools happened after I was making films. There was no such thing as a film school when I was going to school.... To make films, I went to Kansas City and got a job with the Calvin Company."[10]

Calvin made training films, commercials, and documentaries for a variety of organizations and businesses including General Mills, Goodyear, DuPont and the federal government.[11] It was a perfect place to learn by experience, which Altman did, improvising different camera angles and experimenting with sound design, approaches which would often antagonize his supervisors, presaging the hostile relationship he would have with studio executives once he arrived in Hollywood.[12] His work at Calvin led to him making his first feature, *The Delinquents*, in 1957 with some money from a Kansas City businessman. He brought the actors, including future *Billy Jack* star Tom Laughlin, to Kansas City for the filming.[13] *The Delinquents* got him out to California and involved in television. Alfred Hitchcock had seen *The Delinquents* and admired it enough to give Altman a job on his television shows.[14] After working for Hitchcock, he managed to get a lot of work in television as opportunities were plentiful in the growing industry. Altman recalls, "I would keep doing television until I got a film that I really wanted to do. I didn't want to go out and make a feature just for the sake of it and then find out that was the end of it."[15] At this point it was clear that Altman was focused on a career in filmmaking and his time at Calvin allowed him the opportunity to hone his own unique cinematic style.

Tom Laughlin, Pat Stedman, and Richard Bakalayan in Robert Altman's first film, *The Delinquents*, in 1957.

He directed episodes for a variety of television series from 1957 to 1965 including *Bonanza, Combat, Whirlybirds* and *Kraft Suspense Theatre,* whose show he dubbed "bland as its cheese."[16] With this statement and his innovative and meticulous style of filming the shows, Altman began to develop his reputation for being difficult, which would hinder his attempts to break into feature filmmaking. After an aborted attempt to direct the film *Petulia*, which would become a success for director Richard Lester in 1968,[17] Altman managed to direct his first feature film for a major studio, *Countdown,* for Warner Bros., also in 1968. Altman continued his experiments in overlapping dialogue in making the film, which antagonized Jack Warner, leading to Altman's removal from the film and the addition of a much more optimistic ending.[18] Altman's reputation among the executives in Hollywood was only getting worse.

After the conflict at Warners, Altman directed his third feature film, *That Cold Day in the Park,* which was independently produced and filmed in Vancouver because Altman wanted to get away from Hollywood. It was not successful, though it showed that Altman could make a film as economically as possible. His agent George Litto would sound a familiar ring to the distribution and marketing of Altman's films: "It was no hit. It was a small company and they were new and they didn't know how to promote a hit." Altman's films in the future would not be as financially successful as people thought that they could be due to poor marketing and distribution. In this case, he made the film for the small company Commonwealth United, which would not survive much longer after the film.[19] At least *Countdown* and *That Cold Day in the Park* managed to get his name circulated in Hollywood to an extent that when sixteen directors passed on *M*A*S*H* a year later, his name at least came up as an option for Ingo Preminger and Richard Zanuck, who were set on making the film.[20] That film was famously a big success, making Altman a superstar director going into the '70s. He became even more famous once *M*A*S*H* won the Golden Palm at the Cannes Film Festival. This success gave Altman some leeway to make films his own way throughout the '70s. He started his own production company, Lion's Gate. [21]

Most of those films, including *McCabe and Mrs. Miller*, *The Long Goodbye*, *Thieves Like Us*, and *Nashville*, were critically admired and are now considered major works. However, even these films never made much money despite their iconic status. Actor John Schuck typified the response to these films when he said of *Thieves Like Us*, "Pauline Kael just wrote a love poem to Bob and to us individually as actors, perhaps the nicest set of notices we've ever received. But it was released and went in a few weeks." Given that many of Altman's films were experiments in genre revisionism, the studios did not know how to market them. These works subverted an audience's expectations of the way a caper, detective or western film should be. Such approaches require a curious and open-minded population of filmgoers, which seemed to exist in the '70s. Still, such innovation is always a risky commercial prospect, and Altman's film suffered for that. Schuck points out, "*Thieves* was a picture that was so non-mainstream that the studio had no idea how to promote it. They treated it like a bank-robbery movie, which it isn't of course.... It's developed a sort of cult following and it got extraordinary reviews."[22]

Altman's films were often called cult films due to their critical acclaim and small box office returns, prompting Altman to say: "To me a cult means not enough people to make a minority."[23] Still, these films have become the object of much critical scrutiny long after more successful films of the time dropped off of the radar. Also, while these films were not huge moneymakers, they managed to have some success. Vilmos Zsigmond, who was Altman's cinematographer on *McCabe*, recalls, "And even in those days, our movies were successful, basically.... In those days, all movies made money. It cost nothing to make those movies, you know. Not even two million dollars."[24] Zsigmond proves that so-called "cult" films were profitable; they just would not make anybody rich. Still, the little money they cost and the critical prestige they generated allowed Altman the independence to continue making movies in his own way after the success of *M*A*S*H*.

Part of his way of making movies was to give actors as minimal direction as possible, letting them experiment in finding the personality of their characters. He would let the actors improvise the dialogue, much to the resentment of the screenwriters with whom he worked. Studio executives and screenwriters typically conflicted with Altman. However, his actors revered him for giving them the freedom to practice their craft. Rene Auberjonois points out that "most directors don't really trust actors, don't want to see actors acting. That was the difference with Bob Altman. He loved actors and wanted to see acting."[25] Auberjonois' comment is echoed by many actors who worked with Altman, leading those actors to want to work with him as many times as possible, which many did. Like many directors of his time, Altman had what amounted to his own stock repertory of actors. That group changed as some would stop working with him at points or others would join the group. Keith Carradine (who made three films with Altman) maintains that the director was impressed with the craft of acting and "loved to create an environment where he could take people who did that and give them the freedom to do that in their own inimitable way." Carradine adds, "He didn't really cast actors as much as he cast people," indicating that he wanted people who could fit into his type of filmmaking.[26] This technique of directing actors often took the form of improvisation. Altman often gave little-known actors such as Carradine, Shelley Duvall, and Bud Cort their initial chance to be in a major film despite the studio's insistence on hiring someone more well known. Altman fought to keep Tim Robbins as the lead in *The Player*[27] and Cher as the lead in the play *Come Back to the Five and Dime, Jimmy Dean, Jimmy Dean*, which led to her to assert, "You would do things you didn't like because of him. I was crazy about him."[28]

Altman was a gambler in both his personal life and his professional life. He would bet a lot of money on a racehorse he heard about. He would take on actors or film projects based on intuitions or dreams and then somehow find the money for them. Such hazards engendered their share of problems as well as triumphs. Such successes and failures, which are constitutive of the risk in a market economy, influenced Altman throughout most of his life. His life and especially his film career consisted of combining an entrepreneur's sense of survival and an artist's vision of individual creativity. He did not want his films to necessarily earn big money; instead, he was striving to keep doing what he loved doing: making films on his own terms without the crass concerns of the commercially conscious producers. Of course having a major commercial success would have helped him attain this level of independence. However, such a success eluded him. One of his biggest successes was *Popeye* in 1980, a perceived failure due to its cost and schedule overruns. Stephen Altman, who worked on the set design for his father's films, recalls, "It only made sixty million, and of course it cost twenty million to make. So how that translates into bomb, I have no idea. Still, it wasn't the huge success that everybody thought it was going to be."[29]

Popeye signaled the end of Altman's run with Hollywood for over a decade. When the film was released to mixed reviews, Hollywood was changing and the producers were striking back at directors' perceived recklessness in the wake of the failure of Michael Cimino's film *Heaven's Gate* in 1980 which in film industry parlance is synonymous with cinematic failure due to its ultimate cost of $44.3 million and $1.5 million gross.[30] Cimino was seen as the ultimate profligate and pampered director of the '70s who had just bankrupted a studio. Despite *Popeye*'s profiting its backers, it was also seen as a major financial disappointment and Altman was viewed much like Cimino, a director out of control. While Cimino was probably rightly lambasted for his excess, the attack on Altman had a tinge of philistinism. Industry types reacted against any director with a bold vision who went over budget despite the earning potential of the project.

Altman had not had a commercial success in a while and he never liked the heads of the studios, infamously punching one in the nose and knocking him into a swimming pool because he wanted Altman to cut six minutes from *California Split*.[31] Once *Popeye* underperformed along with his commercial failures at Fox that preceded it, the studio heads happily ostracized him. Biskind argues that changes were being put into place even before the *Heaven's Gate* disaster. He points to more commercially oriented executives such as Barry Diller, Michael Eisner, and Don Simpson, who transformed filmmaking towards a more adolescent and television mindset with an eye towards bigger box office receipts.[32]

Either way, by 1981 nobody was returning Altman's phone calls. He had a project lined up called *Lone Star* which was supposed to star Sigourney

Weaver and Powers Boothe. However, it was shelved forever.[33] Altman
was always resourceful. Director Mark Rydell, who appeared in *The Long
Goodbye*, recounts that Altman "went out and got the money to make his
pictures. He rejected the status quo and wouldn't be deterred. If he wanted
to make a picture he would see that it got made. He would fucking get
the money somewhere."[34] However, by 1981 money was nowhere to be
found. Altman entered what Mitchell Zuckoff refers to as his "wilderness"
period in which he sold off his production company Lion's Gate and his
Malibu home; he started directing plays and filming them for the screen;
he became a professor of communications at the University of Michigan
so he could film one of those plays (*Secret Honor*) there for as cheaply as
possible; and he worked in Europe.[35]

He made his famous comeback with *The Player* in 1992. Altman dis-
dained publicly the idea that he had made a comeback because, as he
pointed out, he was working fairly steadily in the '80s,[36] but it was not in
the conditions to which he was accustomed. His films were not the critical
and cultural events that they were in the seventies. Even when a film such
as *3 Women* was commercially unsuccessful, it could still be greeted with
excitement and awards at Cannes and major American critics would review
it and rave about it. Most importantly he could still make a film like *3
Women* within the Hollywood system. Alan Ladd, Jr., who was head of
20th Century–Fox studio at the time, recalls that Altman "was always on
budget" and that he was intrigued by the idea of *3 Women*, so he approved
it.[37] By the '80s, the studios had changed and Altman had gone massively
over budget with *Popeye* and thus he no longer had the power to get a film
made just by offering a studio head a sketch of an idea. At the time Ladd
was the only one who would hire him, pointing out that the "creative community admired him greatly but studios were afraid of him."[38] Still, at
that time he was admired enough that someone like Ladd would hire him.
However, films like *O.C. & Stiggs*, finished by the studio due to Altman's
indifference, and *Beyond Therapy* barely got made and generated little
attention.[39] He bubbled up to the surface with *Tanner '88*, a series made
for HBO, which at the time was newly entering the realm of creative pro-
gramming. He collaborated with Garry Trudeau on creating a fictional
presidential candidate (Michael Murphy) who traveled around campaign-
ing in the 1988 Democratic primaries, often meeting with real presidential
candidates. Altman called it "the most creative work I've ever done — in
all films and theater."[40] The project kept him on the radar, showing that
he was still active and innovating.

After *The Player*, which won the Golden Palm at Cannes just as *M*A*S*H*, his first major success, did, Altman could get films made within the Hollywood studio system. The system was being changed by the rise of independent filmmakers and Altman found his creative independence within the system once again. Peter Biskind compares the '90s to the '70s. He asserts, "Like the 1970s, the 1990s was pregnant with change."[41] Once again ensconced in the Hollywood mainstream, Altman returned to the ensemble genre, making an adaptation of a variety of Raymond Carver short stories, *Short Cuts*, in 1993. He was able to continue to make films in the '90s, experiencing the same studio ambivalence he experienced in the '70s. Fine Line Features did not market the film *Kansas City* in 1996, a film that meant much to Altman because it is about the era of his childhood in Kansas City though it is not autobiographical. It received a mixed reaction from the critics and little success at the box office, somewhat paralleling the reaction his films in the '70s received.[42]

In 2001 Altman had his last shot at winning the Academy Award with a revision of the English manor genre, *Gosford Park*, a collaboration with the actor Bob Balaban. The film was another ensemble piece, following the lives of both the aristocracy and workers of the English manor in the 1930s. The film also includes a murder mystery which is more of a subplot, thus revising the mystery genre. It received multiple Oscar nominations including best picture, best director, and best supporting actress. The campaign leading up to the awards, which occurred the spring after the attacks on the Pentagon and the World Trade Center, prompted Altman to declare, "The movies set the pattern, and these people have copied the movies. Nobody would have thought to commit such an atrocity unless they'd seen it in a movie." He went on to condemn the mass destruction in the very movies that makes Hollywood a lot of money and sinking any chance that he and *Gosford Park* would have had to win Academy Awards. In another parallel to *M*A*S*H*, *Gosford Park* won for best original screenplay. However, Altman never cared very much; he instead prized the independence to say what he wanted to say without caring about the consequences. Losing at the Academy Awards only cemented his image as a rebellious Hollywood outsider.[43] However, despite his seeming indifference, he was quite happy to accept his Lifetime Achievement Oscar on March 5, 2006, eight months before his death. When Harry Belafonte asked him why he attended the Oscar ceremony, he replied: "There's a whore in all of us. It would mean a lot to anything I do from the box-office point of view. But other than that, I don't give a shit.'" Belafonte adds, "It wasn't until the honorary Oscar and the way in which he spoke that I understood the real depth of feeling that he had and what the Oscar meant to him."[44]

Despite the awards, the interest in his work continues after his death. This edited collection is a way to gauge the critical and scholarly direction in Altman studies, pointing to new work in the area of film studies. One area of interest concerns Altman's use of music. Paul Thomas Anderson comments, "Bob loved his music, didn't he? My God, he loved his music. And he used it so well, as good as anybody."[45]

Given Anderson's above comment, this collection includes two essays on his use of music. Krin Gabbard offers a very detailed investigation of the way Altman uses jazz in *Short Cuts*, offering perceptive thematic analysis in addition to a description of the musicians' professional backgrounds before they worked on the film. Gabbard argues that many have not considered the importance of the music in *Short Cuts*. Instead, most of the critical discussion has focused on the use of Leonard Cohen's songs in *McCabe and Mrs. Miller* or the country music in *Nashville*. Of course, as Anderson states, Altman's use of music is always important, and Gabbard shows how valuable thematically jazz is in *Short Cuts*. Unlike Gabbard, Richard R. Ness examines Altman's use of music in an array of films, including *The Long Goodbye*, *Fool for Love*, and *The Prairie Home Companion*. His essay is a rich and broad survey of the various ways Altman employed different types of music and it will serve as a valuable resource for anybody who wants to learn about Altman's filmmaking technique. Moreover, he makes the point that Altman's musical films often involve the subverting of white male patriarchy.

Music is an interest to Altman scholars as it is to many people in society today. Another critical interest clearly perceived in this collection is the relationship between film and history as evidenced by three contributions that deal with this topic. William Graebner has written a perceptive analysis of the way *McCabe and Mrs. Miller* channels '60s discourse on the victim. Graebner investigates the position of women and minorities in the '50s and '60s, examining the different theories of victimization during this period. He then connects these theories to the character of John McCabe, who futilely tries to resist the encroachment of the corporate power which destroys him. Graebner argues that McCabe is not a passive victim of the company; instead, he refuses to cave in to the corporation's demand that he sell out to them. McCabe fights the assassins the company sends, losing, but maintaining his dignity in the struggle against a repressive entity, according to Graebner.

Two essays reference the historical relevance of Altman's own favorite film, *Brewster McCloud*. Marcos Soares argues that *Brewster McCloud* represents the limits of artistic freedom. He maintains that Brewster's failed attempt at flight anticipates the failure of the '70s directors to transform mainstream filmmaking into a more aesthetic art form. He argues that Brewster's rebellion is a mere adolescent prank rather than a legitimate collective resistance to repressive institutions. Soares points out that this lack of a mass mobilization in the film parallels the '70s filmmakers' reliance on individual achievement rather than a unified transformation of Hollywood. In contrast, I connect the narrative of *Brewster McCloud* to the differing interpretations of '60s politics throughout history. I argue that the film satires both the establishment and the counterculture, indicating that the extremes of the political discourse leave an empty space where no legitimate thinking occurs. In my analysis, I reference some of the specific movements and events to which the film makes subtle references.

Jeremy Kaye offers a genre analysis of *The Long Goodbye*, arguing that Elliot Gould's Philip Marlowe reconfigures the character into a Jewish identity as opposed to the traditional version represented by Humphrey Bogart who embodied white Protestant male privilege. Many critics (including Charles Champlin of the *Los Angeles Times*, who is quoted by Kaye) were alienated by Gould's and Altman's interpretation of Marlowe as a wisecracking and slovenly figure. However, Kaye suggests that such an inversion represented the sly ethnic subversion of a clichéd male icon. He contrasts Gould's Marlowe to the Humphrey Bogart represented in *Play It Again, Sam*. In that film Woody Allen is the conventionally nebbishy buffoon in contrast to the fantasy Bogart character, thus reinforcing the image of the foolish Jew and empowered WASP. Altman and Gould subvert that tradition by adding a Jewish sensibility to the hard-boiled Philip Marlowe, indicating the changes taking place in Hollywood as more Jewish and Italian actors were being featured in mainstream Hollywood films. Altman and Gould neither cling to an image of Marlowe as Jewish buffoon or as Bogart tough guy. Gould's Marlowe is a complicated figure, alternating clownish behavior with the gumshoe's ruthlessness. Kaye argues that such complexity challenged audiences upon the film's release, leading to its failure at the time.

Maria del Mar Azcona parallels Kaye in her examination of the multiprotagonist genre. Altman famously made films which typically involved many characters overlapping either within a certain institutional framework or during a certain timeframe. Azcona offers a history of the multiprotagonist film, beginning with *Grand Hotel* in 1932. She proceeds to argue that Altman reinvented the genre through his flexible approach to plot. Azcona points out that Altman follows minor characters or tangential events that do not initially propel the narrative forward. She argues that this results in Altman undermining the standard linear plot line. She offers a detailed analysis of *Short Cuts* to show that Altman's multiprotagonist films resist closure, revealing the interlinking freeways of southern California as the only connections between the various characters.

Robert T. Self, the dean of Altman studies with his two books on the filmmaker's work, contributes a deep analysis of Altman's last two films, *The Company* and *A Prairie Home Companion*. Self indicates that Altman concluded his career focusing on performance. Self notes that in his previous films about performance, Altman exposed the commercial façade around country music in *Nashville* and Wild West shows in *Buffalo Bill and the Indians* among other works. However, in his final two films, Self points out that Altman finds value in both dance and radio performance. Self shows that in *The Company* Altman makes a lyrical and meditative film about the creation of dance performances. Similarly, Self asserts that in *A Prairie Home Companion* Altman finds solace in a community of performers who create a radio program. In that film the program is dying just as Altman was aware of his own mortality. Self points out that these films show Altman's search for meaning in artistic expression.

The title of this introduction is a quotation from Altman's assistant director Alan Rudolph. In explaining the director's personal struggles to get along with certain types of people, Rudolph indicates that the director's anarchic personal and professional life (he was married three times and fathered five children) would catch up to him, creating psychological stress that periodically resulted in antagonistic and polarizing behavior.[46] He lived his mercurial life in order to build his sand castles in the way he wanted to build them. And this independence has led to the creation of works which continue to offer rich critical material for critics, scholars, and audiences. As we continue through the new century without one of America's great filmmakers, we still have his work over which to ponder. For this, we are grateful that he lived the life that he did, to bequeath audiences the quality of his vision for as long as visual media survives. The following contributors offer their insights on the work Altman left behind.

Altman's loyalty to actors he valued continued to the end of his career. I am fortunate to have contributions from Michael Murphy, who probably worked the most with Altman over the years, and Elliot Gould, who Altman helped to make a star in the early '70s, leading to Gould's appearance on the cover of *Time* magazine. He appeared in the closest Altman ever came to a blockbuster, *M*A*S*H*, in addition to three more films, including a cameo appearance in *Nashville*. I will end this introduction with Gould's words: "Robert Altman's legacy will nourish artists and filmmakers for generations to come. He was the last of the great American film directors in the tradition of John Ford, Howard Hawks, Frank Capra, and Preston Sturges. I'll always be grateful for the opportunities he gave me. Bob was my friend."

NOTES

1. David Thompson, ed., *Altman on Altman* (London: Faber & Faber, 2005), 59.
2. Mitchell Zuckoff, *Robert Altman: The Oral Biography* (New York: Random House, 2009), 228.
3. Pauline Kael, *Reeling* (Boston: Little Brown, 1976), 451.
4. Zuckoff, *Robert Altman*, 500.
5. Pauline Kael, *Deeper into Movies* (Boston: Little Brown, 1973), 78.
6. Peter Biskind, *Easy Riders, Raging Bulls: How the Sex, Drugs and Rock 'n' Roll Generation Saved Hollywood* (New York: Simon & Schuster, 1998), 16.
7. Zuckoff, *Robert Altman*, 14.
8. Zuckoff, *Robert Altman*, 19.
9. Zuckoff, *Robert Altman*, 58–9.
10. Zuckoff, *Robert Altman*, 60–61.
11. Patrick McGilligan, *Robert Altman: Jumping Off the Cliff: A Biography of the Great Director* (New York: St. Martin's, 1989), 73.
12. Zuckoff, *Robert Altman*, 63.
13. Zuckoff, *Robert Altman*, 82.
14. Zuckoff, *Robert Altman*, 102.
15. Thompson, ed., *Altman on Altman*, 21.
16. Zuckoff, *Robert Altman*, 123.
17. Zuckoff, *Robert Altman*, 137.
18. Zuckoff, *Robert Altman*, 147.
19. Zuckoff, *Robert Altman*, 154–6.
20. Zuckoff, *Robert Altman*, 164.
21. McGilligan, *Robert Altman: Jumping Off the Cliff*, 255.
22. Zuckoff, *Robert Altman*, 258–9.
23. Zuckoff, *Robert Altman*, 232.
24. Zuckoff, *Robert Altman*, 243.
25. Zuckoff, *Robert Altman*, 175.
26. Zuckoff, *Robert Altman*, 211.
27. Zuckoff, *Robert Altman*, 408.
28. Zuckoff, *Robert Altman*, 415.
29. Zuckoff, *Robert Altman*, 359.
30. Biskind, *Easy Riders, Raging Bulls*, 400.
31. Zuckoff, *Robert Altman*, 296.
32. Biskind, *Easy Riders, Raging Bulls*, 401–2.
33. Biskind, *Easy Riders, Raging Bulls*, 401.
34. Zuckoff, *Robert Altman*, 365.

35. Zuckoff, *Robert Altman*, 363–87.
36. Zuckoff, *Robert Altman*, 421.
37. Zuckoff, *Robert Altman*, 318–19.
38. Zuckoff, *Robert Altman*, 318.
39. Zuckoff, *Robert Altman*, 392–4.
40. Zuckoff, *Robert Altman*, 400.
41. Peter Biskind, *Down and Dirty Pictures: Miramax, Sundance, and the Rise of Independent Film* (New York: Simon & Schuster, 2004), 22.
42. Zuckoff, *Robert Altman*, 452.
43. Zuckoff, *Robert Altman*, 477–8.
44. Zuckoff, *Robert Altman*, 498.
45. Zuckoff, *Robert Altman*, 250.
46. Zuckoff, *Robert Altman*, 294.

1

Working with Robert Altman

Michael Murphy

Robert Altman was a man well suited to his work. He loved being surrounded by people, loved the give and take of new ideas, loved a certain amount of chaos, loved to ... well, *party*. He was a very social guy. He was always relaxed, funny and easy on his sets ... always the great host, completely self-assured (in the best possible way) and extremely generous. People loved to work with him because it was inevitably a very pleasurable experience. He knew that tension was the enemy and he always kept it at bay.

I was part of a group of people fortunate enough to work repeatedly with Bob over the years. I started with him at an early age and he had a profound effect on my life as an actor. He made it all so easy, so much fun, that it gave me the idea, however far fetched, that this was the way movies were made. Over the years, whenever I missed out on one of his pictures, I found myself gritting my teeth mostly because I knew that I was missing a terrific time with a lot of terrific people, all at their best and all orchestrated by the Ringmaster himself.

There has been much discussion about Bob's history of conflict with the studios and with various producers and writers. Well, let's start with the writers. He used to say that he wanted the script to be a *blueprint* of what would eventually wind up on the screen. He was very up-front about that. He was always looking for the immediate response, the look or *take* (or mistake!) that was real and truthful, and he knew exposition when he heard it. Even in his early television days, writers knew to steer clear of him if they were nervous about every article and adverb making it onto the screen. It wasn't so much that he felt the need to make changes in their work, but he knew that a certain amount of paraphrasing made his actors comfortable and immediate and, as a result, real. He was brilliant at bringing the actor and the script together; and, by and large, he got along well enough with the writers ... though some better than others.

As for the studios and some of the producers he dealt with, the conflicts were usually about control and what he considered to be intrusions into what he was trying to accomplish. He was never going to direct programmers or work with storyboards, so some of these people didn't always fathom what was going on as Bob, in his spontaneous manner, worked his way through his films. He was a gambler, dealing in a business that hates to roll the dice. For example, when making *M*A*S*H*, instead of using extras to populate the camp, he famously hired members of a Second City group from San Francisco. These folks were great improvisers and so the "extras" soon became real characters, and these characters added immeasurably to the chaos of the camp and to the success of the film. In retrospect, this turned out to be a marvelous idea, but, at the time, it had a lot of people scratching their heads while watching the dailies. Bob, as usual, had it all in *his* head.

Bob's gambling nature played a big part in how his movies were made. It's been my experience that most people, when embarking on a picture, tend to be as risk averse as possible. And there are always control issues. Producers almost always want things as organized and locked down on the page as is humanly possible. That way, if they can manage to put the script onto the screen with a certain amount of grace and skill, they have done their jobs successfully. Bob's approach was entirely the opposite. He always wanted to take the picture to another level, to ratchet everything up a notch. Well, more than a notch. He loved his actors to surprise him. *Everyone* was always invited along on his somewhat breathtaking ride, and some dealt with it better than others. For example, there is a marvelous scene in *Nashville* in which Ronee Blakeley has a breakdown on stage. In it, she tries to get through a song but keeps interrupting herself with nonsequiturs about her youth, her grandparents and other distant memories. It is very fine work. Before she shot the scene, Ronee went to her hotel room and wrote it, personalizing it to the extent that she felt very comfortable with it. She then went to Bob and wanted to read it for him. But he stopped her. He told her to "just get up there and do it when we shoot and I'll see it then." And that's what Ronee did. It was all over very quickly, as Bob had several cameras going, and she was spectacular. I remember sitting in the audience, completely captivated. Once more he had rolled the dice, trusted his actor absolutely, and come away a winner. Ronee was more than up to the task, which was astonishing when you consider she'd never before been in a movie. I saw this happen time and time again over the years.

Before Robert Altman had set foot on a sound stage, he had, beginning at the age of 19, flown some fifty missions over the South Pacific. As Garrison Keillor reminded us at Bob's memorial, "If you're a guy who has flown fifty missions over Japanese-occupied territory, what the hell can a movie studio do to you?"

I first met Bob on the 1960s-era *Combat!* series at MGM. By then he knew from personal experience the folly, stupidity and heartbreak of war. I was immediately aware of the fact that here was a guy who, although still in his thirties, had grown up fast and attained a kind of maturity for his years that undoubtedly was the result of his wartime experiences. I believe that what he went through as a very young man, flying combat missions again and again over very dangerous terrain, prepared him well for the leadership role he would later assume. He always chafed at authority, whether in the service or in civilian life. So, when he later found himself in an authoritative position, he never used the power that came with it on other people.

Bob was, of course, very skilled in the techniques of filmmaking. Although essentially self-taught, what he did with a camera and with sound was unique and difficult to achieve. He made it look easy, but the camera always seemed to be in the right place at the right time and the audience always heard what he wanted it to hear, often over a jumble of dialogue from other characters. On the set, this was all carried out so smoothly — no fuss, no anxiety about hitting marks or matching moves — that the actors often were unaware of how much was going on as they played their scenes. In fact, sometimes you weren't even aware that you were being photographed. Once, for example, we were making a courtroom drama and the guy sitting next to me actually fell asleep during a take. With great stealth, Bob zeroed in on him with a long lens, and the next day at the rushes we were treated to this very funny, very *real* moment, which ultimately wound up in the film.

In the end, Robert Altman was a guy who *never played it safe.* This, of course, created a certain amount of chaos in his life, but it contributed mightily to the unique and memorable person that he was, as well as the great filmmaker he became.

2

The Hypertext of *Short Cuts*: The Jazz in Altman's Carver Soup

Krin Gabbard

Robert Altman loved jazz.[1] Consider *Kansas City* (1996), in which Altman creates a world where nothing is right except the jazz. The film is Altman's conflicted valentine to his home town, where swing, big band jazz, the blues, and the art of the improviser were all coming together in the early 1930s. In interviews, Altman has even provided material that can connect his youth to that of the revolutionary jazz saxophonist and composer Charlie Parker.[2] Altman has said that as a teenager he would stick around Kansas City's jazz clubs until he fell asleep at a table.[3] At two different moments in *Kansas City*, Altman shows a young Charlie Parker, an alto saxophone hanging from his neck, dozing at a table on the balcony of the Hey Hey Club. According to the film's chronology, Parker would have been fourteen years old, roughly the same age as Altman when he was staying out late at Kansas City clubs.

Also in *Kansas City*, when Seldom Seen (Harry Belafonte) instructs Johnny O'Hara (Dermot Mulroney) on how to appreciate the music of Count Basie, Altman is clearly on the side of Belafonte's black gangster. No one speaks as enthusiastically — nor so clearly with Altman's imprimatur — for country music in *Nashville* (1975). Or for pop music in *A Perfect Couple* (1979). Or for ballet in *The Company* (2003). We can tease out references to jazz and privileged moments of the music throughout the Altman canon, but I would suggest that the director's fascination with improvisation is the key to his jazz connection. Altman regularly turned his actors loose either to develop a character through improvisation during rehearsal or actually to include extended improvisations in a film's final cut. And he has long been attracted to actors who flourish as improvisers. Think of the relatively stiff performances that Elliott Gould often delivers in other directors' films with his free-form exuberance in *The Long Goodbye* (1973) and *California Split* (1974). In these films and in many others, Altman has adapted the skills of the jazz musician to filmmaking.

Short Cuts (1993) may be — in the best sense — the jazziest film Altman ever made, even more so than *Kansas City*. Although Altman and screenwriter Frank Barhydt took their characters from nine unrelated stories by Raymond Carver (all subsequently collected in a single volume[4]), they have added two major figures who might have appeared in the Carver story "Vitamins."[5] In one section of the story, a black Vietnam veteran propositions an attractive white woman sitting nearby at a jazz club. In *Short Cuts*, this portion of the Carver story involves an ex-convict, Joe Robbins (Darnell Williams), and Lois Kaiser (Jennifer Jason Leigh), who is at the club with her husband. But there is nothing in "Vitamins" about the musicians on the bandstand at the venue where the exchange takes place. In the film, however, we learn a great deal about at least one of the performers, Tess Trainer (Annie Ross), a jazz singer who performs throughout *Short Cuts* at the Low Note Club. We also get to know Zoe (Lori Singer), Tess's daughter and a cellist who plays classical music. Tess and Zoe belong entirely to a narrative that cannot be traced back to a specific story by Carver. They appear throughout the film, and more importantly, their music often binds together the several stories intertwined in *Short Cuts*.

By adding Tess and Zoe, and by making their music so essential to the texture of *Short Cuts*, Altman has invited audiences to think of his characters in terms of a dichotomy they embody. As a jazz artist, Tess is an improviser who pieces her life together moment by moment much in the way she constructs a jazz performance. Zoe, by contrast, needs a written score to make music, and she prefers a world where people play by the established rules. When Zoe tells her mother about the death of Casey (Zane Cassidy), Tess is not at all moved. She refuses to accept what Zoe regards as the proper script of mourning. At least in part as a result, the daughter goes home and kills herself. Tess is devastated by her daughter's suicide, but she survives. I find it significant that, at least in Altman's world, the improvisers are likely to survive and even prosper, unlike those who live by a set of pre-conceived rules.

In fact, Altman may have been sufficiently inspired by jazz to build his film around the contrast between improvisers — like himself— and those in need of a stable text. I would even argue that this contrast and its relation to the film's music is the glue that holds the film together. Robert T. Self hints at this reading when he writes, "Or what explains everything may be the significance of art and performance and the jazz and classical music performed by these two women."[6] Typically, Altman himself has made no such claim. Speaking about his adaptation of the nine Carver stories, he told David Thompson, "It says in the credits 'Based on the writings of Raymond Carver,' not on any particular story. I called it a 'Carver Soup.'"[7] Altman is being modest: he has cooked up a much heartier stew then he lets on.

In Carver Country

Nevertheless, many critics have little taste for Altman's confections in general and for *Short Cuts* in particular. Martin Scofield, Kasia Boddy, Glenn Man, and many of the early reviewers of *Short Cuts* evaluated the film primarily by comparing it to Carver's stories. Inevitably they were disappointed. Whatever it was that they liked about Carver they did not find in the film. Scofield believes that Carver has real sympathy for his characters, but that Altman simply ranges ironically from one to another: "The prevailing mood of the film is a kind of buoyant disenchantedness, and energetic delight in survival and the life of the big city and a wry, rueful but never fully engaged sense of individual calamity and tragedy."[8] Contrasting Altman's open endings with Carver's hints at redemption, Man writes, "Altman's changes to Carver's short stories in his cinematic adaptation accentuate his treatment of the family as a site for satire rather than for self-awareness and possible transformation."[9] And Boddy has written that Altman sensationalized Carver's characters with large servings of sex and nudity but allowed few to find real satisfaction: "Almost all the stories in the film are in some way about sexual frustration, and at the film's climax these [*sic*] are released."[10]

Among the writers who are more positive about the film, Robert Kolker may be the most sanguine. He even refers to *Short Cuts* as "Altman's cinema *summa*."[11] For one thing, the film begins with helicopters flying majestically in close formation, a clear reference to the opening moments of *M*A*S*H* (1970) if not to Altman's early work on the television show,

Whirlybirds (1958–59). Kolker sees the film as the culmination of the great themes that Altman had been developing for so many years. He especially admires Altman's sensitivity to characters who are, in the words of one of Tess Trainer's songs, "Prisoners of Life": "he focuses on a broad sample of lower-middle-class and working-class white couples, all of them constricted economically and/or emotionally, some diminished as well by their short-sightedness, their oppressions, their mute despair, their gender panic."[12]

Kolker might have associated his praise of Altman with his love of jazz. Like Tess herself, Altman's films turn away from sentimentality and face the realities of betrayal and despair. Like a jazz solo, *Short Cuts* is always opening onto new possibilities. And like the soloist who can transform a well-known melody by inserting it randomly into an improvisation, Altman delights in riffing on the familiar narrative "melodies" of family, romance, gender, and love. Instead of seeing Tess as the key character, however, Kolker emphasizes Marian Wyman (Julianne Moore), the painter of grimacing nudes. Marian is, after all, one of the four characters on screen as the film ends. After associating Marian with the other painters in Altman's films, including Willie Hart (Janice Rule) in *Three Women* (1977), June Gudmundsdottir (Greta Scacchi) in *The Player* (1992), and most notably, Vincent Van Gogh (Tim Roth) in *Vincent and Theo* (1990), and after connecting both Altman and Carver with the work of Edward Hopper, Kolker writes, "Two distinct voices seem to be speaking these filmic, literary, and painterly discourses. One announces the inevitability of defeat and despair through the hopeless yielding to domination. The other enunciates a freedom of perception, and therefore a control over what is seen, understood, and interpreted."[13] I agree with Kolker's assessment. I would simply add that this second voice can also be that of the jazz artist.

Tess Trainer and Annie Ross

In *Short Cuts*, Altman has enough sympathy for jazz to appreciate the plight as well as the pluck of the working jazz artist. When we see Tess Trainer and her band performing at the Low Note Club, patrons are usually talking, often in loud and obnoxious tones. At home with her daughter, Tess complains about the unruly audiences, even entertaining the possibility of following the large group of American jazz artists who spent portions of their careers in Europe. "I hate L.A. All they do is talk and snort coke.... Think I'll get a job in Amsterdam. They really know how to treat a jazz person there." In two separate scenes, Tess tells the story of Chick Trainer, her late husband and the father of Zoe. She tells Zoe that her father "exploded" when she was six years old. When asked for more details, Tess is concise: "He was a prick. That's the long and the short of it." Later, she is equally candid with the audience at the Low Note Club, telling the customers that Chick made her pregnant in Miami and then "blew his brains out through the hole in his arm."

Tess's unabashed if gratuitous statements about her marriage are consistent with the many songs that present her as a tough and ironic but still vulnerable survivor. The songs have titles such as "To Hell With Love," "I Don't Want to Cry Anymore," and "Punishing Kiss."

Zoe shares a house with her mother but little else. Lori Singer, who is in fact an accomplished cellist, plays Zoe as a woman who would lose herself in her music, often playing with her eyes closed. (Altman rhymes Tess's reception in the noisy club with Zoe's performance in a concert hall where spectators talk among themselves, although at a lower decibel level than at the Low Note.) While Tess lounges about the house drinking Bloody Marys and reminiscing about her dead husband, Zoe seldom speaks, even when she is playing basketball with the young men who join her for a game on her driveway. Zoe takes a special interest in her next-door neighbors the Finnigans when she learns that their son Casey has been hospitalized. When Zoe arrives at the club to tell her mother about Casey's death, Tess is, ironically, in the act of giving one of her most emotionally charged musical performances with "I Don't Want to Cry Anymore," a song recorded compellingly in 1955 by Billie Holiday. As the film comes to an end, Tess sits alone in her house, drinking and singing a blues as she mourns the loss of her daughter.

Before the film has concluded, however, Ross's voice is heard off screen in a reprise of "Prisoner of Life," the song she had sung at the beginning of the film. Then, as the final credits roll, she sings an up-tempo version of "I'm Gonna Go Fishin'," written by Duke Ellington and Billy Strayhorn for the 1959 film *Anatomy of a Murder*. The lyrics were added later by Peggy Lee, one of the few singers who can be considered Annie Ross's peer. Altman and his collaborators surely chose to end the film with this song because it reminds viewers of the fishing trip that is so essential for many of the characters in *Short Cuts*. Ross's final reading of the two songs carries none of the grief that Tess Trainer had experienced moments before as a character in the film. In no way can we understand the singer to be the

Robert Altman, center, directs one of the jazz sequences in *Short Cuts* as singer Annie Ross and an unidentified man look on.

character we just saw at the end of the film. Annie Ross's simultaneously diegetic and extradiegetic presence in *Short Cuts* is not unusual for a jazz artist in a Hollywood film. The same dual role was played by Louis Armstrong in *High Society* (1956) and by Hoagy Carmichael in *Young Man With a Horn* (1950). In both cases, the musicians acknowledge the audience as they introduce and/or conclude the film but also play characters within the story.[14] In *Short Cuts*, there is a similar distinction between the Annie Ross who sings on the soundtrack at the end and the Annie Ross who appears as Tess Trainer. Altman had accomplished something similar several years earlier when he produced Alan Rudolph's *Welcome to L.A.* (1977): Richard Baskin appears as a character in the film while his disembodied voice is regularly heard on the soundtrack. Like Tess in *Short Cuts*, Baskin sings about the disaffected lives of the film's Los Angeles characters.

Altman has said that he added Tess and Zoe to the film because he wanted "a reason for the music. I didn't want the music to come from a sound studio outside and amplify the emotions. And yet I know that music does that.... I just didn't want to *apply* music" (italics in original).[15] Indeed, Altman has let the music play across the film in unusual and ingenious ways. Although Tess Trainer is not an entirely sympathetic character, Altman has apparently named her after Tess Gallagher, the poet who was married to Carver at his death and who worked closely with Altman on the genesis of the film. Gallagher appears to have been pleased with the tribute, calling Tess Trainer "a real gift to me," and saying that she could "recognize some of the widowhood things" from her own life in the singer's behavior.[16] The world-weary but fragile quality of Ross's singing even recalls the tone of many of Gallagher's poems. (See, for example, the poems in *Under Stars*.[17]) There is a matter-of-factness in Ross's delivery and in Gallagher's poetry that stops their sentiments from becoming maudlin or melodramatic. Much the same can be said for the effect of Ross and her group on the film itself.

As a jazz singer, Annie Ross's credentials are impeccable. She first left her mark on the history of jazz in 1952 when she set words to an improvisation by saxophonist Wardell Gray and recorded "Twisted." The song has since been recorded by Joni Mitchell, Bette Midler, Mark Murphy, Anne Hampton Calloway, Jane Monheit, and many others. Ross spent several years with Lambert, Hendricks, and Ross (1957–62), one of the most important vocal groups in jazz history. With the possible exception of the Boswell Sisters in the 1930s, Lambert, Hendricks, and Ross may be the all-time favorite vocal group among jazz audiences.[18] Critics have regularly praised Ross for the extraordinarily broad range of her voice as well as for her ability to communicate emotion. When she left Lambert, Hendricks, and Ross in 1962 because of illness, she returned for a while to her native England. The years with the vocal trio took a toll on her voice, and she lost much of the flexibility and purity of her original sound.[19] Since the 1970s, Ross has moved back and forth between England the United States, working as both a singer and an actress. She has appeared in mainstream films (*Superman III* [1983], *Pump Up the Volume* [1990], and *Blue Sky* [1994]) as well as in low-budget cult items (*Witchery* [1989], *Basket Case 2* [1990], and *Basket Case 3* [1992]). Ross shows her age in *Short Cuts*, but as is often the case with the best jazz singers, including Billie Holiday, Sarah Vaughan, and Frank Sinatra, she has that "authenticity effect" which only becomes more pronounced with the fading of youth's technical prowess.

If Ross possesses an undisputed pedigree as a jazz artist, the same cannot necessarily be said for the Low Note Quintet with which she performs throughout. The band was assembled solely for *Short Cuts* by Hal Willner, a producer who has long excelled as a musical eclectic. He is best known for producing sketch music during thirteen seasons of *Saturday*

Night Live and for the twenty-eight episodes of *Night Music*, a late-night program of jazz and high-life pop that ran on NBC in 1989 and 1990. Willner has also put together a series of records in which a variety of performers record compositions associated with a single individual. Although he built albums around non-jazz artists such as Nino Rota and Walt Disney, he has also paid tribute to the canonical jazzmen Thelonious Monk and Charles Mingus, recording their compositions with performers as diverse as Carla Bley, Joe Jackson, Steve Lacy, Keith Richards, Elvis Costello, Chuck D, Sun Ra, and Henry Threadgill. Altman would call on Willner again to produce the music for *Kansas City*.

For *Short Cuts*, Willner assembled a group of players who have seldom devoted themselves entirely to jazz even though Willner hoped to re-create the sounds of some classic ensembles:

> I based the sound of this band on the mid–50s Miles Davis band with Milt Jackson and Thelonious Monk. But other than the vibes player [Gene Estes], none of the musicians in Tess' band are "jazz" musicians. Terry Adams plays rock 'n' roll piano with NRBQ, Greg Cohen plays bass with Tom Waits. The drummer Bobby Previte is pretty successful playing and composing new music. The trombone player Bruce Fowler worked with Zappa and Captain Beefheart for years.[20]

Willner may have exaggerated the non-jazz background of these performers. Bobby Previte has recorded frequently with downtown New York jazz musicians such as John Zorn, Marty Ehrlich, Tim Berne, and Wayne Horvitz. Bruce Fowler has been involved with the West Coast avant-garde, playing with the Ed Mann Group and on sessions for Vinny Golia's Nine Winds label. Greg Cohen has played with Woody Allen's New York Jazz Ensemble, and Terry Adams has recorded with Carla Bley. The songs in Tess Trainer's repertoire, however, do tend to originate somewhere beyond the established borders of the jazz canon. "Conversations on a Barstool," for example, was originally written for Marianne Faithfull by Bono and the Edge of the rock group U2. "To Hell With Love," "I Don't Know You," and "Prisoner of Life" were all written by Doc Pomus and Dr. John. Before his death in 1988, Pomus had flourished as the composer of rhythm 'n' blues lyrics such as "Save the Last Dance For Me," and "Little Sister." Dr. John, who made some eclectic piano recordings under the name Mac Rebennack in the 1980s, also recorded some mildly psychedelic records about New Orleans witchcraft in the late 1960s. "Punishing Kiss" was written especially for the film by Elvis Costello and Cait O'Riordan. These unlikely vehicles for Annie Ross cause her to reach beyond her usual singing practice, but they mesh surprisingly well with songs by jazz composers Duke Ellington, Horace Silver, and Jon Hendricks, as well as with "I Don't Want to Cry Anymore," written by Victor Schertzinger for the 1940 film *Rhythm on the River* and recorded memorably by Holiday.

Although I know few jazz purists who have celebrated the music in *Short Cuts*, the band maintains a rapport with Annie Ross that was strong enough to survive several sessions of live filming. Unlike what we see in the vast majority of films, the musicians in *Short Cuts* are not miming or lip-syncing to prerecorded music; they have been filmed "in the moment." Altman would have even greater success with live jazz in *Kansas City*, always presenting the music at the Hey Hey Club in real time. He even released a video, *Jazz 34* (1993), made up entirely of live performances filmed on the set of *Kansas City*. In *Short Cuts*, however, Annie Ross gives an extraordinary and unique performance as both an actor *and* as a jazz musician. In preparing Ross to sing as Tess Trainer, Hal Willner told her to use the bottom part of her register to help represent the "darkness" of her life.[21] Although Ross does in fact sing the low notes to great effect, she is clearly reaching at a few points. And she is the same singer who in 1957 made brilliant use of her upper-register in re-creating the trumpet parts on Lambert, Hendricks, and Ross's vocalizations of recordings by the Count Basie orchestra.[22] By going along with Willner's suggestion that Ross sing at the cusp of her comfort zone, Altman is true to an aesthetic he shares with many jazz composers and leaders of ensembles. Charles Mingus, for example, would regularly ask trumpet-players to play extremely high notes knowing that the trumpeters would have to struggle to hit them.[23] Keith Jarrett said that Miles Davis would rather have a bad band playing bad music than a great band playing what they had already played before.[24] Altman understood what jazz writers such as Whitney Balliett meant when they used the term "The Sound of Surprise."[25]

In performance, singers try to project personae that are true to them-selves but that also have a touch of something outside themselves. After all, no singer spends her entire life singing. In this sense, every singer is an actor. But in the moments when singers practice their trade in films, they seldom seem much different from the "characters" they play off screen. To name only two of the most flagrant examples, when Liza Minnelli sings as Francine Evans in *New York, New York* (1977), and when Barbra Streisand sings as Yentl in *Yentl* (1983), they are essentially breaking char-acter, appearing as their off-screen personae rather than as characters in their respective films. Annie Ross's performance in *Short Cuts* is especially remarkable because she is an accomplished jazz singer playing a jazz singer not at all like herself. If nothing else, the real Annie Ross plays to more attentive audiences. When I saw her at Reno Sweeney's in 1979, at the Village Vanguard in 1986, and at Danny's Skylight Lounge in 2005, the audiences were under her spell, including those who had shown up primarily to hear someone who had written a song on a Joni Mitchell album. And the real Annie Ross is much more composed and restrained than the character in *Short Cuts*. Unlike Ross, Tess Trainer works very hard at selling her songs and at projecting a gritty intensity.

Ross has also had a more elaborate love life than what appears to be the case with Tess Trainer: in the late 1940s she bore a child to the great jazz drummer Kenny Clarke while they were both living in Paris; she had long-lasting affairs with Lenny Bruce and Tony Bennett; and she was married to the Irish actor Sean Lynch for twelve years.[26] By adjusting her vocal range and delivery, Ross has created a character whose singing is consistent with her nonmusical behavior. Her acting may be most apparent when she adopts a gruff aspect to interpret "Conversations on a Bar Stool." Seldom has a jazz musician of such stature gone to such lengths to accommodate the vision of a filmmaker. Like so many performers who have flourished within the Altman aesthetic, Ross is at her best as she improvises in character as a jazz improviser.

The Return of the Repressed

The Tess/Zoe contrast is especially useful in pulling together nine Carver stories that were written independently of one another. Unlike a typical Hollywood film, *Short Cuts* has no single plot strain that makes each character's actions comprehensible. Throughout its three hours, audiences must keep track of several discrete plot lines that are almost completely unrelated but come to a shared conclusion through the arbitrary climax supplied by a California earthquake. (No such event appears in any of Carver's stories.) Perhaps in order to give coherence to the multiple, barely related narratives, Altman has suggested that Carver's stories, and presumably *Short Cuts*, can be united by a dark "view of the world" that he shares with the writer. "Somebody wins the lottery. The same day, that person's sister gets killed by a brick falling off a building in Seattle. Those are both the same thing. The lottery was won both ways. The odds of either happening are very much against you and yet they both happened. One got killed and the other got rich; it's the same action."[27]

In the same spirit, Self has traced the chance connections among the characters in *Short Cuts*: "The man who fishes for three days is married to a clown who entertains kids next door to the house where a little boy has been hospitalized because he's been hit by a car driven by a waitress whose daughter is the friend of a telephone sex salesgirl whose husband services the pool of the cello player who lives next door to the dying boy."[28] Altman's addition of Zoe and Tess is consistent with a reading of the Carver stories that emphasizes this same degree of random connectedness. The mother survives while the daughter does not, even though there is no strong reason why this has to be. Would the film have been much different if Tess had been hit by the car instead of Casey?

Because the film is driven much more by character than by narrative, a good reading strategy can be based on the commonalities among the characters. Consciously or unconsciously, Altman and Barhydt may have seen Carver's characters falling into two large groups: those who wear their emotions on their sleeves and those who repress their feelings until, like Tess's husband whose story presages Zoe's suicide, they "explode." As Altman himself has said in the film's production notes, "The cello that Lori Singer plays represents inner feeling — it's more internal and secret — and Annie Ross's jazz is what we express outwardly."[29] In this sense, Tess and Zoe represent the extreme ends of a continuum with virtually all the other characters in between: while the mother rolls with the punches and seldom stifles her emotions, the daughter quietly suffers until she makes a definitive decision and kills herself.

Among the many characters closer to Zoe's end of the spectrum is Jerry Kaiser (Chris Penn), who listens affectlessly to his wife Lois (Jennifer Jason Leigh) plying her trade in the phone sex industry while her children are nearby. At the conclusion of the film, moments before the earthquake strikes, Jerry erupts and kills a young woman who has aroused him sexually. Casey, the Finnigan child who is hit by a car, at first seems oblivious to his injuries and even manages to walk home unassisted after the accident. He never seems to acknowledge the fatal blow he has received. At the hospital where Casey is dying, Howard Finnigan sits silently as his father, Paul (Jack Lemmon), tells him in detail about the incident with his wife's sister that ended his marriage, a story that Howard would clearly prefer not to hear. Only when Howard and his wife Ann (Andie McDowell) confront the baker, Mr. Bitkower (Lyle Lovett), who had been bombarding their house with phone calls, does Howard explode. Stormy Weathers (Peter Gallagher), tolerates the affairs of his estranged wife Betty (Frances

McDormand) until he reaches his limit, gleefully and methodically destroying every scrap of furniture and clothing in her house. Marian Wyman (Julianne Moore) patiently endures her husband's needling until she has had enough; she suddenly and loudly confesses to a long-past, drunken infidelity.

These repressed but explosive characters are contrasted with people such as Lois Kaiser, who is completely uninhibited whether she is arguing with her husband or changing her baby's diapers and simultaneously performing as a dominatrix for a phone-sex customer. Sherri Shepard (Madeline Stowe) is the character most visibly upset by the spraying of malathion over Los Angeles and does not repress her anger at her husband's obvious infidelities. Doreen Piggot (Lily Tomlin) is seldom demure, whether she is expelling her husband, celebrating his return, or desperately attempting to help Casey after she strikes him with her car. Marian Wyman's husband Ralph (Matthew Modine) is consistently aggressive both before and after he finds out about his wife's past. Bill Bush (Robert Downey, Jr.) may be the least repressed character in the film. In an early scene, he jumps out of bed, unflinchingly sips from the previous night's beer can, and with his elbow lands a powerful blow to the face of the lascivious female painted on the slipcover of his couch. Like Tess Trainer, all of these characters are consistently expressive and less prone to sudden outbursts. Regardless of whether or not they are especially likeable, they are surely the most well-adjusted characters in Altman Land.

A Musical Reading Strategy

More importantly, the contrast between Zoe and Tess invites the spectator to see some of the characters as improvisers and others as actors in need of a script. In spite of numerous failures, Altman was always able to continue working at least in part because so many actors enjoyed the creative freedom he offered them on the set. Altman, the life-long jazz fan, surely understands the difference between improvisers and performers who need a text, having regularly faced actors with varying degrees of tolerance for his improvisational approach to filmmaking. If Elliott Gould flourished as an improviser in several Altman films, Paul Newman could barely disguise his discomfort in *Buffalo Bill and the Indians* (1976) and *Quintet* (1979).

In *Short Cuts*, Tess expresses herself with jazz improvisation while

Zoe performs the carefully composed music of Dvořák, Bach, and Stravinsky. The three fishermen (Fred Ward, Buck Henry, and Huey Lewis) seek the predictable script of a fishing vacation away from civilization, refusing to alter it even to report the dead body of a young woman floating in the river. Claire Kane (Anne Archer), who is married to one of the fishermen, is devastated when she hears what happened and carefully enacts the conventional script of mourning for the dead woman. As if to emphasize the performative nature of Claire's actions, Altman films her miming the writing of her name in the guest book at the funeral home. Howard Finnigan, who reads his televised editorials from written copy, must deal with the baker who elaborately improvises his anger over a forgotten cake in a series of telephone calls to the Finnigans. Marian Wyman is a painter, an improvising artist, married to a man who demands that she enact the script of the traditional, faithful wife. Honey Bush (Lili Taylor) tries to abide by the rules of housesitting handed to her by the couple setting off on vacation, while her husband Bill thoroughly explores the apartment and violates his neighbors' privacy. Stormy Weathers improvises the destruction of Betty's possessions while she plays out the script of romance with at least two different lovers. Gene Shepard, the policeman played by Tim Robbins, improvises throughout the film: first he finds a means of dispensing with the obnoxious family dog; he then creates a seduction scenario on the spot by stopping Claire to give her a ticket; and when his wife finds Claire's phone number in his pocket, he throws together an implausible story about a police investigation.

Altman and screenwriter Barhydt created one new character to flesh out Carver's story, "A Small Good Thing," about the boy who is fatally struck by a car.[30] Paul Finnigan, the father of Howard Finnigan and the grandfather of Casey, does not appear in the story, but he is right at home in this cast of improvisers and script-readers. Having adhered closely to the rules of family, home, and work, Paul suffers devastating consequences on the one occasion when his wife's sister offers him a unique opportunity for extramarital improvisation. Perhaps the most tragic example of a character playing by the rules is young Casey, who refuses help from Doreen (Lily Tomlin) after she hits him with her car. She might have been able to save his life, but he rushes away, insisting, "My mom doesn't want me to go in a car with strangers."

Following Roland Barthes,[31] Robert Self would regard this aligning of characters in *Short Cuts* as the function of a "writerly" text, one that leaves much unsaid and invites the reader to supply what is missing. While the "readerly" text follows familiar rules of narrative plausibility and sequentiality, a "writerly" text calls for "the identification of some metaphoric similarity under which to arrange all of the dissimilar situations, qualities, styles, and behaviors that address us from the work."[32] Self calls these types of similarities "hypertexts."[33] Barthes was writing about literature and "the pleasures of the text" when he distinguished between readerly and writerly texts, but as Fredric Jameson has observed, images and musical sounds offer even greater pleasure to those who would add their "writing" to what they experience aesthetically.[34] By leaving the text open on several levels, Altman has invited his audiences to provide connections among scenes that float loosely about each other at the same time that he has surrounded his scenes with musical cues that provoke even more associations.

Indeed, Altman has been extremely sensitive to the allusive possibilities of music. Although Tess and Zoe spend no more time onscreen than the other 20 principal characters in *Short Cuts*, their music is on the soundtrack throughout most of the film.[35] Ross's songs frequently continue into scenes with other characters, and the Low Note Quintet regularly performs instrumental versions of the same songs to accompany the characters' actions. Like all background music in Hollywood films, the *Short Cuts* soundtrack provides continuity, unity, and narrative cuing. But by constantly showing the musicians on camera and allowing their performances to drift in and out of the narrative, Altman has shown little reverence for the standard Hollywood practice of making the music "invisible" and "inaudible."[36] And even when the music does provide continuity, it does not always seem appropriate. On the one hand, a playful instrumental performance of "I'm Gonna Go Fishin'" plays behind Stormy's bizarre encounter with a vacuum cleaner salesman but then continues as Claire Kane grimly drives off to the funeral of the young woman found in the river. On the other hand, the music can be especially successful in gluing together scenes that have more in common than meets the eye. For example, Zoe's suicide is accompanied by the band's introduction to "I Don't Know You," which then continues while Tess sings the song in the Low Note Club. Similarly, an instrumental version of "To Hell With Love" is regularly played behind scenes in which Gene the policeman moves awkwardly among the various women with whom he is trying to maintain or initiate extramarital relations.

The songs of Annie Ross and her sidepeople are not, however, the film's only background music. Mark Isham — who has written music for numerous films including *Reversal of Fortune* (1990), *A River Runs Through It* (1992), *Quiz Show* (1994), *Blade* (1998), *Crash* (2004), and *The Black Dahlia* (2006) — has composed an abstract, often brooding score for the film that frequently alternates with performances by the Low Note Quintet. Isham occasionally mixes the classical sound of a cello with more conventional jazz instruments such as saxophone and vibes. Perhaps he has devised an invisible means to unify the characters of Tess and Zoe, who have otherwise been so carefully distinguished by Altman and Barhydt. Unlike the music of Annie Ross and her group, Isham's score is much more typical of Hollywood practice. At the same time, the New Age aspects of his compositions bring together a jazz and classical ambience that is uniquely appropriate to *Short Cuts*. Isham's music is frequently heard in scenes involving the Finnigans, beginning shortly after the child is hit by a car, when a cello accompanies his walk past Zoe and the basketball players. The same music returns later when Casey's parents are waiting at the hospital for word on the child's progress and when Claire's husband tells her about the dead body near his fishing hole. When Casey dies, Isham's music continues seamlessly as the scene changes to Claire at the funeral.

In one fascinating sequence, music becomes an essential element in the interactions between Tess, Zoe, and characters in the scenes that follow. Coming home early in the morning from the jazz club, Tess enters her daughter's room while she is playing a passage from Stravinsky's *The Firebird*. Tess does almost all of the talking, at one point even humming along with Zoe's music. The mother begins reminiscing about her late husband, eventually singing a bit of Jon Hendricks' "Blue" as she doses off to sleep. The Low Note Quintet plays a few off-camera notes just as Tess is about to begin singing. The instrumentalists then continue without the singer as the camera cuts to a tense scene between Stuart and Claire and then to an emotionally charged confrontation between Doreen Piggot and her husband Earl (Tom Waits). Thanks to the music, the emotional energy in the two subsequent family scenes seems to grow out of the interactions between Zoe and Tess.

Altman's Alternative to "The Jazz Film"

Regardless of how we wish to interpret the presence of Tess and Zoe in *Short Cuts*, there is no question that jazz is a crucial ingredient in the film. But *Short Cuts* has little in common with the many "jazz films" I wrote about in *Jammin' at the Margins*, including *New Orleans* (1947), *The Benny Goodman Story* (1955), *Bird* (1988), and *Mo' Better Blues* (1990). *Short Cuts* is especially unlike Altman's *Kansas City*, which featured the jazz of canonical black artists of the 1930s, such as Count Basie, Lester Young, Coleman Hawkins, Mary Lou Williams, and Ben Webster, played by the best young black musicians of the 1990s, including Cyrus Chestnut, Joshua Redman, Craig Handy, Geri Allen, and James Carter. By contrast, the jazz in *Short Cuts* is several steps outside the mainstream. Annie Ross is not even from the United States. Although she speaks with a solid General American accent in *Short Cuts*, Ross was born in England and has spent a substantial amount of time in that country, at one point even opening a nightclub in London.[37] Furthermore, all of the musicians in Ross's Quintet are white, a fact that Altman seems to present ironically by casting the audience in the Low Note Club as almost entirely black.

Altman has also turned away from Hollywood's conventional script of the jazz artist by avoiding direct reference to obsessions about race, gender, and art, at least in terms of how they affect Tess Trainer. Although Tess, like any entertainer, "performs" her gender, there is no problematization of her performances as in films such as *Young Man With a Horn* (1950), *A Man Called Adam* (1967), and *Lady Sings the Blues* (1972), in which jazz artists fail as performers because of substance abuse and emotional turmoil. Altman is much more interested in the affective potential of jazz, only bringing the music directly into his stories in the scenes with Tess and Zoe but using a large measure of the music to pull together the film's multiple plot elements.

In a brief sequence in *Short Cuts*, Bill Bush (Robert Downey, Jr.) and Jerry Kaiser (Chris Penn) stand on the balcony of the apartment where the Bushes are blithely abusing their privileges as housesitters. Bill and Jerry are smoking pot and drinking beer as they listen to the Low Note Quintet's recording of "Evil California (These Blues)." Jerry says that he likes the music. In a speech that was probably improvised, Bill characterizes the music with the following words: "Yeah, this is good, huh? It's like, it's not ... I don't know, it's different, it's kind of dry ... it's like a dry humping ... some wet ... pussy ... flap." Bill's groping attempt to describe the music is one of the few moments in the film when someone actually talks about jazz. The music is not something the characters can easily classify although Bill Bush has no difficulty associating it with sex. (The connection is not surprising because, if nothing else, the word jazz is probably derived from a slang term for semen.[38]) Later, when the Bushes and the Kaisers walk into the Low Note Club, the hostess tells them to sit by Art Blakey. As the audience sees a large photo on the wall of the late drummer in action, Bill says, "Who's Art Blakey?" In spite of their ignorance of jazz history and aesthetics, the two couples do make the music part of their social activities.

Significantly, other than Tess, no one in *Short Cuts* uses the term jazz. Today the word has much more significance within an institutional context that, on the one hand, valorizes a few artists with recording contracts and concert dates and, on the other, allows for the colonization of the music. For better or worse, this colonization is most apparent in the rise of the academic discipline known as "jazz studies." But like Bill Bush, many people respond to the music outside the discourses that became attached to jazz as it began to develop an elite audience. As for Art Blakey, he himself had no illusions about the audience for jazz. Once, when a French reporter asked him what the American people thought of Charlie Parker, Blakey said, "They never heard of him."[39]

Likewise, Altman and Barhydt have no illusions about the importance of jazz, at least not in *Short Cuts*. They have succeeded in making a couple of good jokes out of Bill Bush's cluelessness about jazz. They have been just as successful in their subtle yet crucial appropriation of jazz, both on the soundtrack and in the "hypertexts" of *Short Cuts*. Perhaps Kolker is correct, and it truly is Altman's "*summa*." It surely represents the director's most complete deployment of a defining element in his aesthetic vision.

NOTES

1. This essay is a revision and expansion of a section of my book *Jammin' at the Margins: Jazz and the American Cinema* (Chicago: University of Chicago Press, 1996), 283–294. © 1996 by The University of Chicago. All rights reserved.

2. Krin Gabbard, "Robert Altman's Jazz History Lesson," in *Black Magic: White Hollywood and African American Culture* (New Brunswick, NJ: Rutgers University Press, 2004), 247–248.

3. Michael Bourne, "Goin' to Kansas City and Robert Altman Takes You There!" *Down Beat*, March 1996, 22–27.

4. Raymond Carver, *Short Cuts: Selected Stories* (New York: Random, 1993).

5. Carver, 28–45.

6. Robert T. Self, *Robert Altman's Subliminal Realities* (Minneapolis: University of Minnesota Press, 2002), 264.

7. David Thompson, *Altman on Altman* (London: Faber and Faber, 2006), 164.

8. Martin Scofield, "Closer to Home: Carver versus Altman," *Studies in Short Fiction*, 33.3 (1996): 391.

9. Glenn Man, "*Short Cuts* to *Gosford Park*: The Family in Robert Altman" in *A Family Affair: Cinema Calls Home*, ed. Murray Pomerance (London and New York: Wallflower, 2008), 162.

10. Kasia Boddy, "*Short Cuts* and Long Shots: Raymond Carver's Stories and Robert Altman's Films," *Journal of American Studies*, 34.1 (2000): 16.

11. Robert Kolker, "Screening Raymond Carver: Robert Altman's *Short Cuts*," in *Twentieth-Century American Fiction on Screen*, ed. R. Barton Palmer (Cambridge: Cambridge University Press, 2007), 181.

12. Kolker, 181–82.

13. Kolker, 190.

14. Gabbard, *Jammin,* 215.

15. Robert Stewart, "Reimagining Raymond Carver on Film: A Talk with Robert Altman and Tess Gallagher," *New York Times Book Review*, September 12, 1993: 42.

16. Stewart, 42.

17. Tess Gallagher, *Under Stars* (St. Paul, MN: Graywolf, 1978).

18. Barry Keith Grant, "Purple Passages or Fiestas in Blue?: Notes Toward an Aesthetic of Vocalese," in *Representing Jazz*, ed. Krin Gabbard (Durham, NC: Duke University Press, 1995), 289.

19. Reg Cooper, "The Art of Annie Ross," *Jazz Journal International*, 32.7 (July 1970): 9.

20. Howard Mandel, "Cutting It," *Sight and Sound*, n.s. 4.3 (March 1994): 11

21. Mandel, 11.

22. Lambert, Hendricks, and Ross, *Sing a Song of Basie* [1957], Audio CD (Polygram B000058A17).

23. Author's interview with Jimmy Owens, March 23, 2009.

24. Keith Jarrett, interviewed in *The Miles Davis Story* (Columbia Music Video, 2001).

25. Whitney Balliett, *The Sound of Surprise: 46 Pieces on Jazz* (New York: Da Capo, 1978).

26. Leslie Gourse, *Louis' Children: American Jazz Singers* (New York: Quill, 1984), 283–92.

27. Robert Altman, "Introduction," in Carver, 9.

28. Self, 257.

29. Altman, 8.

30. Carver, 93–121.

31. Roland Barthes, *The Pleasures of the Text*, trans. Richard Miller (New York: Hill and Wang, 1975).

32. Self, 245.

33. Self, 248.

34. Frederic Jameson, *Signatures of the Visible* (New York: Routledge, 1990), 2–4.

35. *Short Cuts* Soundtrack CD [1993] (Imago 72787–21014).

36. Claudia Gorbman, *Unheard Melodies: Narrative Film Music* (Bloomington: Indiana University Press, 1987), 73.

37. Cooper, 10.

38. Krin Gabbard, "The Word Jazz," in *The Cambridge Companion to Jazz*, ed. Merwyn Cooke and David Horn (Cambridge: Cambridge University Press, 2002), 2.

39. Ralph Ellison, "On Bird, Bird-Watching and Jazz" [1962], in *The Collected Essays of Ralph Ellison* (New York: Modern Library, 1995), 262.

3

"Doing Some Replacin'": Gender, Genre and the Subversion of Dominant Ideology in the Music Scores

Richard R. Ness

From the opening shots of an African American jazz combo perform-ing in a Kansas City nightclub in his first feature film *The Delinquents* (1957) to the final ensemble performance of "In the Sweet Bye and Bye" as the end credits roll in *A Prairie Home Companion*, the films of Robert Altman have foregrounded music and instances of musical performance. Despite Royal S. Brown's claim in his article "Film Music: The Good, the Bad, and the Ugly" that Altman is "a director who, except for *Nashville*, is not generally noted for his music tracks,"[1] it is difficult to think of any filmmaker who has demonstrated a greater willingness to experiment with the possibilities of film scoring or incorporated a wider range of musical styles in his work. The country songs of *Nashville*, folk tunes of *McCabe and Mrs. Miller* (1971) and *A Prairie Home Companion*, the Afro-beat of King Sunny Ade in *O. C. and Stiggs* (1987), the raw jazz of *Kansas City* (1996), the atonal instrumental scores for *Quintet* (1979), *3 Women* (1977) and *The Gingerbread Man* (1998), the British popular songs of Ivor Novello in *Gosford Park* (2001), and the classical ballet selections in *The Company* testify to the variety of Altman's musical choices and his recognition of the importance of the appropriate aural-musical ambience for each of his carefully created, self-contained universes.

Brown's observation may be a response to the fact that while much has been made of the director's use of such techniques as multi-channel sound, zoom lenses and improvisational performance, little attention has been given to his use of music. In part this may be because, unlike established director-composer collaborations such as Alfred Hitchcock-Bernard Herrmann, Federico Fellini-Nino Rota, or Steven Spielberg-John Williams, Altman has not worked consistently with one composer to develop what could be called an "Altman sound."[2] Yet, if the scores for Altman's films only occasionally incorporate similar musical elements (such as the wind chime effects that appear in a range of scores from *That Cold Day in the Park* [1969] and *Images* [1972] to *The Player* [1992] and *The Gingerbread Man*), there is a consistency of approach in the director's efforts to foreground music in much the same way that he calls attention to other aspects of aural discourse. The scores for Altman's films are characterized by a defiance of traditional scoring practices, an avoidance of the musical conventions of various genres, the breakdown of conventional diegetic/non-diegetic barriers, and the use of music to subvert dominant ideology or patriarchal authority. The latter element becomes especially apparent in the four Altman films that deal specifically with musical performance and performers, *Nashville* (1975), *A Perfect Couple* (1979), *The Company* (2003) and *A Prairie Home Companion* (2006), in which the performance space provides a site for challenging the limitations of dominant ideology and which feature autocratic white patriarchal figures whose authority is undermined during instances of on-stage performance by otherwise marginalized voices.

Even in Altman's films that make use of a traditional non-diegetic background score, the director and his composers often eschew conventional scoring practices. In *The Player*, for example, composer Thomas Newman scores an intimate love scene with an aggressive percussion ensemble, the period film *Vincent and Theo* (1990) employs a modernistic score by Gabriel Yared that makes use of "splashes" of dissonant chords to create the aural equivalent of van Gogh's brush strokes, and the growling and clanging noises provided by Mark Isham for *The Gingerbread Man* often seem closer to sound effects than music, even though they are carefully "orchestrated" as part of the overall aural atmosphere. For *Quintet*, one of the most extensively scored of Altman's films, composer Tom Pierson reinforces the game that provides the film's title through the use of five-note clusters and what Brown identifies as a quintuple meter, with the hero's final rejection of the city and defiance of the demands of its patriarchal adjudicator emphasized musically by replacing the five-note patterns with three percussive notes and a cymbal crash.

Much has been made by critics of Altman's deconstruction or sub-version of the conventions of established genres in his early films, including the war film (*M*A*S*H*), the western (*McCabe and Mrs. Miller*), and the hard-boiled detective story (*The Long Goodbye*), but the scores of these films undermine musical conventions in the same way that the narratives invert genre expectations. The opening shots in *M*A*S*H* of military hel-icopters carrying bodies from the battlefield (the closest the film will get to scenes of actual combat) are accompanied not by heroic music or the expected mournful muted horns, but by the folk-like ballad "Suicide Is Painless," with lyrics by Altman's then fourteen-year-old son.[3] As Norman Kagan states, "Immediately warfare as an education into the benefits of society is turned away from, rejected. Visually and aurally, war is shown as the individual's mad choice of isolated death."[4] The song appears again during the staged funeral for the suicidal character "Painless," supporting Altman's visual parody tableau of the Last Supper, and Kagan observes that "again turning the genre upside down, the film's theme now justifies suicide as suicide, not hidden as heroism."[5] Altman's use of music to mock dominant ideological beliefs is also evident in the more conventional march that is heard following the opening credits, as statements by Macarthur and Eisenhower scroll up on one side of the screen while Hawkeye, looking like the anti-thesis of the stoic soldier heroes of earlier war films, walks toward the camera on the right, with the overall effect clearly meant to be taken satirically rather than seriously.[6] Even the American pop songs being song by Asian voices over the loudspeakers add their own comment on the imposing of Western culture on Asian society.

The mock patriotism and use of music to undermine dominant ide-ology that surfaces in the *M*A*S*H* score is even more evident in Altman's follow-up film, *Brewster McCloud*, in which the National Anthem is effec-tively destroyed, first by Margaret Hamilton's off-key rendition and then with its disruption by a black chorus launching into "Lift Every Voice and Sing," the black national anthem, anticipating the undermining of middle class white patriotism by African American musical forces in *Nashville*.[7] The deliberately obsessive monothematic score for *The Long Goodbye* not only serves as an amusing parody of earlier noir scores that employed a similar approach (the lyrics are by Johnny Mercer, who had also penned words to the title tune from the 1944 *Laura*, which contains perhaps the most famous monothematic score in film music history), but suggest the pervasiveness of a dominant power structure and the conformity it imposes.[8] The theme is heard in a variety of settings, from supermarket

Muzak to a Mexican funeral band and even as a doorbell, but as with the hero in *Quintet*, Marlowe (Elliott Gould) finally asserts his independence and individuality from this musical dominance by performing an impromptu harmonica tune at the end of the film.

While the choice of Leonard Cohen songs as the musical accompaniment for Altman's western *McCabe and Mrs. Miller* may have echoes of the use of recurring vocals in earlier genre films such as *High Noon*, as Gary Marmorstein observes in *Hollywood Rhapsody*, they also challenge genre conventions. Marmorstein claims that "the soundtrack had no cracking whip, no thundering string section, no quotations of folk or cowboy songs, no ride-into-the-sunset motifs. It had only a Canadian droning his poetry, owing nothing to silk and silver or the long cattle trail."[9] More significantly, the Cohen songs provide an early example of Altman using music to establish gender distinctions and conflicts, with each of the three numbers becoming identified in the film with specific characters and used repeatedly in the manner of leitmotif: "The Stranger Song" with McCabe, "Traveling Lady" with Mrs. Miller, and "Sisters of Mercy" with the prostitutes McCabe brings to the town.

The incorporation of songs and other musical elements to establish a male/female musical dichotomy becomes even more complex in Altman's version of Sam Shepherd's modern western variant *Fool for Love*, which also demonstrates Altman's penchant for blurring the distinction between diegetic and non-diegetic scoring This study of two lovers who have discovered, after consummating their relationship, that they both have the same father but are unable to control their obsessive attraction, provides another example of Altman making use of two differing and at times opposing musical styles, combining a fragmented, hesitant score by George Burt with a number of country/western songs, mainly by female vocalist Sandy Rogers,[10] but with a few numbers also performed by Waylon Jennings. In contrast to *McCabe*, however, there are no easy character associations established for the songs. Rather, they often serve to overlap and unite the characters.

This unity is established in the opening scenes, which immediately calls into question diegetic and non-diegetic distinctions. The first music heard on the soundtrack is the harmonica played by The Old Man (Harry Dean Stanton) who is later revealed to be the father of both Eddie (Shepard) and May (Kim Basinger), and seemingly establishes his patriarchal authority over both the other characters in the film and the soundtrack. Although first presented diegetically, the harmonica carries over to shots of Eddie driving in his truck, setting up a fight for control of the musical discourse between the patriarch and his children. Eddie turns on the radio in his truck and the song "Let's Ride" by Rogers is heard, introducing the idea of a female voice seeking to take control of the musical elements. The song is interrupted (one of many examples of musical disruption in the director's films) as Altman cuts to May in the kitchen of her cabin at a motel, but returns when she turns on a portable radio. The song thus establishes a link between the two characters that is reinforced later when Eddie tells her they will always be together. Although diegetic sources have now been identified for the song, as Eddie drives into and around the motel grounds it continues to play at levels that seem too intense for either source. In addition to blurring diegetic/non-diegetic distinctions, the song's lyrics confuse visual/sound elements by mentioning the sound of headlights on the ground looking for someone.

The songs by Rogers are often identified with scenes in which May instigates confrontations and the lyrics to songs such as "Why Wyoming," "Go Rosa" and "Love Shy" reinforce both her desire to escape from a dangerous relationship and her need to stay connected to Eddie. "Go Rosa" provides another example of the breakdown between diegetic and nondiegetic music. The song is first presented diegetically, but the references to Mexico in the lyrics inspire a Mexican-flavored instrumental underscoring as Eddie begins to perform rodeo stunts around the motel grounds. The instrumental section grows so naturally out of the vocal that the listener is not at first aware of the transition to non-diegetic scoring.

In his book *The Art of Film Music*, Burt describes how he and Altman worked to introduce the background score so that it would not seem incongruous with the Rogers vocal that opens the film. Burt indicates that his solution was "to use the opening four notes of the main titles song, treating them as a four-note cell and as a basis for variation for the first orchestral cue."[11] The dramatic score becomes more pronounced as the film progresses and the dark secrets of the past are gradually revealed, with the music serving to bridge past and present (recalling the use of the McGuire Sisters songs that serve as temporal transitional devices in *Come Back to the Five and Dime, Jimmy Dean, Jimmy Dean*).

In contrast to the Rogers songs associated with May, male vocals are heard while Eddie is drinking alone in his truck after a violent confrontation with May and immediately after, as he returns to her room to try to assert his control over her, but this masculine dominance of both May and the soundtrack does not last. At the end of the film, the Old Man regains momentary control of the musical discourse, but only after his children have left (separately) and the motel compound has been set on fire. The shattered patriarch plays his harmonica while the flames rise up around him, but as the credits begin to roll the dramatic underscoring that has been associated with both May and Eddie returns and overshadows his music.

The identification of music with gender distinctions and defiance of patriarchal norms becomes particularly evident in the scores for Altman's films dealing with female psychosis. Although scored by different composers, *That Cold Day in the Park*, *Images* and *3 Women* form a kind of musical trilogy dealing with issues of identity and the female psyche. The three films represent a progression, from the focus on a single woman to a woman who seems to be manifesting multiple personalities and hallucinating the presence of a doppelganger to the examination of the lives of three women whose personalities interact and overlap in unusual ways. The score for each film provides an appropriate reflection on the lead characters and development of the narrative construction, from Johnny Mandel's sparse and simplistic use of solo instruments for the single heroine of *That Cold Day in the Park* to John Williams' contrasting musical styles reinforcing the schizophrenic nature of Cathryn in *Images*, to the complex atonal constructions that reflect the intertwining personalities of *3 Women*. In all three films the music is associated almost exclusively with the female characters, who ultimately prove destructive to the males with whom they come in contact. In contrast to Laura Mulvey's concept of a male gaze that visually objectifies female characters in order to reinforce the male position as dominant, Altman in these films privileges the female position and employs music to express aspects of the female psyche that cannot be conveyed through the visual elements. In keeping with the emphasis on a single heroine and a largely straightforward, linear narrative, Johnny Mandel's score for *That Cold Day in the Park* is the sparsest and most simplistic of the three films. Yet even here Irwin Bazelon, in his book *Knowing the Score*, suggests that Altman already is experimenting with music as an expression of the female psyche, noting Mandel's subtle use of "a human voice imitating a musical instrument as part of the ensemble to accompany Sandy Dennis" at various points, adding that "although not readily identifiable, the soft, intimate sound is beautifully expressive and evokes a mood rich in melodic fragments."[12]

Far more complex in employing music as an expression of the heroine's mental state is John Williams' innovative score for *Images*. Williams emphasizes the schizophrenic nature of Cathryn (Susannah York) by contrasting a lyrical theme often associated with her recitations from a children's book she is writing and usually presented on solo piano, woodwinds or strings, with percussive sounds played on sculptures created by the artist Baschet.[13] These avant-garde sounds are augmented by other exotic instruments and musique concrète elements, such as grunting human voices and police whistles. As Bazelon points out, "Combined with avant-garde devices (slides, glissandos, blowing air through the flute) and magnified double-life-size through amplification, echo chamber, and reverberation, the sounds are strange, exciting, and unusual."[14] Bazelon adds that the music serves as a reflection of the heroine's interior states and concludes, "The slightly off-center resonances of the Baschet sculptures, along with other percussive, avant-garde effects, lend themselves perfectly to the hallucinatory atmosphere and, through their alienation from familiar timbres and musical patterns, impress on the viewer her final derangement."[15]

Beyond evoking the heroine's emotional split, Royal S. Brown suggests that the music also underscores the position of women within patriarchy, both in the world of the film and in the filmmaking process itself. In *Overtones and Undertones*, Brown states that the more lyrical (though minor-mode) theme is associated with the heroine's writings, but adds:

> The percussive music, however, is associated with a second set of images, these ones controlled by the male-dominated world. Perhaps the most significant of these is the doubled image of the heroine herself, an image that is the creation of the male gaze.... Whereas a textual interpretation invites the viewer/listener to associate, in these instances, the percussive music with schizophrenic madness, a subtextual hearing/reading reveals a female character battling to free herself from the imagifying male gaze.[16]

Brown expands on this concept in his article "Film Music: The Good, the Bad, and the Ugly," pointing out that the music's stylistic qualities "defy the norms that have dominated Western music both inside and outside of the cinema." Brown states that "each time Cathryn feels threatened by the patriarchal order and its gaze, we hear the avant-garde music" and concludes, "Through the interactions of the music, visuals, editing, and narrative of *Images*, Altman invites his viewer/listeners to free themselves, via the heroine's challenging of the order around her, of prejudices against avant-garde music, and to rethink, via the interactions of the music with the heroine's challenges, the position of women in patriarchal culture."[17]

There would seem to be an inherent contradiction by Brown in associating the avant-garde percussion effects in the score with the male-dominated world, but also indicating that they defy conventions that have dominated Western music, since these conventions would seem to be the product of patriarchal control. These atonal effects are first heard after Cathryn seemingly looks directly into the camera as it slowly zooms in toward her, which Brown identifies as her attempt to challenge and repulse the male gaze, followed by a cut to various inanimate objects that he claims represent the male-dominated environment. But in his description of this opening, Brown leaves out a crucial aural element that calls into question his interpretation. As the camera zooms, a female voice whispering "Cathryn," can be heard on the soundtrack and this is what causes her to look up. Also, it seems to me Cathryn's look toward the encroaching camera is not, as Brown suggests, returning and challenging its gaze so much as looking beyond it at something only she can see. This seems to me even more subversive than Brown's suggestion that she challenges patriarchal control, since it implies that there are limitations to the male gaze and the female character is in a position to see things that it and the viewer/voyeur cannot. In his later analysis of the score in *Overtones and Undertones*, Brown claims that the percussive aspects of the score are associated not with the male world itself as much as with the heroine's perception of it. Thus, both aspects of the score, while seemingly establishing a male/female dichotomy, remain associated with Cathryn and reflective of her mental responses.

The use of music as signifier of the internal states of female characters is further developed in *3 Women*, in which Gerald Busby's fragmented, atonal score continues to challenge the conventions of Western music identified by Brown.[18] Unlike Williams's dual structure for *Images*, Busby's music is designed not to reinforce the division within a single female protagonist, but rather to serve as a unifying force for the three women of the title. In the first half of the film, the music cues are usually instigated by the appearances of Willie (Janice Rule), the first of the women we see, or by images of paintings and/or water, which are associated visually with her. The opening shots of Willie working on one of her elaborate murals on the bottom of an empty swimming pool suggest that what follows may be her creation, a feeling reinforced by her control of the musical discourse in the early stages. Like Elisabet in Ingmar Bergman's *Persona*, which clearly inspired Altman's work, Willie remains silent throughout much of the film and thus the music score functions as her voice, existing free of the semiotic realm of conventional language. The first non-diegetic music cue not instigated by Willie or her visual associations occurs after Pinky attempts suicide and Millie visits her in the hospital more than halfway through the film. This shift in the control of the musical discourse reinforces a narrative shift as Millie begins to take on the mother role. This is also the point at which the previously loquacious Millie rejects the advances of one of the male characters with whom she has been trying to connect in the first half of the film and the shift of musical associations to Millie indicates that she is moving toward Willie's silent strength and resistance to patriarchal power.

A male/female dichotomy is established musically in the treatment of Edgar, the only male character developed to any degree in the film. In contrast to the meandering woodwind themes associated with the female characters, Edgar is introduced by a driving cadence on snare drums that reaches a crescendo as he pulls out a gun (rather obviously parodying the musical cues associated with the kinds of action films Edgar has sought to emulate in his recreational domain, Dodge City). The few instances of diegetic music in the film are identified with Dodge City, or with "normal" society, as demonstrated by the use of a country/western song as background during a poolside party at which Millie's neighbors make derisive remarks about her. In contrast to the graphic killings of male characters in *That Cold Day in the Park* and *Images*, the destruction of Edgar is only indicated in a few lines of dialogue near the end of the film, as it becomes clear that the women have taken control of their environment and the musical discourse, even if the relationships of the three protagonists have been reconfigured.

If *That Cold Day in the Park*, *Images* and *3 Women* demonstrate Altman's association of music with female interiority, the use of music to directly challenge dominant ideology and the patriarchal order becomes most evident in the four Altman films that are structured specifically around musical performance groups. A close examination of the presentation of the musical performances in *Nashville* reveals that the entire arc of the film involves a struggle for control of the musical discourse between the established patriarchal order and outside forces that have been positioned as "other," demonstrated in the two performance scenes that bookend the film. In her discussion of the film, Helene Keyssar observes that "Nashville the city is at least ostensibly controlled by its men, but *Nashville* the movie is made whole and compelling by its women" and that its visual style "specifically calls attention to the gradual dominance of women."[19] Although Keyssar discusses female dominance mainly in relation to Altman's camera work, her comments are equally applicable to the aural elements, which increasingly privilege female voices.

Following a mock advertisement for the *Nashville* soundtrack, which reinforces the capitalistic commodification of artistic endeavor and features a montage of male and female voices singing songs from the film, the first challenge to the established (patriarchal and capitalistic) order is sounded by the loudspeaker from the van of political candidate Hal Phillip Walker, calling for "doing some replacing" as it drives through the streets of Nashville. The dominant order quickly attempts to reassert its authority as the political pronouncements from the Walker van give way to the opening bars of the patriotic bicentennial anthem "200 Years" being recorded in a studio by white-haired country music patriarch Haven Hamilton (Henry Gibson), but the conflict between white male authority and marginalized voices, in terms of both gender and ethnicity, for control of the soundtrack is established during the recording session, as Haven is continually disrupted by outside forces. Although he nearly makes it through the song the first time he is seen recording it, the last word is cut off as he

Haven Hamilton (Henry Gibson) rules the recording studio from a box in *Nashville*.

is distracted by the presence in the recording studio of alleged British female journalist Opal (Geraldine Chaplin), whose gender and nationality pose a double threat to the patriarchal American patriotism of Haven. Haven's authority also is undermined through Altman's construction of the scene by intercutting shots of Haven's attempts to record his song and another recording session in an adjacent booth involving another female character, Linnea Reese (Lily Tomlin) performing with an African American choir (representing yet another challenge to the dominant white power structure).

The scene in the recording studio establishes a pattern in which performances by Haven and the other principal male performers are undercut by outside intervention, whether from other characters or Altman's own aesthetic practices. In Haven's other two solo numbers at the Grand Ole Opry, Altman continually cuts away from his onstage performance to various female characters. During the parodic "For the Sake of the Children"[20] Altman first cuts to Opal in the audience snapping pictures and then to rising star Connie White (Karen Black) arriving backstage to fill in for ailing star Barbara Jean (Ronee Blakely). During Haven's next number, "Keep A-Goin'," Altman pans back to Haven onstage after showing Connie waiting in the wings to go on, but then cuts to the hospital room where Barbara Jean is listening to the program with her domineering manager-husband Barnett (Allan Garfield), reducing Haven's performance to the sound coming from a tinny radio, before cutting back to the Opry and Haven onstage for the last few seconds of the song.

If the performances of Haven and other male characters in the film are continually undercut by the intervention of outside forces and reminders of the presence of female characters, this is not the case for the majority of the female performances. Haven's three solo numbers are paralleled by the three performances of reigning country music queen Barbara Jean ("Tapedeck in His Tractor," "Dues" and "My Idaho Home"), but unlike the treatment of Haven's songs, the solos by Barbara Jean are presented in their entirety, with cutaways only to the audience, rather than to other peripheral events. Whereas Haven is often shown from the back and in long shot during his numbers at the Grand Ole Opry, Barbara Jean's two songs on an outdoor stage at Opryland make heavy use of close-ups, and even the cuts to the audience or other musicians often position her in the frame. Also, the consistent sound level reminds us of her presence, even when she is not visible on camera, in contrast to the sound levels that drop whenever there is a cut from Haven to some backstage activity.[21]

The film's climactic political rally opens with a duet by Haven and Barbara Jean, and then features her in a solo, and the presentation of the two numbers reinforces the differing treatment of male and female performances in the film. The duet is shown largely in long shots, with lengthy cutaways to the crowd as the major characters arrive. But once Barbara Jean takes over, her solo is presented almost entirely in close-ups and the cutaways are mostly to her soon-to-be assassin Kenny (David Hayward).

The most complex of the film's musical performances in terms of sexual politics is "I'm Easy," sung by the narcissistic Tom (Keith Carradine). The song would seem to demonstrate momentary male control of the musical discourse, but as Tom sings Altman cuts to shots of the various women in the audience, including Opal, Linnea, Tom's singing partner Mary (Christina Raines), and the free-spirited L.A. Joan (Shelley Duvall), with all of whom Tom has been (or in the case of Linnea soon will be) involved. On the surface the scene might seem to reinforce sexist stereotypes by presenting Tom as the successful stud being gazed at by his adoring conquests, but the visual construction actually serves to complicate the traditional concept of the male gaze. By virtue of being on stage Tom is put in the position of being looked at, and thus he becomes both objectifier and objectified, especially since the female characters who are both receiving and returning his gaze are aware, to varying degrees, of the impossibility of maintaining any kind of long term relationship with him and thus regard him mainly as an object for immediate sexual gratification. Keyssar even goes so far as to suggest that throughout the entire scene the camera takes a female position, noting that "from the very beginning of this scene the camera seems regendered; it is as if the camera were one of the many women gathered at this club to adore and seduce Tom, the nubile folk-rock hero.... We are also reminded by this sequence that Tom, a man, is and can be a sex object, but he, unlike women in comparable positions in and out of the movies, has control."[22]

Opposing gender positions are evident not just in the presentation style of the musical performances but also in the lyrics sung by the male and female characters. In fact, in many cases songs sung by the women can be seen as responses to those of the male characters. The independence and optimism expressed in "Bluebird" and "Keep A-Goin'" are answered by the helplessness and despair of "Memphis" and "Dues," while the consequences described in "Rolling Stone" are the result of the cavalier attitude expressed in "I'm Easy." Barbara Jean's final number "My Idaho Home" seemingly ventures into Haven's territory in its emphasis on a traditional family environment, though it contrasts with the hypocritical patriarchal position of "For the Sake of the Children" and in its final lyrics reinforces matriarchal control. At the moment when Barbara Jean dares to subvert the patriarchal order by acknowledging her father's dependence on maternal strength, she is killed.

Ironically, the assassination of Barbara Jean results not just in the elimination of the main female character but in the final collapse of patriarchal power, as neither of the two males who have exerted the most control throughout the film, Haven and Barnett, prove capable of protecting Barbara Jean.[23] As a wounded and confused Haven attempts to restore order, control of the musical discourse is suddenly seized by aspiring singer Albuquerque (Barbara Harris),[24] backed by an African American choir, echoing the forces that first challenged Haven's authority in the recording studio at the beginning of the film. Rather than bringing about a restoration of patriarchal order, the sacrificial silencing of Barbara Jean's challenging female voice has instead opened the way for previously marginalized elements to gain control and served as the first step in doing the replacing called for in Walker's political party platform.

Although *A Perfect Couple* narrows the scope of *Nashville* (both thematically and aesthetically since it was shot in a 1.85:1 aspect ratio), it continues Altman's examination of musical performance spaces as sites for challenging patriarchal authority. The film deals with a pair of mismatched lovers who meet through a computer dating service, and their opposing lifestyles are reinforced through contrasting musical associations. Alex (Paul Dooley) is from a wealthy Greek family and has a sister who plays cello in the Los Angeles Philharmonic, while Sheila (Marta Heflin) is a lead singer in a rock band, Keepin' 'Em Off the Streets, that also serves as her communal family.[25] As more than one critic has pointed out, the irony in Altman's film is that the allegedly free-spirited rock group is shown to be every bit as much a patriarchal construction as Alex's family, and its lead singer/manager Teddy (Ted Neeley) rules the band with a ruthless authority that matches that of Alex's father. Brown emphasizes this point in his discussion of the film in *Overtones and Undertones*:

> What is particularly interesting in *A Perfect Couple* is the association of music, both classical and pop, with bullying, patriarchal figures.... The narrative/visual images of *A Perfect Couple*'s rock band as a kind of hippy commune and 1960s counterculture image projected by their music stand in strong contrast to the authoritarian manner in which the leader runs the group. But it is precisely this patriarchal authoritarianism that takes on the responsibility for maintaining those images.[26]

Brown claims that in the film's finale, which involves Alex and Sheila reuniting while attending a concert at the Hollywood Bowl in which the rock band performs with the L.A. Philharmonic, "Classical music and rock have … resolved their differences to become a perfect (postmodern) couple."[27]

What Brown does not address in his analysis of the film, and the way music functions in it, is the degree to which patriarchal authority is subverted. As in *Nashville*, this subversion is demonstrated through disruption of the musical performances by the male authority figures. Both autocratic male leaders are introduced in musical sequences that both establish and challenge their authority. Alex's father is first seen in his home, conducting with a baton in front of a bank of speakers and stereo equipment, with his family formally gathered around him as though attending a live concert, though this "performance" is soon disrupted, first by the return of Alex and a short time later by Alex's sister Eleousa (Belita Moreno).

Teddy is first seen during a rehearsal of "Something's Got a Hold On Me," acting the role of proud patriarch as he kisses his wife Star (Melanie Bishop) and their baby, and interacts with various band members. Despite Teddy's presence, however, the entrance of the song on the soundtrack is instigated by the return of Sheila to the band's loft after her first date with Alex and carries over to shots of her in the rehearsal space and then to a post-rehearsal gathering, ending as Teddy asserts his authority by turning off the tape recorder from which the song is now playing and demands of Sheila "Where the hell have you been?"[28]

The pattern of disruption of male-dominated musical sequences continues in the performance of "Hurricane," in which Teddy takes the lead vocal but stops the performance when he hears Sheila sniffling and admonishes her for showing up at rehearsal with a cold. Rather than remaining on him when the performance begins again, the camera follows Sheila as she leaves the rehearsal space. Later, Teddy also interrupts a performance of "Weekend Holiday," in which he again has the lead vocal, to criticize the band. It is only when Sheila takes the lead vocal on "Won't Somebody Care" that a song is allowed to be played in its entirety for the first time in the film.

As the relationship between Alex and Sheila grows stronger, Teddy retreats to the background, taking a supporting role on stage during performances at a press party and later in scenes of Alex accompanying the group on the road. When Alex eventually becomes frustrated with the casual lifestyle of Sheila and her band mates and leaves, Teddy's reassertion of his patriarchal authority is signaled by a shot of him striking a gong at the end of one of their performances after Alex has departed.

Brown's claim that the finale at the Hollywood Bowl concert resolves the conflicts between the two musical styles in the film would seem to celebrate, rather than defy, patriarchy since these styles have been identified throughout the film with autocratic male authority figures. It is clear, however, that by this point both Sheila and Alex have decided to leave their respective family structures. Although throughout the film Teddy is continually heard telling Star to "put down the goddamned baby" the final musical number opens with Star sitting on stage behind the piano player holding her child. As the music continues Sheila emerges from the wings and the camera follows her in an unbroken shot when she walks off stage and out into the audience, crossing to the box where Alex is sitting. Only after they are together does Altman cut back to the stage as the rest of the group joins to perform "Goodbye Friends." During the performance Teddy is no longer foregrounded, but becomes just another contributor to the ensemble as male and female voices unite (along with an African American presence through the appearance of guest vocalist Ren Woods), and the song emphasizes Teddy's relinquishing of authoritarian control as he acknowledges through the lyrics Sheila's need to go off on her own.

Although aspects of musical performance can be found in many of Altman's films following *A Perfect Couple*, most notably *Short Cuts* (1993) and *Kansas City*, the overall plots of these films do not center specifically on the preparation of these performances and it was only in his final two films that Altman returned to the concept of performance groups as his main focus. Of all of Altman's films, *The Company* most closely resembles *A Perfect Couple* in its streamlined plot, emphasis on preparations and performances, and depiction of the communal living and working relationships of the performers. Here Altman carries his free-form style to extremes, reducing plot elements to a few sketchy romantic relationships and the usual dance film dramatics of twisted tendons and shattered dreams, and instead emphasizing an almost documentary exploration of the rehearsal process and the beautifully photographed performance sequences. Yet even this least plot-driven of all the director's films equates musical performance with gender differentiations and challenges to patriarchal authority.

From the outset of the film Altman establishes the gender divide within the company by cutting between the female and male dressing rooms, and Altman employs this strategy of using editing to both separate and parallel male and female characters most directly in a later scene where he juxtaposes shots of the central character Ry (Neve Campbell) returning home after a long day of rehearsals with images of one of the male performers practicing in an empty studio. While the male directors and choreographers may dominate the rehearsal sessions and offstage business meetings, women are given primacy in the actual performance sequences, which often feature either solo female performers or position the female dancers in the center of the stage/frame supported on either side by the male company members. Even a pas de deux during an outdoor performance that, in a direct parallel to the rained out opening concert in *A Perfect Couple*, plays out during a thunderstorm, begins with the female dancer taking the lead and dictating the movements for her partner to follow.

Altman provides another of his autocratic patriarchs in the form of Alberto Antonelli (Malcolm McDowell), musical director of the company, who reinforces his patriarchal position by referring not only to the dancers but also to his staff members (many of whom are older, retired performers) as "babies." Alberto holds court during the rehearsal scenes, leaning on the back of his designated chair as he watches the performers with a piercing critical eye, rising occasionally to bark orders or provide superficial observations about the nature of the piece they are performing. Even when he is not present at the rehearsals, his authority is felt. When a new choreographer makes the mistake of sitting in Alberto's chair as he starts the session, he is quickly warned by the company members that he has violated a sacred space. Whereas the male authority figures in *Nashville* and *A Perfect Couple* keep being disrupted by outside forces, in *The Company* Alberto is the one who brings an end to conversations in which others disagree with him, often dismissing the dissenter with a curt "We're done here." At one point he watches silently as one of the older female dancers argues repeatedly with her choreographer about putting some steps back into the performance, but when she finally addresses Alberto to try to get his support he simply stands up, walks to his assistant who is holding Alberto's coat at the ready and walks out.

Alberto appears to demonstrate the most control of Altman's autocratic performance leaders, in part because, unlike Haven or Teddy, he is not actually a performer himself and therefore does not run the risk of his authority being undermined onstage.[29] But whereas Teddy lives with the group as well as acting as its director, Alberto's control is limited to the rehearsal space and Altman emphasizes his detachment from the troupe by cutting from Alberto in meetings or watching run-throughs to scenes of the dancers getting together outside of work, including a company Christmas party where one member does an imitation of Alberto, mocking his overbearing manner. Also, like Altman's other patriarchal figures Alberto ultimately cannot control what happens on the stage once the actual performance begins, and during these sequences he is reduced to being just another member of the audience.

If *The Company* effectively bookends *A Perfect Couple*, many critics noted that Altman's final film, *A Prairie Home Companion*, returned to the musical and performance milieu of *Nashville*, though it actually bears even more similarities to a largely forgotten skeleton in the Altman closet, a 1951 film called *Corn's A-Poppin'* that Altman co-wrote but did not direct, which deals with an attempt to present a broadcast of a country/western oriented musical program (in this case on television rather than radio) as corporate types are scheming behind the scenes to ruin the show (the program is sponsored by the Pinwhistle Popcorn Company, a name that would not be out of place in one of *A Prairie Home Companion*'s faux radio spots).[30] As the host and creator of *A Prairie Home Companion*, Garrison Keillor[31] is presented as the least authoritative of Altman's patriarchal performance leaders. He is first presented in the rather undignified position of putting on his pants backstage and appears to be just another member of the ensemble. Although it becomes apparent that the show revolves around him, his lack of control is evident during the offstage scenes. A running bit involves his ever-changing stories of how he got started in radio constantly being interrupted. At one point a female crew member even tells him to hush when he and Lola Johnson (Lindsey Lohan) break into a spontaneous rendition of a jingle backstage, eventually putting her hand over Keillor's mouth to silence him. The attempts to undermine his authority become even more apparent in the sequences onstage. As in Altman's previous performance based films, the stage becomes a space for challenging and undermining patriarchal dominance, particularly by the female cast members.

The main opposition to Keillor's authority is provided by singer Yolanda Johnson (Meryl Streep), with whom he once had a romantic relationship. Not only does Yolanda clearly still harbor resentment over their breakup, but she also objects to Keillor's refusal to make any kind of on-air statement about this being their final show. The tension between them plays out during their performances, as each attempts to take control of the show. Before going on, Keillor informs her that he wants them to perform "Gold Watch and Chain" (a song which has resonance for their own relationship) but appears to concede when she suggests "Red River Valley" instead. Once onstage, however, he introduces their duet by claiming a listener has requested "Gold Watch and Chain." In retaliation, Yolanda and her sister Rhonda (Lily Tomlin) steal the show away from Keillor by egging on the sound effects man when Keillor drops his script while doing a commercial and has to improvise. The sequence ends with Yolanda turning the public performance into a personal argument with Keillor by talking about the postman bringing a letter from an ex-girlfriend who has been dumped, and (in an echo of *A Perfect Couple*), emphasizing her sonic control by angrily hitting a gong as she leaves the stage.

Throughout the film Keillor's stoic individualism is contrasted with the more familial collective matriarchal spirit of the Johnson sisters. Recalling Barbara Jean in *Nashville*, Yolanda and Rhonda make reference to their mother in introducing both of their performances, and much of their backstage banter revolves around family. Recalling Altman's handling of the female performers in Nashville, although there are cuts to backstage activity when the Johnson sisters perform their first number the sound level remains consistent, but during Dusty and Lefty's first appearance the sound levels drop during the cuts backstage to Keillor and Lola talking. Gradually, matriarchal forces take control of the program, as Yolanda succeeds in securing a solo spot on the broadcast for her daughter Lola. Even death itself is presented in the form of a mysterious woman in a trench coat. The loss of patriarchal power is affirmed in the finale, in which the ensemble performs Yolanda's requested "Red River Valley" and Keillor is absorbed into the group, harmonizing with Yolanda, Rhonda, and Lola.

The film's epilogue takes place a few years later, after the theatre has been demolished and the station sold, as the surviving members of the troupe gather in a diner to reminisce and discuss future plans. Keillor's published script ends in the diner as the female figure of death enters, but in the concluding moments of the film Altman, for the last time, reinforces the significance of musical performance, as he cuts back to the ensemble on stage singing "In the Sweet Bye and Bye." Fittingly, female voices dominate the rendition, and in the last images Yolanda drags Keillor back onstage and kisses him, but then separates from him and is seen being consoled by the company of women.

Although Altman once claimed in an interview with David Wilson that "music is like a prop,"[32] it is clear from the manner in which it has been foregrounded in his films that it has much greater significance. Music, when and where it is used, becomes as important an element of the discourse as dialogue and the visual elements, and provides another means through which Altman not only subverts cinematic and genre conventions, but also challenges the dominant patriarchal power structure. Perhaps the best summation of the value of music in the director's work is provided by Molly Haskell in her review of *Nashville* for *The Village Voice*: "While some characters are more 'major' than others, they are all subordinated to the music itself. It's like a river, running through the film, running through their life. They contribute to it, are united for a time, lose out, die out, but the music, as the last scene suggests, continues."[33] Thirty years later, Haskell's observations could have applied equally well to Altman's final production, *A Prairie Home Companion*. In the film's concluding moments the director even uses music to momentarily transcend death itself and we are reminded that although Altman himself may be gone, the films and their music will continue.

NOTES

1. Royal S. Brown, "Film Music: The Good, the Bad, and The Ugly," *Cineaste* 21 (1–2): 66.

2. Altman tended not to work more than twice with the same composer on any of his feature film productions, and those composers who did double duty for the director often worked on back-to-back projects involving wildly disparate subject matter and musical approaches. The result has been such unusual pairings, both musically and thematically, as *That Cold Day in the Park* and *M*A*S*H* (both scored by Johnny Mandel), *Images* and *The Long Goodbye* (John Williams), *Nashville* and *Buffalo Bill and the Indians* (Richard Baskin), *Secret Honor* and *Fool for Love* (George Burt) and *Beyond Therapy* and *Vincent and Theo* (Gabriel Yared). Altman also has shown a tendency to draw on other than established Hollywood composers for his background scores, such as Gerald Busby for *3 Women*, David A. Stewart for *Cookie's Fortune* and Lyle Lovett for *Dr. T. and the Women*.

3. In Fred Karlin and Rayburn Wright's *On the Track: A Guide to Contemporary Film Scoring* (New York: Schirmer, 1990), Mandel describes the origins of the song, noting that Altman told him he wanted something that sounded "real stupid" because it was going to be sung and played in the film by GIs who only knew a few chords on the guitar. Altman originally planned to write the lyrics himself but told Mandel he could not come up with anything stupid enough so he turned it over to his teenage son. Mandel claims Altman originally set the lyrics to a song by Leonard Cohen, indicating the director's awareness of Cohen's music before it was selected for the *McCabe and Mrs. Miller* soundtrack.

4. Norman Kagan, *American Skeptic: Robert Altman's Genre-Commentary Films* (Ann Arbor, MI: Pierian, 1982), 29.

5. Ibid., 36.

6. Notably, Altman's later serious war films, *Streamers* and *The Caine Mutiny Court-Martial*, make limited use of music, providing only a few diegetic songs from a radio in the former and brief sounds of military marches outside the makeshift courtroom in the latter.

7. Altman has often employed musical styles associated with African American performers to challenge middle class white society. Altman's first directorial effort, *The Delinquents*, opens with a performance of "A Porter's Love Song to a Chambermaid" by Julia Lee being disrupted by a gang of white thugs. In *O. C. and Stiggs,* the teenage heroes employ the music of King Sunny Ade and His African Beats to disrupt a theatrical production in which one of their mothers is appearing. The Alberta Hunter songs heard on a radio in *The Laundromat* emphasize the incongruity of a white middle class woman, also named Alberta

(Carol Burnett), in such a location. The Paris fashion shows in *Ready to Wear (Prêt-à-Porter)* are dominated by hip-hop and rap numbers.

8. Like the main theme in *Laura*, the title song in *The Long Goodbye*, as Diane Jacobs observes in *Hollywood Renaissance* (Cranbury, NJ: A. S. Barnes, 1977), is never played through to completion.

9. Gary Marmorstein, *Hollywood Rhapsody: Movie Music and Its Makers 1900 to 1975* (New York: Schirmer, 1997), 305.

10. In a doubtless unintentionally disturbing parallel to the incest theme, singer/songwriter Rogers is playwright/star Sam Shepard's sister.

11. George Burt, *The Art of Film Music* (Boston: Northeastern University Press, 1994), 73. Burt's text also includes a discussion of his working relationship with Altman during the editing and mixing sessions for *Fool for Love* (222–224).

12. Irwin Bazelon, *Knowing the Score: Notes on Film Music* (New York: Van Norstrand Reinhold, 1975), 86.

13. For a detailed account of the music and how it was developed, see Bazelon's interview with John Williams (*Knowing the Score*, 202–206).

14. Bazelon, 94.

15. Ibid., 95.

16. Royal S. Brown, *Overtones and Undertones* (Berkeley: University of California Press, 1990).

17. Brown, "Film Music," 67.

18. Although *Three Women* is the only film Busby scored for Altman (and indeed appears to be his sole contribution to film music), the composer also appeared as a performer in *A Wedding*.

19. Helene Keyssar, *Robert Altman's America* (New York: Oxford University Press, 1991), 159.

20. The song both reinforces and satirizes Haven's patriarchal role by presenting him as a dedicated father but also a womanizing lout who is dumping his lover in the interest of keeping the family together.

21. Connie White's "Memphis" number also employs several close-ups and is presented complete, with only a few brief cuts to the audience.

22. Keyssar, 160–162.

23. Although Barbara Jean is murdered by a male character, it has been established that he has a mother complex and his actions seem to be triggered at least in part by the references to home and motherhood in her final number.

24. Albuquerque's previous attempts at vocalizing were silenced by male intervention, as demonstrated by her attempt to sing at a racetrack where the sounds of the cars speeding by completely drown her out.

25. For a detailed account of Altman's attempt to market the rock band in conjunction with the film see Rory O'Connor, "Sound Track: Strike Up the Band," *American Film* 4/4: 64–65.

26. Brown, *Overtones*, 248–249.

27. Ibid., 249.

28. The progression of the song from seeming underscoring for Sheila's reaction after being kissed by Alex, then carrying over to the rehearsal and continuing in a seamless transition from live performance to recording is the first of many examples of the breakdown of diegetic/nondiegetic scoring distinctions that Brown regards as such an integral and intriguing aspect of the film's musical construction.

29. It is undoubtedly no accident that he is referred to by members of the troupe as "Mr. A." which obviously also could stand for "Altman," and one senses his position as surrogate for the director not only in his interactions with the performers during rehearsals, but also in his debates over budgets and possible projects with other members of the ballet's administration.

30. The no-budget production has a cityscape seen through one office window that is obviously a painting. Aside from serving as a forerunner of Altman's performance oriented films, the production's most interesting element is a musical number containing a lyric referring to Cinemascope, which may well be the first reference to the widescreen process in a popular song.

31. In an echo of *The Company,* the other cast members usually refer to Keillor only by his initials.

32. David Wilson, "Robert Altman," in *Close-Up: The Contemporary Director,* ed. Jon Tuska (Metuchen, NJ: Scarecrow, 1981), 179.

33. Molly Haskell, *"Nashville," The Village Voice,* 11 June 1975, 60+.

4

The Company's Coming:
The Hero, the Survivor, and the
Victim in *McCabe and Mrs. Miller*

William Graebner

Today, some forty years after its 1971 debut, Robert Altman's *McCabe and Mrs. Miller* is widely understood as a work of considerable artistic and social merit. Scholars have given the film its due, shedding light on its contribution to a wide variety of issues and movements: the revisionist westerns of the 1960s and early 1970s, including the ways in which the film incorporates or reflects the new western history of Richard White, Patricia Nelson Limerick, and others; the issue of violence and its relationship to the American past; the fragmentation of American community; the image of women in film and the film's understanding of and contribution to second-wave feminism and to the captivity narrative; the western hero; changing concepts of masculinity; modernist narrative; and the counterculture.[1] And this list hardly exhausts the ways in which scholars from several disciplines have explored, interpreted, and contextualized this complex film.

With the exception of Julie Christie's portrayal of Mrs. Miller as a strong woman with links to feminism, critics have focused on the film's dark side, from its depiction of a mining frontier driven by gambling and prostitution to its treatment of big business as immoral and implacable. Indeed, in the latest reading, even Mrs. Miller loses much of her allure as she is reduced to McCabe's captive, eager to move from the brothel to the boarding house, but unable to do so without McCabe's assistance — that is, without McCabe's survival.[2] Efforts to *explain* the film's darkness have

59

been prudent and reasonable; they include (working on the aspects above) the new western history, with its less mythic, more realistic take on the frontier; the New Left/counterculture hostility to big business; and frustration with the pace of second-wave feminism.

While there is truth in these explanations, and in others of a similar nature, they stop short of appreciating the substratum of ideas that grounded and shaped the film and the story it told and were collectively responsible for its bleak pronouncements on everything from small town community to the American dream. The search for that substratum takes us back to 1959 and the publication of Edmund Naughton's *McCabe*. The basis of the screenplay and subsequent film, and from there, backward and forward, from William H. Whyte Jr.'s *The Organization Man* (1956), to Erving Goffman's *Asylums* (1961), Bruno Bettelheim's *The Informed Heart* (1960), Stanley Elkins's *Slavery* (1959), Betty Friedan's *The Feminine Mystique* (1963), and Hannah Arendt's *Eichmann in Jerusalem: A Report on the Banality of Evil* (1963).[3]

To be sure, these works covered very different subjects: Whyte was writing about big corporations, Goffman about prisons and asylums, Bettelheim about World War II concentration camps, Elkins about slavery, Friedan about women in the postwar suburbs, and Arendt about German bureaucracy — not a mining camp in sight. What they shared was a belief in the power of institutions — the prison, the concentration camp, the suburb, the plantation — to dominate their "inmates," to shape their behavior and values, to corrode and undermine a sense of individual (or group) efficacy and, perhaps above all, to produce the victim or, at best, the mere survivor. Among the film's victims and survivors are a weak and broken Sheehan welcoming the Company; a foolish and misguided McCabe, dying for a community that isn't one and for principles that no longer exist; and a defeated Constance Miller, huddled in an opium den, escaping from what she can't change.[4]

Of all these texts, Whyte's *The Organization Man* was easily the most optimistic and perhaps the most misunderstood. Although the title seemed to suggest the dreary prospect of modern man at the mercy of powerful organizations, Whyte's goal was to make Americans aware of the power of the organization in the hope of generating resistance to it. "The fault is not in organization," he wrote in an existentialist vein, "it is our worship of it.... Organization has been made by man; it can be changed by man." Even so, Whyte was deeply concerned about the decline of the individual and the rise of people who had not only *worked* for the organization, but *belonged* to it, whether as civil service bureaucrats, corporate trainees, "engineering graduates[s] in the huge drafting room at Lockheed," or as residents of the "packaged villages" of the "new suburbia." Indeed, Whyte seemed in despair over a new generation of men that had given themselves to the presumed benevolence of the organization: "Once people liked to think, at least, that they were in control of their destinies, but few of the younger organization people cherish such notions. Most see themselves as objects more acted upon than acting — and their future, therefore, determined as much by the system as by themselves." Given this widespread acceptance of the organization, Whyte — and his readers — could only wonder where resistance was to begin, or from what source — other than his book — it might emanate.[5]

If *The Organization Man* was a call for resistance, Goffman's *Asylums* was an effort to explore the nature of what he called "total institutions," institutions such as the prison and the mental asylum, where "like-situated individuals" lived and worked, "cut off from the wider society for an appreciable period of time," [leading] "an enclosed, formally administered round of life." Their "total character," Goffman explained, was "symbolized by the barrier to social intercourse with the outside" and by barriers to departure — the inability to leave the institution — that included "locked doors, high walls, barbed wire, cliffs, water, forests, or moors." While some total institutions — prisons and POW camps, for example, were designed to sequester those understood to be a danger to the community, others were essentially workplaces: boarding schools, army barracks, and work camps — including remote logging camps.

Among the characteristics of total institutions, one was the absence of spaces where an individual could take refuge in an effort to withstand an institution's assault on the self, on the individual qualities that make people unique and sustain them in places and circumstances that otherwise restrict their roles and behaviors. Here Goffman contrasts civil society, in which an individual in need of shoring up the self might "crawl into some protected place where he can indulge in commercialized fantasy — movies, TV, radio, reading — or employ 'relievers' like cigarettes or drink, with total institutions," in which "these materials may be too little available."[6]

While Goffman's goal was to produce a taxonomy of total institutions by examining the lives of mental patients and prisoners in detail, others — Bettelheim, Elkins, and Friedan, all publishing major and influential books within a four year period at the end of the 1950s and the early 1960s — were more interested in describing the experiences of particular groups, past and present, caught up in coercive, controlling institutions or life experiences. Moreover, as Kirsten Fermaglich notes in *American Dreams and Nazi Nightmares* (2006), these writers either wrote directly about the crushing and dehumanizing experiences of the Jews in Nazi concentration camps (Bettelheim) or they employed analogies based on the camps to explain and appreciate the nature and degree of the oppressive experience they were studying.[7]

Elkins, writes Fermaglich, was strongly influenced by Bettelheim's view of the camps as having emasculated and infantilized an inmate population of formerly "autonomous individuals," and he wrote that view of human behavior under conditions of extreme stress into *Slavery: A Problem in American Institutional and Intellectual Life*, his influential and controversial history of the impact of American slavery. In a slave environment not unlike that of the concentration camp, Elkins argued, slaves were transformed into docile, "helpless dependents." Freidan's target was the American housewife, adrift in the vapid and vast emptiness and isolation of the postwar suburbs, her sense of self at risk, coming to identify with the enemy, reduced to a dependent, passive, child-like non-adult. The women who "adjust," who accept their circumstances and roles, are, Friedan wrote, "in as much danger as the millions who walked to their own death in the concentration camps."[8]

This body of work, which emphasized the fragility of the individual and the power of the institution, was enormously influential at the time of publication and remained the dominant view until the mid–1970s, when new perspectives took hold, emphasizing resistance, agency, and dignity. Elkins's *Slavery* went out of print in 1976, having been superseded by John Blassingame's *The Slave Community* (1972), which described the many ways in which plantation slaves had managed to maintain a sense of themselves, distanced from their owners. Freidan's *The Feminine Mystique* remained popular, but many feminists now rejected its more extreme depictions of women as victims of concentration camp-like suburban environments. Something similar occurred in the scholarship of the concentration camp that had served as the foundation for the more specific discourses of victimization. Terrence Des Pres's *The Survivor: An Anatomy of Life in the Death Camps* (1976) represented the turn, arguing that despite the enormous pressures of life in the death camps, and the "terrible damage" they caused, inmates somehow survived: "sane, alive, still human."[9]

Here, then, were two perspectives. One, dominant at the end of the 1950s, when Edmund Naughton's *McCabe* appeared, and carried forward into the late 1960s, was about the weakness of human beings in extreme situations and, especially, when up against the power of the institution; this view was about producing the victim, about victimization. The other, prominent by the mid–1970s, was about the strength of human beings, about their ability to emerge from extreme situations with dignity intact; this view was about producing the survivor — or even, in some cases, the hero. *McCabe and Mrs. Miller* appeared as one of these sets of ideas was morphing into the other, and one of its functions was to negotiate these conceptual frameworks. Later, we'll examine how the film accomplished that task.

The same period that produced these studies of victimization also produced an important study of those who committed "evil" acts — an issue of more than passing significance in the novel *McCabe* and in Altman's film. Reporting for the *New Yorker* on the 1961 trial of Nazi functionary Adolph Eichmann, who had arranged for the deportation of hundreds of thousands of Jews to the gas chambers, Hannah Arendt found a man whose "deeds were monstrous. But the doer ... was quite ordinary, commonplace, and neither demonic nor monstrous." Based on her observations, Arendt framed Eichmann's conduct with the phrase "the banality of evil," an idea she developed at length in *Eichmann in Jerusalem*, published in 1963. As Arendt explained, the "banality of evil" referred to "monstrous" acts committed by people who were neither wicked, nor stupid, nor profoundly self-interested, nor pathological, nor possessed of deep ideological conviction. Instead, the perpetrators were shallow, thoughtless, and unthinking — that is, unable to engage in the sort of thinking that would give them a moral perspective on their actions and help them avoid doing wrong. "We resist evil," she argued, "by not being swept away by the surface of things, by stopping ourselves and beginning to think, that is, by reaching another dimension than the horizon of everyday life."[10]

There is little reason to believe that *McCabe and Mrs. Miller* was intended to be understood as an allegory of the Holocaust. Nonetheless, interest in the phenomenon might be inferred from the film's treatment of religion. The most revealing line, which appears in the McKay/Altman screenplay but not in the film, is delivered by McCabe as he leaves Presbyterian Church for Bearpaw and a meeting with the lawyer. As he passes the church and the sneering Reverend Elliot, McCabe says, "God's dead, you prick." We can't be sure why the line was removed, but it was certainly reasonable to do so, given that the God-is-Dead controversy was a recent phenomenon, its literature dating to the early 1960s and brought to broad public consciousness in April 1966, when the cover of *Time* featured the question, "Is God Dead?" The movement had a variety of causes or influences, but one of them was the Holocaust. God must be dead, so the argument went, because a living God would not have tolerated the murder of six million Jews. Altman deleted McCabe's brazen remark, but he did not dispense with the sentiment. Indeed, the film is unremitting in its claim that God is dead in Presbyterian Church.[11]

The film is perhaps even less direct in its treatment of the "banality of evil." However, Eugene Sears and Ernie Hollander, representatives of the mining company and charged with negotiating with McCabe (and having the power to decide that he should be killed), track Arendt's argument in certain respects. Like Eichmann, they are bureaucrats, situated *between* their victim (here, McCabe) and the Company, which is something of a phantom, having a small office in Bearpaw but otherwise existing in an imagined space elsewhere.[12]

Although the decision to give up on McCabe and bring in hired killers seems "monstrous" (using Arendt's term), Sears and Hollander do not at first seem to be thoughtless people; indeed, Sears's first approach of McCabe is that of the reasonable businessman, eager to strike a deal with another businessman and move on. When McCabe's responses to this and a second offer make this easy resolution unlikely, however, Sears and Hollander become thoughtless agents of evil. Discussing the situation at Sheehan's saloon, Sears thinks they can still close the deal, while Hollander is adamant that McCabe is too foolish and stupid to warrant going further with the talks. In words that value his own impatience more highly than another man's life, Hollander announces that he's going back to Bearpaw. "After 17 years," he says, "I think I deserve something better than being sent out on a goddamn snipe hunt like this. He's [McCabe's] impossible!"

> SEARS: Yeah, okay, I guess you're right. We tried. [rising from the table] Do you think that meat was all right? [pause] God, if it wasn't rancid. That's all I need on a trip like this is a case of the runs.[13]

This exchange is especially chilling in the way it suggests Sears's quick and easy acceptance of what amounts to a death sentence for McCabe, and in how it reinforces the shallowness of the two men as they move casually from death to the perils of diarrhea. Sears and Hollander are not evil at the core, and they lack the ideological motivation and the defined self-interest — we have no idea what they stand to gain from the McCabe negotiations — that would make McCabe's death vital to them. But they are shallow men and men incapable, in Arendt's terms, of thinking through the problem before them and understanding the moral meaning of their acquiescence. Their act is monstrous, yes, but also the product of banality.

The Harrison Shaughnessy Mining Company, the company behind McCabe's murder, has little concrete presence in the film. It is represented, albeit briefly, by Sears and Hollander, whose demeanor and tone marks them as representatives of a corporate culture; less directly, by the three men sent by the Company to kill McCabe, who stand in for the Company only in their actions (rather than their demeanor and tone) which the Company, through Sears and Hollander, have authorized; by the Company offices at Bearpaw, which we see only briefly and which appear as a small town façade for genuine corporate power; and by the bar owner Sheehan, a weak man who early on decides that his best interests lie in accommodation to the looming corporate presence.

Sheehan is a natural company man, a rough, frontier version of Whyte's "organization man," running his own business while yearning to be a part of the emerging corporate world. Although he seems to participate in the same culture of individualism as McCabe and the miners who drink in his saloon, his enthusiasm for corporate-like suppression of competition is apparent from his first real conversation with McCabe, when he "proudly" (in the language of an early shooting script) asks the gambler to join him in a partnership that would "keep any outsider from coming in here and building other saloons."[14] While McCabe's response is instinctively entrepreneurial and individualist — "Deals I don't mind. It's partners I don't like" (and, in an earlier version of the screenplay, "I don't like company towns") — Sheehan is indefatigable in his desire to *be* the Company, to merge his self with the corporate entity. This characteristic of Sheehan is affirmed most clearly late in the novel, when the gunfight has begun and Sheehan, cowering in his saloon, asks his manager to look out the window and see what's happened. When the manager replies, "I won't see nothing," Sheehan explodes: "Goddamit, when I talk it's the Snake River Mining Company, Incorporated, that's speaking. Now look out that window!" "Anyone who heard Sheehan," writes Naughton in anticipating this scene, "could tell that the Snake River Mining Company was the true church to him: he was awed by the Company."[15]

By and large, the mining company is not vividly presented or pictured in the film; Sears and Hollander are as close as the film takes us to the corporation, and their attitude is sufficient to make us fear the corporation itself. However, this virtual absence should not be misunderstood. To give the Company more screen time — say, by showing corporate officers in

Seattle scheming over how to acquire Presbyterian Church — would seem needlessly obvious, even corny. Despite its shadowy presence, the Company motivates everything on screen, in the way that the horror film stalker, without ever being seen, is understood to be "out there." Put another way, without the Company there is no film: no tragic weaknesses revealed, no problem to be solved, no threat to overcome, no love thwarted. In short, the Company is more central to the film than it might seem to be.

This centrality is especially clear in the novel, a form that tolerates abstract discussion in a way film does not. While film requires that we learn about power (in this case) by being *shown* how it operates, the novel more easily supports a *discourse* that explains power's reach and methods. Admittedly, Naughton's *McCabe* would be a better book without the heavy ideological description of corporate evils, which in this regard is reminiscent of Upton Sinclair's indictment of the meat industry, *The Jungle*.[16] Nonetheless, the novel is helpful in understanding the corporate enemy as it appeared to social critics in the late 1950s — that is, a version of Goffman's total institution.

Even before the Company showed interest, Presbyterian Church had some of the characteristics of a total institution. It is a work camp (one of Goffman's categories), historically a place of regimentation and exploitation, its inhabitants "cut off from the wider society." And, as the film makes clear, it is a community that lacks the private spaces necessary to sustain the self. Most every scene is crowded, often with people who have widely different perspectives and interests; McCabe's tragically unsuccessful "negotiations" with the Company all take place in public spaces where distractions are plentiful and concentration difficult. As a survivor, Mrs. Miller understands the value of privacy better than McCabe, finding moments to read and smoke in her room, fending off McCabe's interruptions and violations of her wish to be apart. In Naughton's book, the first words Mrs. Miller speaks to McCabe are: "I want to talk to you. Alone."[17]

As the film's opening scene reveals, the town is thoroughly isolated, distanced from the closest settlement by miles of forest and muddy and snow-covered trails that function, in Goffman's phrase, as "barriers to departure." Goffman's barriers were real, concrete ones — barbed wire, locked doors, and asylum walls among others — and the barriers that contain the people of Presbyterian Church are not of that extreme sort. Yet there is something curiously restrictive about the town that binds and limits the mobility of even its most entrepreneurial residents: McCabe and Mrs. Miller. On the surface both are upwardly and outwardly mobile;

Mrs. Miller makes it clear that she is in Presbyterian Church only temporarily, while she saves money to open a boarding house in San Francisco, and in crucial situations she encourages McCabe to get out of town — to go down the mountain with Webster, perhaps to participate in the "boom around the fort," later to "just sell out and go someplace where people are civilized." The signals we get from McCabe are mixed; on the one hand, he seems to want to make a deal for his holdings, at some price, which would imply the desire to move on; on the other hand, he enjoys being the big man in town, and his "reputation" and "principles" bind him to the community.[18]

In the end, of course, the forces holding our protagonists to this mining camp prove overwhelming. McCabe's decision to stay in Presbyterian Church and fight the Company isn't much of a decision at all; as he tells the Bearpaw lawyer in the early screenplay, "I don't have no other place to go." McCabe will be buried there, and with his death goes the deal that might have freed Mrs. Miller to open her boarding house. They have been contained and, as Naughton explains, contained in ways that reflect Freidan's "comfortable concentration camps" of the American suburbs and echo novelist Richard Yates's *Revolutionary Road*, published in 1961 and representative of the mood of stasis that characterized the last years of the 1950s. Like *Revolutionary Road*'s Frank and April Wheeler, Naughton's John McCabe and Constance Miller revel in their superiority to the people around them.

In language that imagines the turn-of-the-century mining frontier as a postwar suburb, Naughton explains the curious distance between the values McCabe and Mrs. Miller articulate and the actions they take: "The last thing they ever wanted was to be like them Main Street people hog-tied together by a stable of kids like the kids was a mortgage that kept them in the same house.... They would lie in bed and ... compare themselves with other couples in town ... they would imagine how the married couples were in bed and snicker at them. They ... made jokes about the ineptness of each couple in each house." Despite this talk — and again like Frank and April Wheeler — they never did the things that would get them beyond the town. "He kept saying he would sell out and go back East," Naughton writes of McCabe, "and Mrs. Miller said she was saving to go to San Francisco. But they never left." Although the screen version is not as explicit about this containment project as Naughton's novel, it presents McCabe as a man who talks big and thinks small (in a paraphrase of Constance's line), and its trajectory moves from openness and possibility to the tragic confinements (death and the opium den) that mark the end of the film.[19]

Naughton's "voice" on the larger issue of the total institution is that of the "Socialist Swede," the owner of the livery stable. When the town gathers to consider rumors that the Company has an interest in Presbyterian Church, the Swede presents the Company as an all-powerful, irresistible force. The Company "would take the mines and the town for nothing, if it wanted to," he argues. It "owned all the courts," and "the legislature too," and "all the newspapers," and so the Company could "kill everybody in the town and nobody in the East would say a word about the Company." "There was nothing anyone could do against it," the Swede claims. "Nobody could stand up to them." "Any resistance will be worse than useless. We will just have to wait for the verdict of history."[20]

To be sure, Naughton achieves some distance by putting these words in the mouth of a socialist and a Swede (that is, a socialist twice over). But the Swede's cynical view of power is confirmed by the Chinese, who understand their own helplessness completely, and it is underscored by McCabe, who doesn't speak at this meeting but ponders the future the Company will bring: round-the-clock hours, prohibitions on hunting and prospecting, company dormitories, company houses, company stores for food and clothing and hardware, company scrip, company doctors, company permission required to leave town, company coffins — and, given what we know about Sheehan, he might have added company saloons.[21]

As noted, the film is much less precise than the novel with regard to the power of the mining company and the anticipated consequences of its takeover of Presbyterian church. Aside from the perspective we get from Sears and Hollander, and the anti-company interjections of both McCabe and Mrs. Miller (who in the film appears to have some previous knowledge of the Company's reputation and proclivities), we don't learn much. However, what both novel and film share is an understanding that the Company's intimidating power produces McCabe's isolation. That is, the Company motivates the plot and produces the film's dramatic conclusion. Indeed, the novel makes this explicit: "A silent agreement was made between McCabe and Presbyterian Church that anything that had to do with violence was for him to settle."[22]

The company's power, and the community's vulnerability and helplessness before it, are foregrounded in a striking scene that brings Butler and his fellow killers into Presbyterian Church. The scene opens with a representation of communal fellowship: a dancer jigs and shuffles to the tune of a fiddle on the glimmering ice of the water course beneath Sheehan's saloon, its windows warmly illuminating a dozen men watching and clapping from the porch and around the pond, a fire glowing in the foreground. Into this idyllic scene ride Butler and his associates. The camera's attention is on Butler, an enormous, burly man ("the sonofabitch must be seven feet tall"), and on his weapon, a huge, holstered rifle, and as his presence is noticed, the fiddle stops, the dancer stops, and the area empties, the community in fearful retreat. "The mining company," writes Robert Merrill, "is presented as the one truly evil presence in Presbyterian Church, the one reality no one can do anything about."[23]

How are we to understand those who find themselves confronted by extraordinary power, whether it is a total institution or the Company? Our vocabulary for that evaluation includes the words "victim," "survivor," and "hero," and the one we find most appropriate depends on the historical moment. *McCabe and Mrs. Miller*'s moment lay at the intersection of the 1960s, when the "victim" was in vogue, and the 1970s, when historical developments — Watergate, a severe recession, a defeat in Vietnam — favored the "survivor" or, as the decade wore on, the "hero." Watching the film, one naturally wants McCabe to succeed, to kill all three of the gunmen and to live to tell about it, and one can imagine understanding McCabe as a "hero" if he were to produce that unlikely result. Indeed, Altman tempts the viewer to buy into that scenario, as if the film were an inquiry into the possibilities of heroism, a staple of the Western genre. Although McCabe's "heroism" (his decision to fight the Company) is motivated by naïveté and a deep need for approval that distorts his priorities — hardly the qualities one expects from the hero — Altman puts him out there, testing our willingness to imagine McCabe as something he can't and shouldn't be.

Fantasies aside, this isn't a story about heroism. It isn't that McCabe isn't capable of being the last man standing; he is that, if only barely. But even if that were to happen, without McCabe dying in the process, the Company — all-powerful and unscrupulous — would still be there, and the community would again shrink in fear or sublimate its anxieties in irrelevant, frenetic activity, as it does in fighting the church fire at the end of the film. Although the last scene could be read as indicating Altman's preference for a community invested in opposing the Company, the only voice of resistance is the lawyer's, and it is highly ironized, lacking all credibility. "Know who the real villain is," he asks McCabe in the McKay/Altman script, "Not the Company — the people who let the Company roll over them."[24]

The Company is the future. Mrs. Miller knows that, and more than

The church in the town of Presbyterian Church burns near the end of *McCabe and Mrs. Miller*.

once she encourages McCabe to make a deal with the Company or, failing that, to leave town — that is, to take the position of the survivor. Mrs. Miller is a strong and realistic woman; her considered evaluation of the circumstances and available options is worthy of attention. And Mrs. Miller's position, as her end-of-film opium retreat suggests, is that of the survivor. It aligns her not only with the Chinese, who represent the epitome of powerlessness, but with withdrawal and resignation. "I'd rather be a Company whore," says Mrs. Miller in a line that didn't make the final cut, "than a dead Madame." That stance makes good sense with the Company on the scene, but that threat aside, it also represents the limited expectations of the average American as the sixties gave way to the seventies; for all her business savvy and combativeness, Mrs. Miller remains a woman of limited vision and ambition.[25]

The book ends differently from the film, with McCabe and the gunmen dead but Mrs. Miller outside with a shotgun, waiting to blow a hole in Sheehan, as if that act might define her own brand of survival as somehow different from his, her own burden of guilt in some way lesser. As McCabe describes Sheehan in the novel, "he had never been the man to

Warren Beatty as the entrepreneur McCabe *in McCabe and Mrs. Miller.*

take no kind of chance," and the film develops that characteristic, presenting the saloon keeper as the great pragmatist, the ultimate compromiser, a weak and valueless man who wants only to get by and keep living — the quintessential survivor. Tellingly, in the novel both these survivors apply the word "hero" to McCabe, and each does so with caustic irony. "He had to make himself a hero," says Mrs. Miller. And Sheehan adds: "The great hero. The big gunman."[26]

McCabe as survivor (imagine him abandoning Presbyterian Church, hidden under a tarp in Webster's wagon, as Mrs. Miller suggested) seems sensible and pragmatic and, above all, life-saving, yet that resolution of McCabe's dilemma is inconceivable; it would not only reduce the character to cowardice but deprive the film of the tension that drives the plot. McCabe as hero, as we have seen, is little more than a tease. Significantly, one possible outcome, that McCabe would die, but in defense of values and "principles" that include the "free enterprise" system, is identified with the Bearpaw lawyer, a character that lacks respect and credibility. Although the film is clear enough on this point, the McKay/Altman script is even more direct, reducing the lawyer to simplistic absurdities: "Everybody dies," he pontificates, "but you're going to die with dignity." The solution he proposes involves something akin to suicide. In his mid–1970s search for a better way of understanding concentration camp behavior, Des Pres suggests that the suicide solution — the foolhardy act that inevitably leads to death — is Bettelheim's solution — that is, a solution that emphasizes the abject powerlessness of concentration camp inmates.[27]

No, at bottom McCabe is neither survivor nor hero, but rather that familiar creature of the late 1950s and 1960s: the victim. By the mid– and late 1960s, it was commonplace to affix the label "victim" to society's unfortunate. Women were understood as victims of sexism and sex discrimination; students at the University of California at Berkeley as victims of impersonal, bureaucratic, education factories; the poor as victims of a "culture of poverty"; welfare recipients as victims of an impenetrable system that denied them the benefits they rightfully deserved; the elderly as victims of thoughtless neglect and age discrimination. By the late 1960s, it was common even to understand *criminals* as victims — victims of abuse, or poverty, or race, or ignorance. Although this analysis was weakening, when *McCabe and Mrs. Miller* appeared in 1971, it remained the dominant discourse for analyzing behavior, and it was momentarily fortified by the publication that year of two books, one a best seller, the other widely read.

The best seller was *Beyond Freedom and Dignity*, behavioral psychologist B.F. Skinner's classic of determinism. "In the traditional view," Skinner writes, "a person is free. He is autonomous in the sense that his behavior is uncaused. He can therefore be held responsible for what he does and justly punished if he offends. That view," Skinner concludes, "must be re-examined." For Skinner, environment is everything, and guilt — Mrs. Miller's or Sheehan's or McCabe's, or even Butler's guilt, or the Kid's, or the Company's — is beside the point. For Skinner, all the film's characters are simply victims (he would have used the word products) of their genetic and environmental endowments; they are outputs based on inputs, acting out their destinies.[28]

In typical 1960s fashion, William Ryan's cult classic *Blaming the Victim* assumes the existence of victims: victims of poverty, of racism, of ghetto housing and ghetto schools, of substandard health care. Nonetheless, Ryan argues, even the most socially progressive liberals engage in a subtle process of "blaming the victim," in which victims are believed to have qualities that explain their victimization. In this discourse, they are products of weak communities, of dysfunctional families, of rural, Southern backgrounds that ill prepare them for life in the big city, of a "culture of poverty." Hence even well-meaning progressives, while displaying deep concern for victims, engage in what Ryan labels an "evasion"; they come to believe that victims are "different." They are "less competent, less skilled, less knowing"; they "cling to different values, seek different goals, and learn different truths"; they haven't learned the "rules" or haven't learned how to "keep to them." In short, they "unwittingly ... cause their own troubles." The solution? To "change the victim."[29]

Ryan's duality—the acknowledged victim, the victim blamed—reveals *McCabe and Mrs. Miller* to be a meditation on 1960s liberalism. On the one hand, Altman positions McCabe as a victim of the Company, an institution so powerful and so indifferent to human life (akin to slavery, or to the German concentration camps) that abject concession to its demands seems the only reasonable position. But McCabe does not concede, and for that he is blamed, and blamed by none other than Mrs. Miller, the film's most thoughtful, most progressive (health and cleanliness are her causes), and most "liberal" character. It happens more than once. The first time occurs early in the film, before Sears and Hollander come to town, when Mrs. Miller, frustrated in her efforts to make her own deal with McCabe, anticipates his later failure with the Company: "I haven't got a lot of time to sit around and talk to a man who's too dumb to see a good proposition when it's put to him." The last time is in Mrs. Miller's room, immediately before Cowboy is gunned down on the bridge, foreshadowing McCabe's death. McCabe has returned from Bearpaw brim full of high ideals and personal concerns—"principles" and "reputation"—that Mrs. Miller finds inane: "What's Presbyterian Church to you?" she asks. "You just got to sell out!" Naughton is more direct: "It was his fault, she thought."[30]

Moreover, in not conceding, McCabe exhibits many of the traits of the blamed victim; in Ryan's terms, he is "less competent, less skilled, less knowing." He misunderstands the Company, studiously ignoring Sears's first greeting and later, Hollander's impatient earnestness. He confuses and irritates its representatives with tasteless jokes and an offer of prostitutes, and he misjudges their willingness to continue with the talks. By the same token, his confidence in the gambler's bluff remains unshakeable, even late in the game when Butler is in town to kill him, and when it ought to be clear that the Company's patience has been exhausted. Throughout the film, he exhibits a variety of character flaws—flaws, at least, when it comes to dealing with the Company or saving his life. He is vain and arrogant, vulnerable to the flattery of subordinates ("You handled them beautifully.

They knew they weren't dealing with no tinhorn") and the Bearpaw lawyer, who massages McCabe's ego to pump him full of insipid ideas about "justice" and trust-busting, "freedom" and "free enterprise," ideas irrelevant to the dilemma he faces and that he doesn't believe in or really understand. As a viewer, one cannot help but imagine that things might have been or would be different if McCabe had more common sense, or were less self-absorbed, or better understood power (and evil), or just didn't have too much to drink at the wrong time.[31]

In short, Altman invites us to blame the victim or, at least, to think about the problem of blaming the victim, perhaps to better understand how foolish that game is. Although nominally possessed of free will, McCabe's freedom, like that of *Revolutionary Road*'s Frank Wheeler, is illusory, circumscribed by McCabe's deficiencies or, better put, by his ineluctable self. Yes, McCabe fights back — Altman's tease, and Hollywood's requirement — but he does so against enormous odds, without realistic hope of success and, most important, without having freely chosen the course of resistance; in that, too, he is a victim of forces beyond his control: of his own bullheadedness, of his need to perform for Mrs. Miller and others, of his susceptibility to the silly ideas of a glib Bearpaw lawyer and, above all, of the Company. A character created in the late 1950s and brought into the 1960s, McCabe is some version of Bettelheim's concentration camp Jew, Elkins's slave, Freidan's suburban woman, Goffman's asylum inmate, each traumatized, each helpless (or nearly so) to deal effectively with a dominant institution or setting, each confronting a version of Arendt's "banality of evil." McCabe's nemesis is the Company, to which there is no satisfactory response. Too little space for genuine heroism, too much for an unappealing survival, and just enough to contain and diminish the actions of John McCabe, as he flails through this ultimate challenge as prototypical protagonist of the 1960s: the victim.

NOTES

My thanks to Robert Rosenstone and Rick Armstrong for their comments on earlier versions of this essay.

1. Robert T. Self, *Robert Altman's McCabe and Mrs. Miller* (Lawrence: University Press of Kansas, 2007), 46–90 (new western history), 118–26 (second-wave feminism), 76ff (captivity narrative), 119, 67–68 (masculinity), 140–41 (modernism), 101–109 (the counterculture); Ralph Brauer, "Who Are Those Guys? The Movie Western During the TV Era," *The Journal of Popular Film* 2 (Fall 1973): 389–404 (violence); Helene Keyssar, "The Unconquered: The Feminization of Altman's Films," *Robert Altman's America* (New York: Oxford University Press, 1991), 180 (community), 175–201 (feminism); Lillian Gerard, "Belles, Sirens, Sisters," *Film Library Quarterly* 5 (Winter 1971–72): 16 (feminism); Alan Karp, *The*

Films of Robert Altman (Metuchen, NJ: Scarecrow, 1981), 74 (western hero); Jack Nachbar, "Riding Shotgun: The Scattered Formula in Contemporary Western Movies," *The Film Journal* 2 (September 1973) (masculinity, the hero).

2. Self, *Robert Altman's McCabe and Mrs. Miller*, 76–90.

3. Edmund Naughton, *McCabe* (1959; New York: Berkley Medallion, 1960); William H. Whyte, Jr., *The Organization Man* (1956; Garden City, NY: Doubleday Anchor, 1957); Erving Goffman, *Asylums: Essays on the Social Situation of Mental Patients and Other Inmates* (Garden City, NY: Anchor, 1961); Bruno Bettelheim, *The Informed Heart: Autonomy in a Mass Age* (Glencoe, IL: Free, 1960); Stanley M. Elkins, *Slavery: A Problem in American Institutional and Intellectual Life* (Chicago: University of Chicago Press, 1959); Betty Friedan, *The Feminine Mystique* (1970; New York: W.W. Norton, 1963); Hannah Arendt, *Eichmann in Jerusalem: A Report on the Banality of Evil* (New York: Viking, 1963). I am indebted to Kirsten Fermaglich for her pioneering work in conceptualizing and contextualizing this literature. See Kirsten Fermaglich, *American Dreams and Nazi Nightmares: Early Holocaust Consciousness and Liberal America, 1957–1965* (Waltham, MA: Brandeis University Press, 2006).

4. Without interrogating the texts used in this essay, Robert T. Self arrives at a similar conclusion: "*McCabe and Mrs. Miller* ... depicts debilitated individuals living in constrained circumstances of powerlessness and subservience ... caught in irresistible systems...." Self, *Robert Altman's McCabe and Mrs. Miller*, 141–42.

5. Whyte, *Organization Man*, 13, 14 ("worship of it"), 3 (belonged to it), 4 (Lockheed), 10 ("new suburbia"), 437 ("people liked to think").

6. Goffman, *Asylums*, xiii ("total institutions"), 4 ("the barrier," barriers to departure), 5, 10 (logging camps), 70 ("crawl into").

7. Fermaglich, *American Dreams and Nazi Nightmares*.

8. Bettelheim and Elkins, quoted in Fermaglich, *American Dreams and Nazi Nightmares*, 22 ("autonomous individuals" [Bettelheim]), 26 ("helpless dependents"[Elkins]). Also Fermaglich, 60, 66 (on Friedan); Friedan, *Feminine Mystique*, 294 ("concentration camps").

9. Des Pres, *The Survivor*, v ("still human").

10. Arendt, quoted in Bethania Assy, "Eichmann, the Banality of Evil, and Thinking in Arendt's Thought," http://www.bu.edu/wcp/Papers/Cont/ContAssy.htm, accessed July 17, 2009, 1 ("neither demonic nor monstrous"), 2–3 (avoid doing wrong), 4 ("beginning to think").

11. On the larger controversy, see Thomas W. Ogletree, *The Death of God Controversy* (New York: Abingdon, 1966), and John Warwick Montgomery, *The 'Is God Dead?' Controversy: A Philosophical-Theological Critique of the Death of God Movement* (Grand Rapids, MI: Zondervan, 1966). McCabe's line is in "*THE PRESBYTERIAN CHURCH WAGER*," based on the novel *McCabe* by Edmund Naughton, screenplay by Brian McKay and Robert Altman (David Foster Productions, July 27, 1970), online at www.awesomefilm.com, accessed July 1, 2009, 73. Hereafter referred to as McKay/Altman Script. The *Time* cover is *Time* 87 (April 8, 1966); it also appears in the 1968 film *Rosemary's Baby*.

12. Not unexpectedly, of the more than 100 production stills in the *McCabe and Mrs. Miller* collection at the Margaret Herrick Library, none are of Sears or Hollander. The Warner Bros.' *Pressbook* makes it clear that the picture was marketed as the story of "a gambling man and a hustling woman." *Pressbook, McCabe and Mrs. Miller* collection, Academy of Motion Picture Arts and Sciences, Margaret Herrick Library, Los Angeles.

13. Soundtrack, *McCabe and Mrs. Miller*, VHS (1971; Burbank, CA: Warner Home Video, 1990) ["snipe hunt," "runs"]. In addition to the Soundtrack, I have consulted and cited "McCabe and Mrs. Miller Script — Dialogue Transcript," http://www.script-o-rama.com/movie_scripts/m/mccabe-and-mrs-miller-script.html, accessed July 1, 2009 (here, 49). Although this transcript contains errors and does not identify the speaker, it is useful for locating scenes and dialogue. Hereafter referred to as Transcribed Film Script.

14. Soundtrack, and Transcribed Film Script, 16 ("other saloons"), 27 ("proudly").

15. Soundtrack, and Transcribed Film Script, 17 ("partners"); McKay/Altman Script, 14 ("company towns"); Naughton, *McCabe*, 141 ("look out that window"), 43 ("awed by the company").

16. Upton Sinclair, *The Jungle* (New York: Doubleday, Page, 1906).

17. Naughton, *McCabe*, 16 ("Alone"). See also Self, *Robert Altman's McCabe and Mrs. Miller*, 143. Robert Kolker argues that "the cutting of the film and its crowded, fragmented spaces and sound create a sense of pervasive isolation in the midst of community." Robert A. Kolker, *A Cinema of Loneliness: Penn, Stone, Kubrick, Scorsese, Spielberg, Altman* (New York: Oxford University Press, 2000), 327–28, quoted in Self, *Robert Altman's McCabe and Mrs. Miller*, 159.

18. Soundtrack, and Transcribed Film Script, 34 (San Francisco), 54 ("around the fort"), 69 ("just sell out," "reputation," "principles").

19. McKay/Altman Script, 75 ("place to go"); Richard Yates, *Revolutionary Road* (1961; New York: Vintage, 2008), especially 62–63; Naughton, *McCabe*, 23 ("jokes"), 19 ("never left"); Transcribed Film Script, 34 ("you think small because you're afraid to think big"). On Yates's novel, see the rich discussion in Blake Bailey, *A Tragic Honesty: The Life and Work of Richard Yates* (New York: Picador, 2003), 229–34. Note also that Naughton's novel takes the form of a flashback, a staple of *film noir* and a device that emphasizes the inevitability of events and the impossibility of transcendence. See also Brauer's 1973 essay, "Who Are Those Guys": "McCabe's town gives way to the corporation town: to Homestead and Park Forest and Levittown" (124).

20. Naughton, *McCabe*, 33 ("take the mines," "all the courts," "kill everybody," "against it," "stand up"), 38 ("verdict").

21. Naughton, *McCabe*, 35–36.

22. Naughton, *McCabe*, 38 ("for him to settle").

23. Robert Merrill, "Altman's *McCabe and Mrs. Miller* as a Classic Western," *New Orleans Review* (Summer 1990): 82, 83 ("truly evil presence"). Writing in *Newsweek*, P.D.Z. linked the film's "message of corporate menace" with the anti-corporate campaigns of consumer advocate Ralph Nader. P.D.Z., "Virgin Wood," *Newsweek*, July 5, 1971, accessed in *McCabe and Mrs. Miller* Production File, Academy of Motion Picture Arts and Sciences, Margaret Herrick Library, Los Angeles.

24. McKay/Altman Script, 77.

25. McKay/Altman script, 95 ("Madame").

26. Naughton, *McCabe*, 86 ("no kind of chance"), 80 ("make himself a hero"), 84 ("big gunman"). The town shares this discourse of survival. The McKay/Altman script notes the signs that dot the town, reflecting the community's 1970s-level expectations: "Always Tomorrow," "Starvation Hole" (5).

27. McKay/Altman Script, 77; Transcribed Film Script, 65–69 ("free enterprise," "principles," the Bearpaw lawyer scene); Des Pres, *The Survivor*, 161 (Bettelheim).

28. B.F. Skinner, *Beyond Freedom and Dignity* (New York: Alfred A. Knopf, 1971), 19, 160 ("traditional view").

29. William Ryan, *Blaming the Victim* (1971; New York: Vintage, 1972), 5 ("culture of poverty"), 9 ("evasion," "less knowing"), 10 ("learn different truths"), 13 ("keep to them"), 5 ("own troubles"), 8 ("change the victim"). On the idea of the victim in the 1970s, see Alyson M. Cole, *The Cult of True Victimhood: From the War on Welfare to the War on Terror* (Stanford, CA: Stanford University Press, 2007).

30. Soundtrack, and Transcribed Film Script, 23 ("too dumb"), 69 ("got to sell out"); Naughton, *McCabe*, 80 ("his fault").

31. Soundtrack, and Transcribed Film Script, 48 (bluff), 50 ("no tinhorn"), 65–67 ("free enterprise").

5

Brewster McCloud and the Limits of the Historical Imagination

Marcos Soares

"We have gone through a long, dark night of the American spirit.
But now that night is ending. Now we must let our spirits soar
again. Now we are ready for the lift of a driving dream."
— Richard Nixon, campaign speech, 1971.

"The rules of the global economy are like the laws of gravity. They
are not American rules."
— Bill Clinton to Boris Yeltsin, Moscow, 1998.

Coming after the enormous (and unexpected) critical and box office
success of *M*A*S*H, Brewster McCloud* (1970) represented a daring move
on the part of director Robert Altman. The very peculiar context in which
it was made would never quite repeat itself in Altman's future career, but
remained a model which in many ways he would always try to approximate.
The increasing difficulties involved in the attempt had to do, of course,
with the fact that neither the social nor the cinematographic revolution
for which the country seemed to be ready at the beginning of the '70s
went beyond very narrow limits, if compared with the ambitions of the
previous decade. But here I may be advancing myself and formulating
what may be the central theme of *Brewster McCloud*: the dreams of freedom
of the period and their historical limits.

The exceptional conditions that characterized the production methods
of the industry in the second half of the 1960s have been amply discussed

by the specialized literature, which went to great lengths to create myths around the alleged creative freedom that marked the "Hollywood renaissance." To once more advance myself, *Brewster McCloud* is, among many other things, a film about the "lost illusions" of the era, which promised an unheard-of level of freedom to its young directors, whose rebellious work saved the industry from the worst crisis of its long history.[1] Most accounts of the period begin with the "fact" that the generation which had been born in the post-war period and that now came of age, already weary of the "classical language" of the traditional studio system endlessly reproduced and trivialized by television productions, demanded a cinema more in consonance with the rebellious spirit of the era. This may, of course, be true, but it is also true that the industry itself likes to emphasize how the all-powerful viewer is able to determine what it produces. So, while huge conglomerates were taking over the studios in 1970, *Life* magazine triumphantly announced in its cover story:

> Involved youth, raised in a crisis society and educated by saturation communication, had become 75% of the moviegoing public. They wanted relevant movies reflecting reality as *they* saw it, and they got them: a rash of "small films" like *Easy Rider*, made on location for peanuts.[2]

Such accounts, which emphasize the power of the audience to direct the course the industry takes, usually avoid questions of ownership (corporate and state domination). On the other hand, the rebelliousness of the audience was itself already under the scrutiny of the more demanding minds of the period, mainly in relation to the perspectives of the student movement: was it determined by its (petit bourgeois) social origins or did it represent a peculiar social function, with more radical interests? The difficulty involved in moving beyond this ambiguity, both from a practical and a theoretical perspective, divided the cinematographic production of the period into two broad, but recognizably diverse, fields: on the one hand, the various celebrations (often nostalgic) of the glories of the 1960s, when "everything was still possible"; on the other, the public confessions (often abject) of the failures and missed opportunities that characterized the decade.[3] The originality of *Brewster McCloud*, as I will try to demonstrate, resides in its avoidance of both errors.

One of the greatest screenwriters of the "golden age" of Hollywood, Ben Hecht, had summarized the general attitude of the period towards the aging studio system in his 1953 memoirs, when he stated that "one basic plot only has appeared daily in their fifteen thousand theaters: [...]

that there are no problems of labor, politics, domestic life or sexual abnormality but can be solved happily by a simple Christian phrase or a fine American motto."[4] The target of the new generation of filmmakers will be precisely the incredible spectacle of social anachronism that characterized the American 1950s: in practically every area of social life, the richest and most modern country in the world was trying to overcome the embarrassing conservatism that marked a great part of the ideology of the previous decade. Thus, the new films — "contemptuous of mediocrity, conformity and 1950s-style groupthink"[5] — gave American society an image that was more in tune with the spirit of the new era.

The rest of the story is well-known: the model of young European auteurs such as Truffaut (the confessed idol of many of the aspiring American directors), Godard, Fellini and Antonioni, among others, who had demonstrated that the new audiences were ready for new levels of daring formal experimentation and political radicalism, fueled the imagination of the young generation, who went on to form its own peculiar standards of international taste, giving rise to a revolution at the center of the most powerful cultural industry in the world. For many of the budding American auteurs of the era, the confluence between the new "art cinema" and the industrial apparatus did not seem to produce discomfort or contradiction: after all, as a whole generation of European cinephiles liked to insist, it was the models of American auteurs (Nicholas Ray, Howard Hawks, and others) working under the pressures of an industrial system that had inspired the European revolution.

Thus, the American "new wave" produced two immediate effects that rekindled the market and saved the industry from ruin: on the one hand, it sounded the death knell for the traditional studio system, placing the responsibility and a large part of the creative decisions (as well as the risk of financial losses) on the shoulders of the new independent producers and directors, who sniffed the "new tendencies," sold their ideas to investors interested in enlarging their field of interest and looked for the support of the marketing, distribution and exhibition departments of the major studios. On the other hand, in the more properly aesthetic field, the new films created innovative forms of great visual exuberance and introduced themes of interest, which would have been largely frowned upon by the more conservative audiences of the previous age. The graphic violence and the thematic novelty of the "film-manifesto" of the new age, *Bonnie and Clyde* (1967), indeed created what Rick Perlstein called a truly "public symposium over the meaning of the present."[6] In hindsight, the films of the "Hollywood renaissance" constituted a vision of the "period," identifying and helping to create common styles, ways of thinking and behaviors which, retrospectively, we have learned to identify with "the 1960s." Though the production of the period was diverse and cannot be summarized by a reduced number of categories, one can detect in some of its best films the attempt to take up aspects of the best political art of the 1930s, interrupted by post-war affluence and political conservatism, either by emphasizing the "elective affinities" between past and present moments of radicalism (e.g., the Great Depression in *Bonnie and Clyde*) or by building daring analogies between supposedly different areas of social life (e.g., the confluence between the culture industry [radio, television, cinema], the counter-culture [the happenings], militarism [the soldiers on the bus to NYC] and real estate speculation [the squatters] in *Midnight Cowboy* [1969]).

But what to say of the "formal borrowings" that these films made of the most advanced European cinema of the era? The question has been addressed by a number of critical works, many of which privilege the vision of the new directors as true American auteurs who were able to enrich the language of the traditional studio system and create landmark films in which they expressed a highly personal vision *despite* the pressures of the industrial apparatus.[7] According to this account, the new directors were in touch with the radical production of the modern European auteurs and were able to "trick" conservative producers into allowing them to create critical visions of the process of filmmaking and of society as a whole. There is a great deal of truth in this account, and indeed it may help to explain the unparalleled quality of this *generation* of American artists, even though the emphasis on the figure of the auteur may quickly slip into visions of individual grandeur (the themes of *Brewster McCloud* keep on intruding themselves) which mask the collective nature of film work (the fact that a whole new generation of filmmakers were able to make radical films must surely mean that they could count on a vast network of (mostly) progressive technicians, actors, and other workers who made it possible for the "auteurs" to express themselves). These narratives often emphasize the (real or imaginary) willingness of the auteurs to go back to some sort of golden age, sometimes a pre-technological past, when the "true art of film" was untainted by the new industrial interests. On the other hand, this vision of individual talent working against the odds finds a parallel in the focus that most of the new films place on questions of individual agency.

Indeed, this may be a good moment to remind ourselves that many of the new directors retained an emphasis on "special individuals" (though not necessarily of heroic stature) typical of the industrial models perpetrated in Hollywood. In Europe, in the aftermath of 1968, political radicalism and the related attempt to interpret their characters' values within the context of the whole society led a number of European directors to confront more directly what critic Peter Szondi calls the "dramatic model" and its emphasis on individual action[8] (one may think of Godard's move from *À Bout de Souffle* [*Breathless,* 1960] to, say, *La chinoise* [1967] or the difference between Fellini's *La Strada* [1954] and *Roma* [1972]).[9] Seen from this slightly different perspective, the new techniques borrowed by the new auteurs can be understood as moments of "formal sophistication" employed (sometimes) cosmetically in films that obey, despite localized transgressions, the demands of the character-based construction of the plot (one immediately remembers some of the emblematic sequences filmed in the period such as the great shooting scenes at the end of *Bonnie and Clyde* and at the beginning of *The Wild Bunch* or the car chase sequence in *The French Connection*). Such embellishments, or localized demonstrations of technical virtuosity, are not necessarily exempt from relevant historical information and analysis (e.g., the innovative use of the subjective camera in the swimming pool scene in *The Graduate* as an image of the claustrophobia of the family setting), while their capacity to subvert the rules of the "well-made story" is more debatable,[10] as the contrast with practically any of Altman's films and their multiple narrative strands clearly shows.

As for *Brewster McCloud,* an analysis of the original screenplay by writer Doran William Cannon[11] will suffice to show its affinities with the script of films such as *The Graduate* and how Altman's approach (the final shooting script is markedly different from Cannon's work) represents a major breakthrough in the work of the "American renaissance." *The Graduate* cannot be said to be strictly linear in terms of narrative structure due to its innovative use of montage, which builds an elliptical, episodic storyline. However, each individual "episode" clearly contributes to the development of the main protagonist, whose struggles make up the whole of the film so that the final result stands somewhere between an allegorical thrust (Benjamin as a representative of a whole generation) and the very specific concerns of one individual character. Something of the same order happens in the original screenplay for *Brewster McCloud*: the episodes that follow each other keep the main character as the center of the narrative, including samples of "psychological analysis" (a flashback in which Brewster is bullied by his classmates). As I hope to demonstrate, Altman's approach entails a multiplication of (socially relevant) themes which far exceed the demands of the well-made screenplay and its emphasis on the development of well-defined individuals. In this sense, Brewster's progression throughout the narrative may be more properly seen as an "excuse" (something akin to the Hitchcockian "MacGuffin") for other types of contents to emerge.

The (sometimes awkward) combination of the more traditional (industrial) demands (focus on well-defined individuals, frequently played by big stars) with the selective use of the conquests of the vanguard (the use of elliptical montage, expressionist devices, etc.) does not restrict itself to this period. Back in the 1940s Bertolt Brecht liked to say that the industrial procedures (in his case, embodied by the producers of the UFA studios) tended to break down the repertoire of demanding artists into autonomous components, use some parts, often disfigured and transformed into their opposite, and eliminate others, transforming the political views of their authors into "eccentricities."[12] Something of the same order can be said to have taken place in the 1970s as the industry slowly came out of its crisis. Although this process was not indigenous to the United States, it reached here its advanced industrial formulations, which transformed the conquests of the "Hollywood renaissance" into a profitable business. For individual filmmakers the contradictions are complex and often impossible to avoid: is it possible to be radical in the "interstices of the system," or are the limits and pressures insurmountable? Is one working to subvert the system or to renovate it and give it new strength? The truth probably lies somewhere in between the two extremes, with artists testing the limits of the culture industry while the industrial apparatus is ever ready to use new talent as a laboratory of new forms which can be marketed with the label "radical" attached to them as a selling point.[13] In an essay analyzing a similar indigenous cultural phenomenon taking place roughly at the same period in Brazil (the rise of a radical musical movement known as "tropicalismo"), Brazilian critic Roberto Schwarz attempted to generalize his findings: he claims that all too often the cultural vanguard of the Western world, whose main concern was the dismissal of capitalism (but not necessarily the dynamics of revolutionary action) saw the rebel ideology of the period helping to solve the problems of capitalism by selling marketable symbols of the revolution which were readily and triumphantly welcome by the industry and the audiences in general. In a similar vein, American essayist Thomas Frank has written an important book where he analyses the ways in which the new visual forms of the counterculture of the 1960s were employed profitably by the advertising industry.[14]

What we witness in the period, in fact, is the construction of a new "international taste" (combining diverse national film traditions under the ever watchful eyes of the Hollywood producers), whose rules were strengthened by the expansion of the American film market in the period, reinforced by Nixon's tax policies which supported the industry. Internal tax cuts (the famous "Schrieber Plan") and the end of the gold standard (and the consequent devaluation of the dollar, which made foreign currency more valuable, nearly doubled the influx of American films into the international market and produced a paper gain of about $34 million a year in overseas film and television sales) greatly strengthened the connections between the film industry and international financial capital.[15] The "new quality" demanded from the new films, which had to cater to the tastes (and investments) of an incredibly large worldwide audience, may be said to have opened the way for the abstractions of postmodernism (the blend of high art and popular culture, the mix of genres and traditions, the idea of a new international space without a center, etc.). One of the first important post-modern American auteurs, director Brian De Palma, is a fitting example, with his combination of the conventions of the thriller with celebratory quotations from the great auteurs of the past (especially Hitchcock, but also Eisenstein), minus a great part of the critical edge that had characterized the "American renaissance." The "sophisticated" visual style that marked many of the films of the period is one of the central critical targets of *Brewster McCloud*. However, to cut a long story short, the rise of the blockbuster era with the films by George Lucas and Steven Spielberg put an end to the more radical hopes of the period and signaled the end of the career of many a talented director.[16]

But at the beginning of the 1970s things seemed to be looking up for Altman: the success of *M*A*S*H* (the third box office success of the year, behind the, say, more conventional *Love Story* and *Airport*) gave him some money as well as credibility in the industry, which allowed him to create his own production company (Lion's Gate) and to hire the actors, producers and technicians that had best adapted themselves to his peculiar working methods in the previous film. Temporarily freed from the pressures of the "star system" (most of the actors in the new film were either relatively unknown or non-professional), Altman made an attempt to create the conditions for real "ensemble work" in the place of the "false collective" of the culture industry (where each professional does his/her own part). In retrospect, even the best of Altman's subsequent films serve as re-elaborations if not as planned regressions of themes first developed in *Brewster*

McCloud. The rise of the New Right, the economic crisis and the very complicated ideological climate of the country, all framed by a strong anti-intellectual atmosphere, worsened the conditions of production and reception of his films, far beyond what the sinister beginnings of the decade promised.

This evaluation of the importance of *Brewster McCloud* may seem a tall order for a film replete with every type of zany and even idiotic moments, silly bird-shit jokes, banal chase sequences and other comic clichés. Robert Kolker, for one, commenting on the film's "demented assemblage" claims it is "a film of adolescent shenanigans and excremental humor that Altman continues to stumble into, in *O.C. and Stiggs*, and again in *Prêt-à-Porter*."[17] Indeed, much of the film seems to flirt with a cheeky and adolescent "bad taste," if not with the "banality" normally associated with slapstick. Nevertheless, the accumulation of crazy moments that constitute the adventures of the "main character" is compressed between an enigmatic prologue and epilogue, which seem to deviate from the tone of the film, perplexing viewers and critics. Altman's own evaluation of the film only increases the confusion: he often declared that from his more than 40 films, *Brewster McCloud* was his most cherished work, though the statement can be seen as an eccentricity or a joke. However, as Altman's jokes were always very serious, one might as well take the clue seriously.

What I have called the prologue of the film covers the sequence that starts with an image of MGM's lion and ends with the camera zooming in to reveal the news about Vice-President Spiro T. Agnew ("Agnew: Society should discard some US people"). It builds an arch that covers the presentation of the initial credits, juxtaposing a number of places and groups of characters, linked each time by sound bridges that suggest relationships between them. The opening with the MGM lion-logo is an appropriate emblem for a film about domestication and imprisonment, while the dubbed voice that replaces the lion's roar ("I forgot the opening lines"), introduces a parodic approach that persists throughout the film. But does the insubordination gesticulate within or outside the limits of the industrial paradigms? In other words, is the gesture radical or part of the clichés of the industry, which, after all, has frequently encouraged some level of (well-behaved) self-criticism?[18] The initial few seconds already indicate the limits of an industrial cinema as opposed to the virtual freedom of the auteur film, whose development in the United States the directors of the "Hollywood renaissance" had proposed. However, at this moment the rebellious gesture runs the risk of vanishing into a mere adolescent joke, an example of a naive humor devoid of ambition, the irony of which disappears at the very moment of its formulation. Thus, the problem that insinuates itself right at the outset suggests an impasse that demands our scrutiny.

In what follows, the lecture of the professor (René Auberjonois) presents the theme that "we will deal with [...] for the next hour or so." Although the tone is clearly satirical — the parody is reinforced by the skeleton of the large bird that shakes its head approvingly while the professor speaks — it is with a mix of perplexity and interest that the audience listens to the professor, whose ridiculous figure does not invalidate the importance of the question proposed or of the diagnosis offered. The change from a long to a medium shot indicates the reinforced attention of the camera which, like a good and well-behaved student, comes closer to be able to hear better. The terms used in this rather peculiar class zero in on two key questions: initially, the attempt to establish the similarities between human beings and birds and then to better understand the reasons for man's dream of flying (the "isolation of the dream"): is the dream to attain the ability to fly or is the dream the freedom that true flight seems to offer? After that, the professor goes on to ask himself about the future consequences of man's destructive intervention in nature and about the doubtful solidarity he would show towards the birds in the case of a natural catastrophe. In this second part, the voice is superimposed over the images in long shot of Houston in the background, while a pan shot reveals the Astrodome, the "cage" where most of the action of the film will take place. The relative isolation of the Astrodome from the urban conglomerate of Houston, which is separated from the former by a green stretch of trees and vegetation (which, in its turn, barely manages to distract us from the urban pollution that hovers above the city) does not manage to invoke the usual ideas of isolation or refuge from the city: the immense expanse of concrete that encircle the Astrodome suggest, on the contrary, a continuity, in a world in which sports and physical activities have themselves become part of show business[19] and where "real nature" has been entirely colonized by new forms of urban planning. In this way, the abstractions of the professor's lecture about mankind and nature are placed historically in the midst of the ugliness and monotony that characterize the vast majority of large cities worldwide, creating some sort of dissonance between the images and the eloquence of the professor's statements, which include references to European high art (the "German poet Goethe").

But the prologue does not stop here. In what follows, the camera focuses on the ceiling of the Astrodome, panning slowly down, without any cuts, to reveal a rehearsal: a woman on the stage sings "Star Spangled Banner," in a counter-illustration of the beauty of the singing of birds. Her unbearably strident voice, which does not miss a single chance of getting a note wrong, is accompanied by a band of black musicians, who play slowly and mechanically, while a group of women are frozen in a step of the choreography that will embellish the presentation. Meanwhile, we see part of the initial credits, which divide the screen with the singer, positioned on the left of the frame, while the credits appear slightly dislocated, on the center-right. The singer (we will soon learn she is the "socialite Daphne Heap," played by *The Wizard of Oz* actress Margaret Hamilton) interrupts the rehearsal, walks angrily in the direction of the musicians and complains that they are out of tune. In the tones of the enraged lion of the beginning, she reminds the musicians that she bought their uniforms and is paying their salaries. She then makes two demands: the improvement of the playing and the use of the electronic panel, which is supposed to be on while she sings. But to whom is this last demand directed? Surely not to the musicians, who have little say in the general organization of the spectacle. As one of the cameras places itself in the midst of the musicians during the singer's verbal attack, observing the owner of the show from below, we are led to see in this convergence of points of view the insinuation that she is telling both musicians and the director off, while the latter aligns himself with the victims of the onslaught. The continuation of the sequence seems to confirm this hypothesis, for not only do the musicians resume their work, with no noticeable improvements, but the director also remakes the presentation of the initial credits, this time placed right in the center of the screen. In making this "correction," the film mimics the "technical perfection" demanded by the industry, which frequently wastes its money and the energy of creative workers in the improvement of details of this type, creating a fetishistic relationship with techniques (or shall we say, following Brecht, the "tricks" of the trade?) used mechanically to follow "norms of perfection" that have been emptied out by its repeated and formulaic use.

This tension between the submission to the rules of the culture industry and the attempt to expose its internal logic and mechanisms critically is constitutive of the most progressive art of our era and is central to an understanding of Altman's work. Initially disconnected, the three sequences (the image of the lion, the sequence of the professor and of the singer) build a narrative that asks the audience to sketch in their minds what they have in common, demanding a high degree of awareness of the persistence of central themes and forms as well as the need to transform them into formal principles that begin to establish themselves here. Let us say, while we do not go any further, that these initial sequences both adhere and expose the industrial forms that have become nearly universalized (or shall we say "naturalized"?) at this stage of the history of the industry.

But what saves the film from a reduction of its anarchic impulse into a mere "textual gesture" is the contrast that marks the continuation of the sequence: the opposition between the collective mutiny of the black musicians, who refuse to resume the torture session to which they were being submitted and Brewster's individual initiatives: our "hero" (Bud Cort) appears for the first time, observing the events *through the television set* while he develops his own plans of freedom. This contrast, suggestive of a more general order, will help to explain Brewster's defeat: his obvious sympathy for the victims of an order that he also abhors falls behind his actual capacity of analysis and ability to act. It is at this moment that we also see the "fallen angel" (Sally Kellerman), that observes the musicians' mutiny from a distance, framed by two gigantic Texaco logos. If, however, the news about Agnew's plans of "social cleansing" on the floor of Brewster's hide-out remains invisible to both, the same is not true for Altman's camera, which zooms in to reveal it, reinforcing the alliance between the film and the spectators, who have access to certain levels of meaning which remain outside the field of vision of the characters.

But let us go back to the beginning: in the first sequence it is the professor who establishes the narrative point of view of the film. As the deranged fable that follows is full of names of birds in improbable places (such as car plates), can we infer that Brewster's adventures are part of the lecturer's class, sharing with the former an obsession with the universe of the birds? Would the "fallen angel" that will help Brewster in his mythological ventures be a degraded version of Goethe's Mephistopheles? Could we also conclude that the gradual transformation of the professor into a bird is a compensatory strategy that makes up for Brewster's failure?

The emphasis of the professor's comments on the natural processes that will serve as mottos for many of the episodes of the film should not distract us from the essential: the release from prison, the dream, the conquest, the attempt to dominate nature: the chosen terms describe human practices, specific relationships between human beings. The fluidity between the description of natural processes and historically determined practices is confirmed at each step, when, for instance, the motto used to comment on Mr. Wright's behavior refers to "social hierarchies" and to a "definite order of social distinction" that characterizes the relationships between birds, or when Daphne Heap scares away a crow which she callously calls a "nigger bird." Here, as in the rest of the film, there is a convergence between the vocabulary used to describe natural phenomena and social conflicts. We still need to determine what direction the relationship will take as the film unfolds: will the natural sciences be understood historically, or will the human situations be naturalized?

But the professor, far from insisting on a rigid separation between the natural and social spheres, passionately emphasizes the comparison and its power of revelation and, indeed, many of the comparisons strike us as "correct": Mr. Wright's greed, Daphne Heap's racism, Frank Shaft's vanity are all illuminated by the comments. As the film advances, these comments reappear sporadically, establishing a comparison between the birds and a great variety of social types, whose weight in the narrative varies considerably. There follows the sequence of events showing Brewster's escape from the Astrodome guard, the events in the camera store, Louise's protective actions, the conflict with the corrupt cop in the zoo, the murders of obnoxious enemies, among other events. Each time the comments help to create a high degree of fragmentation, typical of certain kinds of comedy in which the vertical interruption of the gag predominates over the horizontal organization of the plot: as the suspense is not very serious and the "hero" not exactly prone to create identification with the audience, it is not the identity of the murderer or his methods that engage the viewer, but the parade of the ridiculous behaviors of the characters, whose exposition far exceeds the demands of the central plotline.

Although the endless digressions and the resulting narrative dispersion — coupled with the flagrant disrespect for the rules of realism (which frequently verges on the absurd, as when the stolen film is transformed into shampoo bottles) — may suggest that the central narrative structures resemble those of the dream-work, part of the iconography and narrative organization of *Brewster McCloud* may be closer to the homogenizing aesthetics of television (though, as I will argue, this is done for parodic purposes). I think Raymond Williams was one of the first critics to insist that mainstream television should not be seen merely as a collection of individual programs, but in terms of *flux* (the ultimate post-modern text), where the mingling of different genres, rhythms, heroes, villains, secondary characters and advertisements levels all those elements down to some sort of massive undifferentiation, a repetition of pre-packaged clichés and com-modities whose indistinct fluxes preclude special emphasis.[20] *Brewster McCloud*'s peculiar, episodic and apparently random blend of adventure, comic sketches, love scenes and endless car chases may indeed be seen as a parody of the chaotic flux of television which Altman knew from personal experience.[21]

In *Brewster McCloud* Altman takes the parodic use of the blend of genres to its extremes: differently from the language of television (with its multiple cinematic derivatives) and its establishment of general equiva-lences, the film's prologue, which encourages the audience to establish homologies between disparate elements, already signals the progressive role the spectator is called upon to perform. To go back to the metaphors of nature used throughout the film, there is nothing "natural" in the language of television. Again it was Raymond Williams who warned his readers against what he called "technological determinism" (or Darwinism applied to the study of the modern media) so common in the field of media studies: against the teleological narratives that posit that more advanced technolo-gies "naturally" supersede older ones. With the flux of television program-ming embodying mimetically the "rhythms of modern life," Williams insisted that specific uses of technology are socially directed.[22] Even the individual type of reception (remember Brewster's watching the musician's mutiny on TV) to which television seems so "naturally" to adapt itself, with its ever smaller sets, can be said to respond to a social logic of frag-mentation and social anomie: after all, there is nothing *in the technology* that necessarily requires individuals to watch television on their own.

As for the persistence of "natural" elements, the images of the film show a world where there are not natural and untouched areas left: the Houston we see is made of large expanses of concrete that have little to do with the poetic, scientific or philosophical reveries of the professor and the only areas of "natural beauty" that we glimpse are the fanatically man-icured gardens in Daphne Heap's private property (where the socialite and her scissors build a parody of the innocent rural world of *The Wizard of Oz*), the small squares and lawns that break the unbearable monotony of the driveways, the intensely commodified green areas in the service sectors (the zoo and the cemetery) and, finally, the amusement park, where "nature" is transformed into a motif used in the boat ride through the Dis-neyfied version of the "jungles of the Third World" (at that moment being heavily bombarded by the American troops in Vietnam).

At each step the contradictions between the world of nature and the human forms of sociability become more complex. On the one hand, the inutility of the efforts of man to imitate the wisdom of nature seem obvious and Brewster's final defeat has an apocalyptic tone, not distinct from the various versions of the end of the world popular at the beginning of the 1970s (until those "theories" found a more "practical" function in the call for the return of order that marked the rise of the New Right).[23] In fact, *Brewster McCloud* shows a world where the developments usually associated with the 1960s seem to have gone unnoticed: the emergence of the new collective "identities" and "subjects of history" that marked the decade are sadly ignored: at best we see some of the "typical" behaviors of the period being turned into "styles," as in the hippie party thrown by Haskell Weeks (William Windom). The most progressive aspects related to the Civil Rights movement and the struggle of feminism appear inverted: the social division is brutal, with blacks occupying clearly inferior roles (apart from the sequence of the musicians, the rage of the black driver provides other moments of social comment), while the situation of the widow (Angelin Johnson) who marries Hines (Corey Fischer) shows a woman who moves quickly from a violent and unhappy marriage to another that could lead to similar situations. The success of the strategies of neutralization of the progressive aspects of the 1960s is best demonstrated by Suzanne (Shelley Duval) and her former boyfriend Bernard (William Baldwin), the first to embrace the new political possibilities of the period by having a hair cut, assuming a more "respectable" demeanor and finding a job as an assistant of a politician involved in the traffic of influences. At the same time, Suzanne persists in the adoption of certain behaviors which are closer to the rebellious ideologies of the era — in the extravagant clothes and make-up, in the flagrant disrespect for private property (she steals a car) and for religion (the statue of the Virgin Mary is fashionable), in the heady confrontations against law and order and in sexual promiscuity — but channels her energy and "creativity" into the function of guide to the Astrodome, a second-rate job by the standards of the culture industry and the show business. Her ambitions are best revealed, of course, by her plans to create patents for Brewster's wings.

The forced "pacification" and the systematic erasure of so many of the conquests of the 1960s were part of a larger and more varied frame of changes with a view to the "re-establishment of order" whose political side is not absent from the film: the newspaper on the floor of Brewster's laboratory refers to Agnew's defense of policies of social Darwinism whose effects we witness until today (the dismantling of the Welfare State, which in the conservative version of the period helped "bums and lazy people" to survive at the expense of the public money). In fact, the taxpayer's money had more "important" uses in the period, mainly in Texas, where the local oligarchy, heavily subsided by the State, took over some of the most important political decisions in the country (but also the "cultural" life in Houston: according to Suzanne, the Astrodome is the "only place you can go that far underground in Texas and not strike oil").[24]

But the film also shows a more "attractive" type of selection: the murders committed by Brewster and his "bird assistant." It is not without some pleasure that we watch obnoxious types such as Mr. Wright, Daphne Heap, the corrupt policeman (Bert Remsen) and Billy Joe, the owner of the car driven by Suzanne, being eliminated. Yet, despite the obvious imbecility of these people, they represent more or less harmless types, at least from the perspective of Brewster's plans. Mr. Wright's bad humor, Daphne Heap's awful singing (already dealt with successfully by the black musicians), the police officer's threats (not taken seriously by his colleagues, who knew he was "a bad cop") and Billy Joe's aggressive behavior (ridiculed by the Porky Pig T-shirt) justify our pleasure in watching each one of them being summarily executed, but in themselves create little sympathy towards Brewster, whose status depends on our evaluation of his aims. Going back to the question asked in the prologue: what is the "nature of the dream" and what is the real mechanism that justifies his actions?

In the comparison between man and nature that the professor proposes, it is Brewster that stands out as he deliberately studies and imitates birds, even if Houston is hardly the most appropriate place for the development of mythological narratives. His project may be the product of a lunatic's delirious mind, but it is somewhat touching for the ascetic purity it demands (including the denial of the corporeal and of sexuality) in a world where there are few ideals left (as the professor reminds us at the beginning). The commitment with which he devotes himself to the realization of his dream regulates every aspect of his existence, and even his job as a chauffeur functions only as a strategy to get hold of a precious book which will reveal the secret of an ancient dream, realized a thousand times in man's imagination.

In fact, a great part of Brewster's appeal has to do with the fact that they point to another old dream, that of a type of labor that demands creativity, imagination, intelligence and involvement, that is, non-alienated labor. One needs only compare the images of Brewster's efforts with literally every other image of people working (the musicians, the black driver, the guides, the policemen, etc.) to see the difference. One needs only remember another phenomenon of the period, the proliferation of a number of theories of "scientific management," in another example of the combination between "science" and society, to understand the utopian resonances that Brewster's activities conjure up.[25]

But where can he fly to? Or, to put it in another way, what sort of solution can one expect from Brewster's plans? Hegel liked to remind his readers that the concept of "individual freedom" was a fallacy: freedom must be universal in order not to see itself degraded into privilege. Surely something of this order is at stake here and in this sense Brewster's plans resemble the dreams of the celebrity (ridiculed in the figure of Frank Shaft), whose ideological limit consists of an individual solution that overcomes the unbearable banality from which one wants to escape, while keeping intact the same conditions that created the problem in the first place.[26]

But Brewster's plans also point to another problematic solution: the reversal to a simpler, more "hands-on" approach to labor, which goes back to the origins of human history (the old book) to restore some supposedly more organic order destroyed by the new forms of technology. This (regressive) return to handicraft and other "more human" types of labor are invoked again and again in newer artistic practices and theories, which see in the new technologies an evil that must be ignored or destroyed.[27] Against all the efforts to define and defend the "specificity" of the more traditional forms of artistic expression, Brecht had already explained the regressive side of the struggle against the new means of production. His main statement on this question is worth quoting at length:

> Those who advise us against using these new apparatuses concede to them the right to work badly and out of sheer objectivity forget themselves, for they accept that only dirt is produced for them. Yet from the outset they deprive us of the apparatuses that we need in order to produce, because more and more this kind of producing will supersede the present one. We will be forced to speak through increasingly complex media, to express what we have to say with increasingly inadequate means. The old forms of transmission are not unaffected by the newly emerging ones nor do they survive alongside them. The film viewer reads stories differently. But the storywriter views films too. The technological advance in literary production is irreversible. The use of technological instruments compels even the novelist who makes no use of them to wish that he could do what the instruments can, to include what they show (or could show) as part of the reality that constitutes his subject matter, but above all to lend to his own attitude towards writing the character of using instruments.[28]

Seen from this perspective, *Brewster McCloud* may be read as a statement against the adoption of anti-modern tendencies of so many ideologies of art and the artist as a solution for the problems created by the "modern" approach of the "Hollywood renaissance." (Incidentally, Altman films Brewster's dream — the sequence in which he dozes in the bathtub and "flies" — with a camera obviously attached to a plane, a solution Brewster would clearly frown upon. As for the hippie version of the same myths, the inclusion of Suzanne and Bernard makes Altman's view perfectly clear).

Brewster's individual attempt to provide a solution for the generalized imbecility of the world may be moving, but its lack of a collective basis which could lead to its realization gives his dream a complacent and megalomaniac nature, whose true limits become evident when he postpones the attempt in order to conquer more "concrete" aims, which turn out to be contrary to the initial intentions (the alliance with social-climber Suzanne). As a diagnosis of the many "failed dreams" that characterized the sixties (and so many efforts of the left, which often abandoned its radicalism to enjoy more "feasible" possibilities), there is no other more devastating portrait in the American culture produced in the period.

But as I observed at the beginning, the narrative point of view does not restrict itself to the perspective of the professor, but activates it in order to expose it critically. The duplicity of the narrative focus indicated previously reveals another active formal structure at work, one that begins with the professor's generalizations to move beyond them. In fact, the images of the film always show some sort of "excess" in relation to the comments that function as the "theme" of each part. Indeed, many of the professor's comments are correct and even his final diagnosis (the futility of the imitation) is wise: with such short-sighted dreams, conjured up within a ceiling that radically reduces their vision, there is little chance of real freedom. If, on the one hand, the comments generalize the nature of the events, on the other, it is undeniable that they reveal some truth: this is a world that sold its dreams for peanuts and there is great power of revelation in the "bad taste" of the film, which reigns supreme in real life.

But the mere exposition of the catastrophe, however useful, can lead to the same despondency and hopelessness expressed by the professor at the end of the film. Let us say, maybe prematurely, that the modernist sensibilities of *Brewster McCloud*, Altman's attempt to make the familiar new through the adoption of a distancing approach, turns the film into a veritable exercise in cognition. For a demonstration of how the modes of composition of the film presuppose a cognizant viewer, let us go back to the detailed analysis of the film where we left it: the end of the "prologue." The first chapter of the professor's lessons shows Mr. Wright as an illustration of the social hierarchies that regulate the life of every flock of birds. The following sequences will show McCloud working as a chauffeur, taking the millionaire in his round of visits to the retirement homes he owns. At each stop, he ruthlessly mistreats his employees, while he collects the monthly rent. The tour is accompanied by various connecting elements between the scenes, notably the voice of the radio, which tells the viewer/listener about the sequence of murders that had occurred recently in Houston and the arrival of San Francisco "super cop" Frank Shaft. This narrative voice summarizes the elements that constitute the universe of the typical detective film and ironically introduces a large part of the information that makes up the original screenplay (with slight modifications). This source of information, whose center is the typical plot formation in its industrial formulation (the radio — or rather, this particular use of the radio — as an extension of the demands of the culture industry), and which the spectator is not encouraged to take seriously, is superimposed on a series of images (the visits) that contribute very little (if at all) to the suspense that a traditional detective story would demand.

Here the emphasis falls on the constant humiliations suffered by McCloud and on the repetitive and mechanical nature of his job, an aspect reinforced by the editing, that strengthens the feeling of reiteration by juxtaposing short scenes linked by quick cuts. Apart from the emphasis on the alienated nature of Brewster's work (which will give weight to his plans of escape), the sequences also point to another theme previously introduced by the newspaper on the floor: the theme of social Darwinism, already at an advance stage of development here. The film shows that the "survival of the (un)fittest" is only of interest if it can generate money for people such as the owners of the homes for the elderly, although the former have sometimes to deal with "unfortunate inconveniences," such as delays in payment (here the guilty part is a "client" who died before the end of the week without paying the rent). The thesis is contemporary and highly explosive: poverty is no longer seen as a "failure of the system," but as an integral part of the social systems of multiplication of capital. On the other hand, Brewster's action and Mr. Wright's punishment do little, if anything, to alter the structural order of things: individual actions (as opposed to the collective actions of the black musicians) have, at best, short-term results. Finally, Mr. Wright's punishment is commented on by a song which we hear as his wheelchair runs down a busy street.

This integration between scene and commentary is greatly amplified in the next part, when detective Frank Shaft arrives in town. This part starts with a series of comments: first the statements made by the professor (about the vanity of peacocks), then the voice of the radio (of a non-diegetic type) which glorifies the professional abilities of the California police. Meanwhile, the camera, in flagrant disrespect for the aural information introduced by the comments, contradicts the radio by zooming in on the combinations of colors that constitute Shaft's main worry (his shoes, belts, bags, and sweaters). Besides, the details of the décor also work as comments on the scene: the peacock at the head of the bed, the over-elaborate frames of the mirror and, later, the flowery wallpaper that frames Shaft's face, everything lets us in on the narcissistic and kitsch personality of the detective. Following the sequence, it is Johnson (John Schuck), the detective's assistant, who will function as a narrator: he tells the details of Daphne Heap's murder, which had already been summarized by the radio news and that we see for the first time in flashback. Moreover, it is not only Johnson's voice that will link the hotel room and the scene of the crime, but also the background music ("Over the Rainbow" from *The Wizard of Oz*), which reminds the audience of the presence of actress Margaret Hamilton, while the zoom in on the dead woman's shoes suggests a relationship between her and the detective, whose concern with his shoe colors we had witnessed only moments before. These procedures taken together — the juxtaposition of scenes and various narrators and commentaries — produce relationships that far exceed the demands of the constitution of the plot but which nonetheless demand our attention. In contrast to the norms of the culture industry, according to which diverse levels of the constitution of the scene (music, acting, dialogue, and décor) must produce redundancy (different means of expression saying the same thing), here the semi-autonomy of the various procedures employed define a formal principle that will be central in the disruption of the industrial Hollywood plot.

To this complex web of narrative voices, whose main function, it is worth repeating, is not the constitution of a well-made plot or storyline, we must add another formal principle that will become a hallmark of Altman's style: the presence of internal observers within the scene. In the sequence of the visit to the elderly homes, the unfriendly behaviors of Mr. Wright are cut by shots of the elderly, but also Altman himself, who appears reflected in the window of the car among the victims of the millionaire's abuses during the first visit. In another sequence, no effort whatsoever is made to hide the real life observers who watch the filming of Mr. Wright's ride on his wheelchair. These internal points of view produce a multiplicity of contents that are not external to the film: if the visits are looked at from the point of view of the elderly, it is the social disaster produced by social Darwinism (its human cost) that stands out; if seen from the millionaire's perspective, it is the winners' version of history that will surface. Each time *it is the language of social conflicts that determines the internal structure of the scene.*

These internal observers will find their peers throughout the film: the tourists in the Astrodome and in the amusement park, the reporters and curious bystanders at the zoo, the guests at the burial of the corrupt police-man and, of course, the spectators at the Astrodome. In each case, they constitute a crowd of spectators that remain passive, unable to react or intervene in the course of the observed events. But the process that vic-timizes the observers also destroys the life of what is observed. For Frank Shaft, who behaves like a star, the presence of an audience is virtually ubiquitous and constitutes the center of his existence: he only exists to be seen. It was Guy Debord who shrewdly observed that the star "passing into the spectacle as a model for identification, [...] renounces all autonomous qualities in order to identify himself with the general law of obedience to the course of things."[29] Alienated labor, seen from its most glorious perspective (that of the star) shows its dehumanizing face.

Therefore, we can see *Brewster McCloud* as an analysis of the one point of view that tries to impose itself universally in the cultural scene: the point of view of show business. And since we are dealing with a film about flying, it is worth remembering that one of the earliest theoretical formulations about cinema involved the attempt to praise its "bodiless eye."[30] But within the "internal" history of film theory it is possible to map out a gradual change from some of the earliest formulations — the new medium and its capacity to adopt and confront many points of view, the ease with which it could tell many stories at the same time — to the "naturalization" of one type of film, which became the model for industrial production: the film in which the "bodiless eye" was able to adopt only the "best" points of view in order to tell a story, without "unnecessary deviations." It is against this limit of the medium, this ceiling that threatens to reduce the scope of what film can show, that Altman's cinema will rebel.

But *Brewster McCloud* suggests that this rebellion should not aim at the "refinement" of the taste of the audience: as Brecht liked to say, "The public's public taste will not be changed by better films but only by chang-ing its circumstances."[31] The productive side of "bad taste," therefore, lies not in its embellishment, for it is in bad taste that reality resides: the horror of social life that spies from behind the mask can only be disguised by thicker layers of illusion. The use of the slow motion and the addition of music in the chase sequence in which the cars "fly" hardly cover the banality of the scene. But it is in the gesture of pointing to its own mask that resides the strength of *Brewster McCloud*, where "bad taste" appears without disguise so that the film can proceed to its de-naturalization through the intelligence of the spectator.

In the 1970s the industrial production in Hollywood would create and market a number of narratives of "naturalization," the main one being the "scientific" study of the popular taste aided by the transformation of marketing departments into the nervous system of the production process (for the first time in the history of the industry the capital involved in the research, marketing and publicity of films exceeded the costs of production).[32] As one of the most successful strategies used to bypass the financial crisis was the pre-selling of exhibition rights to television networks, the statistical study of "what people want to see" became a central concern. But as everyone that follows the struggle of television channels for the attention of audiences knows, the industry cannot predict everything and frequently makes mistakes. The advantage of the culture industry does not lie in its ability to predict what people want to see, but simply in the fact that it has more capital and can run risks and (sometimes) cover the losses.

The end of *Brewster McCloud* shows the victory of show business. But also shows the cost in human lives, which decreases a large part of the glories of victory. If the final sequence is a quotation of Fellini's *8½*, one might as well point out the differences. Fellini's silent circus showed a director that made every effort to submit a number of artists and workers to the tyranny of his personal memories, whose violence the film maps out. In Altman's film, the violence of the spectacle counts upon a cheery and large audience that transforms, to take up Debord's extraordinary formulation, the spectacle into the language of unification between the eye and the conscience. But the final battles have not yet been fought and Altman's films count on (and try to create) another kind of spectator.

NOTES

1. According to David Cook, between 1969 and 1971 the losses of the industry totaled approximately $600 million. In 1970, again according to data provided by Cook, 40 percent of all Hollywood directors were unemployed. See David Cook, *Lost Illusions* (New York:

Scribner, 2000), 3. Mark Harris, on the other hand, points out: "In the early 1960s, the American studio film had bottomed out: even many of its own manufacturers and purveyors felt they had dragged the medium to a creative low point in the sound era." See Mark Harris, *Pictures at a Revolution: Five Movies and the Birth of the New Hollywood* (New York: Penguin, 2008), 9.

2. Quoted by Toby Miller, et al., *Global Hollywood 2* (London: British Film Institute, 2005), 5.

3. Fredric Jameson, "Periodizing the Sixties" in *The Ideologies of Theory* (London and New York: Verso, 2008).

4. Quoted by Rick Perlstein in *Nixonland* (New York: Scribner, 2008), 208–9.

5. Harris, 11.

6. Perlstein, 210.

7. Orson Welles remains, of course, the uncontested model of such narratives, as can be attested by recent publications such as Clinton Heylin's suggestively titled *Despite the System: Orson Welles and the Hollywood Studios* (Chicago: Chicago Review, 2005).

8. See Peter Szondi, *Theory of the Modern Drama* (Chicago: University of Minnesota, 1987).

9. As a matter of fact, even Godard's *Breathless* cannot be said to focus on well-defined individuals. Its gangster-hero, a concoction of quotations from American gangster and noir movies, is not really a "character" in the usual (psychological) sense of the word, but rather a narrative device that Godard employed to discuss the modernization (or Americanization) of postwar France. Likewise, Fellini's *Casanova* focuses less on the development of the character's motives and more on the "decadence" of ancient Rome as an allegory of the "radicalism" of the 1960s.

10. Geoff King makes a similar point in Geoff King, *New Hollywood Cinema: An Introduction* (New York: Columbia University Press, 2002).

11. Published in C. Kirk McClelland, *On Making a Movie: Brewster McCloud* (New York: New American Library, 1971).

12. See Bertolt Brecht, "The *Threepenny* Lawsuit," in Marc Silberman, ed., *Bertolt Brecht on Film and Radio* (London: Methuen, 2000), 178.

13. Of course, so-called radical films can be politically conservative, whereas supposedly conservative films can provide a much richer map of important ideological problems.

14. See Roberto Schwarz, "Cultura e política, 1964–69" in *O Pai de Família* (Sao Paulo: Paz e Terra, 1978), and Thomas Frank, *The Conquest of the Cool* (Chicago and London: University of Chicago Press, 1997).

15. Cook, 516.

16. See Ryan Gilbey, *It Don't Worry Me: Nashville, Jaws, Star Wars and Beyond* (London: Faber and Faber, 2003); Peter Biskind, *Easy Riders, Raging Bulls* (New York: Touchstone, 2003), and Jean-Baptiste Thoret, *Le Cinema Américain des Années 70* (Paris: Editions Cahiers du Cinema, 2009).

17. Robert Kolker, *A Cinema of Loneliness* (New York: Oxford University Press, 2000), 339.

18. Just to illustrate my point, in the 1970s directors such as Mel Brooks built a career on relatively harmless parodies of a number of Hollywood conventions.

19. Some of the great British working-class essayists of the first half of the twentieth century argued that the practices of certain sports were typical working-class events in which new types of sociability, based on a competition that included feelings of camaraderie and differed markedly from a more properly capitalist competition, could be enjoyed. See, for instance, Richard Hoggart, *The Uses of Literacy* (New York: Pelican, 1981), and George Orwell, *Essays* (New York: Everyman's Library, 2002). Clearly, such utopian components of the practice of sports seem to be wholly absent from the universe of Brewster McCloud. They occasionally resurface in recent films such as Ken Loach's *Looking for Eric* (2008). John Sayles' brilliant *Eight Men Out* (1988) uses the working class ethos of baseball to illus-

trate the ways in which "residual" types of solidarity and communal sociability are destroyed by the incorporation of baseball by finance capital.

20. Raymond Williams, *Television and Cultural Form* (London: Wesleyan University Press, 1992).

21. Films such as *Star Wars*, with its mixture of pop-existentialism (the battle between Good and Evil) and its "omnibus generic text" (western, comedy, science fiction and love story) can be said to constitute a counterpoint to *Brewster McCloud*'s parodic use of the blend of genres typical in the period.

22. Raymond Williams, "Culture and Technology" in *The Politics of Modernism* (London and New York: Verso, 1994).

23. For an analysis of the various narratives about the impending end of the world in this period, see Perlstein, *Nixonland*, 541–544.

24. According to Mike Davis, the Vietnam War indirectly led to various improvements in California, Washington, Florida and Texas, as the military industry sponsored the growth of electronic and other industrial complexes in those states. This, added to the presence of oil in Texas, turned it into one of the most important states in the country and transformed its elite into the most influential from a political perspective. More for detailed information see Mike Davis, *Prisoners of the American Dream: Politics and Economy in the History of the U.S. Working Class* (New York and London: Verso, 1999).

25. The classic book on this subject is, of course, Harry Braverman's *Labor and Monopoly Capital* (New York: Monthly Review, 1988), written only a few years (1974) after *Brewster McCloud* was made.

26. According to Hegel, the sublation that produces a "solution" for the dichotomies of the initial situation while keeping the constitutive elements of the dichotomy intact is a "negative sublation [Aufhebung]." See G. Hegel, *Phänomenologie des Geites* (Berlin: Nabu, 2010).

27. I think Heidegger was one of the first modern defenders of what he called "spiritual handicraft," a concept that combined his taste for the archaic with the defense of the national-socialist cultural and educational program. See especially his *Introduction to Metaphysics* (New Haven: Yale University Press, 2000).

28. Brecht, 161.

29. Guy Debord, *La Société du Spectacle* (Paris: Gallimard, 1972), 56.

30. See, for example, Vsevolod Pudovkin, "On Editing" in Gerald Mast, Marshall Cohen and Leo Braudy, eds., *Film Theory and Criticism* (New York and Oxford: Oxford University Press, 1992).

31. Brecht, 168.

32. Miller, et al., 1–49.

6

Brewster McCloud's '60s Hangover

Rick Armstrong

In *Robert Altman's America* Helene Keyssar asserts, "Altman's films are profoundly historical, but that is less a matter of their competence in capturing particular times and places in American history than it is of their focus on the kinds of decisions that shape an American identity."[1] Altman made some films set in times different from his own: *Thieves Like Us* (1974) takes place during the Great Depression; *McCabe and Mrs. Miller* (1971) is a western; and *Gosford Park* (2001) is a thirties costume drama set at a British manor house. While these films show Altman working in different time periods, Keyssar's comment can be truly applied to films that Altman made about his own time in which he depicts a variety of people's compulsions, obsessions and personal pathologies. Given his mosaic style in which a variety of characters' lives randomly intersect like atoms in an unstructured universe, Altman offers a sizable canvas on which he depicts the behaviors of a large group of people, revealing the collective impulses of many Americans at a given time in history.

When Altman made his films, they were not historical films per se; he was just revealing what he saw around him. However, seen from a distance of thirty to forty years, his films take on the patina of historical documentation. A viewer far removed historically from a mosaic style film such as *Nashville* (1975) can get a sense of Americans' values and concerns on a writ large scale in the mid-seventies. Robert Kolker asserts, "Altman's best work is an ongoing process of representing a cultural and political milieu he sees as ridiculous at best, barren and cruel at worst."[2]

Robert T. Self points out that Altman's work is deeply embedded in the tradition of the international art film as opposed to the classical Hollywood approach to filmmaking. Self asserts that Altman's art films "appropriate the modernist force of the art cinema to convey in inventive form the radical complexities of the modern world."[3] Using the definition of modernist literature, Self explains that one aspect of the "modernist force" concerns the awareness of the tragedies that history brings. For the literary modernists of the twenties, a key subject was the alienation of the individual from society, others and the self, especially after the carnage of World War I.[4] Regarding this sense of alienation, Self asserts, "Between a modernist point of alienation and the postmodern celebration of being lost in the funhouse, these films locate marginal characters working stoically and ineffectively to succeed in a world beyond their knowledge of comprehension."[5]

Self argues that the alienation of social outsiders constitutes Altman's form of cinematic modernism, locating that modernism in a particularly historical perspective. He builds on Keyssar's conception of Altman as a historian of his time. Altman made his first theatrical film *The Delinquents* in 1957. As a low budget movie about teenage gangs, *The Delinquents* has its own value for examining fifties paranoia. However, Self's insight really applies to Altman's seventies films, depicting characters living with the results of the social and political changes brought by the sixties. In films such as *M*A*S*H* (1970), *Brewster McCloud*, *The Long Goodbye* (1973), and *Nashville* among others, Altman depicts the two influences brought by the sixties. As Self says, Altman showed the "lost in the funhouse"[6] (to quote postmodern novelist John Barth) element of characters wandering freely, pursuing their own inclinations in an America that was absurd, chaotic, and conspiratorial.

Self hints that Altman uses absurd comedy to communicate the postmodern sense of play in a nation that was losing its bearings amid assassinations, political corruption and economic stagnation. While Altman's films entertain by revealing the patent silliness in seventies America, they also reveal alienated characters lacking a cultural, philosophical or institutional perspective to guide them. The doctors in *M*A*S*H* rely on male hedonism to cushion the horrors of war and Brewster McCloud counts on the dubious goal of flying away from human greed and venality. In *The Long Goodbye*, Philip Marlowe is left with his own code of ethics after learning that his friend Terry Lennox is a liar, adulterer, and murderer and the various characters in *Nashville* pursue empty dreams of fame, power and sexual gratification.

For the purpose of this study, I will investigate the historical signifi-
cance of *Brewster McCloud*. The film was shot from May to July 1970 and
released later that same year which means it was completed after Altman's
fame skyrocketed due to the critical and commercial success of *M*A*S*H*.
The conflicts of the sixties were still alive as the film was being made.
Protests against the Vietnam War were still occurring, leading to the Kent
State killings in May of 1970 as *Brewster McCloud* was in pre-production.
And Richard Nixon, a symbol of the fifties and sixties establishment, was
president. Robert Kolker was the first to see the historical themes in *Brewster McCloud*, asserting that the film "examines some of the contradictions
in the 'youth rebellion' of the late sixties — its inherent aimlessness and
dependence on the existing social-political order." He further highlights
the complex nature of the film, stating that Altman reveals "the stupidity
of the prevailing order"[7] while showing the difficulty of overcoming that
order. However, Kolker dismisses the film's historical importance as irrelevant due to its aesthetic shortcomings.

Kolker is not the only critic to dismiss the value of the film. Noted
Altman backer Pauline Kael, fresh off her enthusiastic praise of *M*A*S*H*,
derides the film as an example of "schoolboy humor." She sees some meaningful potential in the film's ideas and stylistic innovation, "It's disconnected in a way that could be explained as social comment or as a new free
style, but I don't think it is either."[8] Similarly, Vincent Canby writing in
The New York Times calls the film "dim and pretentious" lacking in wit.[9]
Perhaps Canby and Kael were too focused on the moment to see either the
social significance of the film or its narrative innovation. Kael does not
value the film's fragmented narrative; however, such a style has been emu-
lated many times since the film's release. She considers the social relevance
of the film, but dismisses its importance immediately given its elusive plot.
Kolker has some historical distance, writing in the early nineteen eighties,
and thus sees more of the film's thematic relevance to the sixties. Still, his
dismissal of the film's artistic virtues limits his ability to perceive the historical relevance of the film.

A discussion of *Brewster McCloud*'s history lesson necessitates an
explanation of the methodology involved in using a narrative feature film
as a historical artifact. Much has been written on the idea of film as a historical document, mostly focusing on films that are overtly historical, such
as films about the Vietnam War or the Holocaust. However, there has
been a small subset of scholars who value films about their own time as
sources for historical investigation into the values, ideologies, and beliefs

of a certain period. This form of investigation is less popular than discussing films about the past in terms of their historical value. However, it is a vital field with much debate in it. John E. O'Connor was an early proponent of using film in historical research. He wrote about historical films; however, he also saw movies as a useful source in understanding a particular time. In 1979 he and Martin A. Jackson (who started the journal *Film & History*) edited a book entitled *American History/American Film* in which various historians (including O'Connor and Jackson) analyze various films in connection to their historical contexts. In their introduction O'Connor and Jackson assert that a film "documents American social history and captures the state of mind of the American people at the time it was released for popular distribution."[10]

O'Connor and Jackson contrast newsreels to what they call "the entertainment film" which is valuable because such a film indicates some of the ideas or emotions that interested and moved people as opposed to merely documenting the events of the time. Such films are not merely documentations of the past, but offer what an audience would have consciously turned to for personal engagement and heightened visual experience.[11] When analyzing a film in relation to its historical context, O'Connor and Jackson point out that the scholar must consider the film's "surface content and its deeper implied meanings." Also, the scholar must examine the film "in relation to the specific conditions which led to its production," for example the director's style or the film's financial limitations. The scholar must also understand "the broader social and political context from which it took shape…, and the audience for which it was intended" whether it is a broad commercial audience or a smaller niche market.[12] *Brewster McCloud* was produced by MGM for a general audience. It followed on the success of *M*A*S*H* which led its makers to expect a box office triumph. As actor Michael Murphy recalls, "I thought 'It can't miss.' Bob was flying and there was much enthusiasm. Of course, nobody came to see it. It was a flop. Floperama."[13]

Despite the high expectations for the film, it failed to find a mass audience which does not deter from its importance as a historical document. Although O'Connor and Jackson's points are valuable, Robert Sklar reveals the way some of their categories are problematic especially for a film like *Brewster McCloud* which was not financially successful in its time. He asks, "How is popular acceptance judged?" and continues, "Raw data on box office receipts, attendance, or viewing cannot tell us whether spectators accepted, agreed with or even paid attention to what the media works communicated." Sklar uses this concern to pose the larger question of how to know if a film or television show is worth studying as a historical document. He asserts, that "what seems commonsensical and straightforward based on our intuitions and perceptions, becomes problematic when subjected to scholarly inquiry." He concludes, "In delineating our field of study, we must not only construct a method, but also articulate the theories that are the bases of a method."[14]

Sklar proceeds to present three theories that have influenced the use of film as a historical document: the psychological, the aesthetic, and the ideological/cultural paradigms. The first involves using films of a certain time period in order to understand a particular nation's mindset at a particular time. This approach was largely influenced by Siegfried Kracauer's book *From Caligari to Hitler: A Psychological Study of German Film* (1947) in which Kracauer argued that the roots of Nazism could be found in the German films of the twenties. This argument was disputed by many critics and filmmakers including Fritz Lang whose films Kracauer examines. Also, Sklar points out that Kracauer's American followers "were careful to avoid his metaphysical language and his claims to the "'retrodictive' power of film analysis."[15] The second paradigm comes out of the European auteur theory which posits the director as the "author" of the film through the use of distinctive camera work and sound effects.

The aesthetic paradigm extends the auteur theory by asserting that a film represents the director's distinctive analysis of his society. Sklar points out that the films "were to be read as statements to, or interpretations of, a culture and it was not necessary to connect them to the collective mentality of their spectators or the economic circumstances of their production or reception."[16] The aesthetic paradigm builds on O'Connor and Jackson's concept of the entertainment film. Given that they are looking at a film as a historical and social artifact, they did not consider it as an art form in which the director is reflecting on his society in a particularly unique way. Marxist analysis informs the third approach, viewing film as a form of what Louis Althusser claims is an "Ideological State Apparatus" like the church or the schools which serve to reinforce state power by reproducing the prevailing industrial conditions in people's consciousness, thus distracting them from the conditions of their existence.[17] Hollywood could be considered one of these apparatuses.

Sklar acknowledges that certain debates occurred within Marxist thought concerning the power of the Ideological State Apparatuses. Althusser argues that individuals become subjects of the state, produced by the ideology of the dominant institutions. However, Sklar mentions Raymond Williams who believes there are certain ideas that can "somewhat stand outside the domain of the hegemonic — some of these he calls emergent, pertaining to innovative practices." Sklar further points out that in his analysis Williams returns to the auteur theory, given his focus on artists' ability to examine their culture. While Sklar acknowledges that Williams' theory is more elaborate, he argues that his viewpoint does not differ very much from the aesthetic paradigm.[18]

All three of these perspectives will be useful in analyzing *Brewster McCloud* in relation to sixties discourse. While the psychological approach can overestimate the connections between films and the social developments of a certain era as Kracauer did, the general idea of certain films as representative of certain social conditions is the foundation of film as historical study. *Brewster McCloud* was filmed at the end of the sixties with a chaotic and absurd cinematic style that parallels the irreverence of the counterculture. Moreover, the plot about an eccentric young man operating outside of social boundaries exemplifies the preoccupation with youthful rebellion that characterized much of the sixties. Given these connections, a historical reading of the film is appropriate. The aesthetic paradigm is also valid because Altman was part of the sixties and seventies Hollywood "new wave" that redefined mainstream American filmmaking. Robin Wood points to "the centrality of Altman's work to the development of the modern American cinema." He continues by stating that Altman's films exemplify the main themes of modern filmmaking two of which include "the growing sense of disorientation and confusion of values, with the consequent sapping of any possibilities for affirmation."[19] Wood takes issue with Altman's films; however, his statement shows that Altman was a filmmaker very much embedded in his time both cinematically and philosophically, thus indicating the historical relevance of Altman's films.

Williams' idea of a group of artists carving out a space outside of the ideological state apparatuses works here given that Altman was part of the Hollywood new wave along with Martin Scorsese, Arthur Penn, and Francis Coppola though he was much older than the majority of that group. In *Brewster McCloud* Altman is investigating the impact of the nineteen sixties on American life in a comic way which leads the film to be complicated ideologically. While Altman clearly parodies establishment figures, the counterculture is both seriously considered and mocked.

The nineteen sixties has been one of the more debated times in recent American history. People of different political persuasions try to define the

Bud Cort as title character Brewster McCloud at work on his project of flying.

decade to fit their political perspective. These differing interpretations have existed since the decade itself. Writing in 1970, the same year that *Brewster McCloud* was filmed and released, Charles A. Reich offered an extremely optimistic viewpoint of the counterculture, heralding "a new conscious-ness" that rejects the sterile concept of linear thought that supports a stifling status quo.[20] Reich's insights find some parallels in Altman's film. Writing a year earlier, Theodore Roszak also sees the repressive elements in Amer-ican society that drove the counterculture. However, he offers a more skep-tical take on the youth movements of the time, pointing out that the counterculture represents a preoccupation with "childlike enchantment." He points to the hippies' fascination with the hobbit world created in the novels of J.R.R. Tolkien.[21] The character of Brewster (Bud Cort) parallels this point, existing in a childlike state and watched over by a guardian angel figure, Louise (Sally Kellerman), who chastely bathes him and sings him lullabies while both are naked, existing in an Edenic state, reflecting the film's fairytale qualities. He is a young naïf, building his wings and focused on his mythical goal of flying away from the tawdry materialism of American culture, a fantasy of escape shared by many in the counter-culture.

Over the years the battle to define the sixties has raged on as time passes and the era recedes from historical view. In the late nineteen eighties former political radicals Peter Collier and David Horowitz published *The Destructive Generation* in which they portray the political dissent of the era as irresponsible and reckless. Collier and Horowitz assert, "It was a time when innocence quickly became cynical, when American mischief fermented into American mayhem." They continue, "While we wanted a revolution, we didn't have a plan. The decade ended with a big bang that made society into a collection of splinter groups ... whose only common belief was that America was guilty and untrustworthy."[22] These types of criticisms appear indirectly in *Brewster McCloud* long before the neo-conservative criticism offered by Collier and Horowitz. Strikingly, these ideas coexist in the film with similarly anti-establishment satire.

In the film Brewster attempts to enact the revolutionary idea of humans flying as he spends his days in the fallout shelter of the Houston Astrodome, building his personal wings and exercising so he will be strong enough to fly. Brewster is a young man who wears large owlish glasses and oversized striped polo shirts which indicates that he eschews the sixties youth focus on fashion. In his celebration of youth values, Charles Reich argues that clothing was a crucial part of counterculture values.[23] Similarly, Alice Echols describes the essential role clothing played in the hippie life of Haight-Ashbury: "Beautiful people dressed to underscore their freaki-ness.... Being beautiful was more than copping a look, though; it was an attitude, a stance, a vibration. Weirdness mattered, and so did a mellow vibe."[24] Given these descriptions, Brewster is simultaneously emblematic of and uniquely unlike sixties youth. Brewster's look is more absent minded professor than beautiful hippie and he lacks the type of self-awareness that the hippies possessed. He is more immersed in his project of flying rather than engaged in striking a "a beautiful" pose.

Brewster is a good place to start in analyzing the sixties themes in the film. While his dream of escape parallels the anti-establishment direction of the time's youth movement, Brewster's goal is not political or utopian; he envisions no new community of shared values. Altman's film is a com-plicated historical document because it is not a realistic take on contem-porary conditions. The film is a fusion of different elements: fantasy, slapstick comedy, detective story, and Greek tragedy. Altman uses a variety of cinematic approaches to evoke these elements: zooms, close-ups, jagged

Brewster (Bud Cort) dumps the rapacious Abraham Wright (Stacy Keach).

edits. Michael Murphy who plays Frank Shaft, a parody of Frank Bullit, says, "It was one of those movies where it just got wilder by the minute. I mean I haven't seen the movie in many, many years, but I don't know if anybody has a clue what any of it is about. I don't remember if it was drug induced or what."[25] The drug reference invokes the chemical exploration of the time while capturing the unpredictable, playful, psychedelic aspect of the film which shows Altman using the visual style of the counterculture in portraying a wide range of ideas about the conditions of youth culture. In casting Bud Cort, Altman told him, "'You're going to play a mass murderer and its going to be a whole reaction to how sick society is right now.'"[26] Altman indicates that he saw the film as a commentary on current social conditions; however, he never clarified in what part of society he saw the sickness which muddies his overall point about the decade, leading the film to undermine both the establishment and hippie perspectives.

While Brewster is a young man engaged in a visionary program, he stands outside of society, living in the Astrodome, only interacting with the world outside of his own when he needs something. The film begins with him working as a chauffeur for Abraham Wright, the third Wright brother, indicating the film's theme of flight. Wright is an infirm octogenarian whom McCloud must drive and push in a wheelchair. He gropes young women while feverishly collecting cash from the retirement homes he owns. Brewster initially tolerates Wright's verbal and physical abuse that includes calling McCloud "a fag" and others "a dirty pinko." Wright exemplifies the corrupt and rapacious establishment given his use of reactionary insults of the time and his wearing an American flag pin, a prophetic view of the ersatz patriotism of the early twenty-first century. Wright's caricatured portrayal and his subsequent murder by McCloud — speeding down a street in his wheel chair covered in bird droppings — would indicate that Altman's sympathies lie with the revolutionary spirit of the time. However, McCloud remains emotionless in his dealings with Wright and the murder occurs more due to Wright's threatening of Brewster as opposed to any stated social justice aims. Also, Wright is a cartoon figure as are many of the establishment people in the film. His rapaciousness is so caricatured as to hardly be taken seriously. Caricature is based on empirical behavior and Wright's depravity and death indicate Altman's contempt for petty greed. However, the way he presents Wright's death does not equate to the sixties type of revolutionary perspective. Brewster is not enacting social justice by killing Wright; in fact he stands by as Wright fleeces poor retirees of their money and fondles young women. Only when Wright threatens to fire McCloud, the latter kills him.

While those who are killed throughout the film are hypocritical establishment figures, their primary sin within the narrative of the film equates to attempting to stop Brewster from his single minded focus on flying. Brewster simultaneously represents and contradicts late sixties youth experience due to his marginal social position, somewhat dropping out and following his own dreams as the hippies wanted; still he is socially detached from others. He never engages in large scale civil disobedience activities, preferring a solitary non-conformity which Charles Reich maintained in 1970 was an aspect of youthful rebellion.[27] Still, Brewster does not practice the activism of the sixties.

Like the hippies, Brewster believes in experimentation and not conforming to mainstream society given his illegally living in the Astrodome's fallout shelter. One of the film's recurring jokes is Brewster being chased by a rotund white security guard whom he constantly eludes in returning to his hidden residence. Altman enacts the sixties youth's evasion of authority as a type of zany slapstick, turning a defiance of authority into a type of cartoon, undermining the counterculture's sense of importance. Members of the counterculture used ironic humor as a way to communicate their ideas, creating their own wacky events to make their points about the corruption of the American system. The Yippie (Youth International Party) was famous for stunts such as dropping dollar bills on the floor of the New York Stock Exchange. The Yippies tried to fuse the counterculture's emphasis on lifestyle with the New Left's direction of radical politics.

Alice Echols quotes Yippies Abbie Hoffman and Jerry Rubin as agitating for "'a blending of pot and politics ... a crossfertilizaton of the hippie and New Left philosophies.'"[28] Reich argues that the counterculture's goal was to create a politics out of a non-conformist lifestyle, using Bob Dylan's artistic independence as a model for this type of sensibility.[29] Writing in 2008, Gerard De Groot echoes Reich when he states, "The Yippies would believe that the Establishment would crumble under the weight of nonconformity."[30] The Yippies hoped that the general public would follow their example of disregarding the status quo. Brewster too could function as such a role model given his own eccentric behavior though rather than crushing the establishment, he just wanted to leave it and all of society behind, anticipating the seventies, a decade in which many withdrew to their own interests. While the Yippies' stunts were witty and transgressive, such acts do not necessarily mobilize people to a particular program and could be seen as adolescent pranks. This point parallels Pauline Kael's criticism of the film's "schoolboy humor" which is valid. However, Kael missed the film's reflection on the infantile behavior of the Yippies. Unsurprisingly the Yippies failed in their revolution, as represented by Abbie Hoffman's suicide in the eighties, partly due to his irrelevance, and by Jerry Rubin becoming a businessman.

This emphasis on an irreverent lifestyle and the attendant immaturity that such acts imply can be easily transformed by skilled professionals into a market. Many recent historians of the era assert that a youth market is the most enduring sixties legacy. This issue was already a concern for activists of the time such as Todd Gitlin and Peter Coyote who worried that such lifestyle politics could mean "'spend any way you choose.'"[31] Recently Gerard De Groot asserts that in the sixties "the most profound revolution that occurred was the emergence of a consumer society."[32] The film all but predicts as much. Not only is much of Brewster's rebellion silly and individual, lacking the political pretensions that both the New Left and the Yippies had while paralleling the Yippies' immaturity, but Altman ends the film with a circus. After Brewster's dream of flight has crashed on the floor of the Astrodome, the actors parade out in circus costumes being introduced by name. The scene is an obvious tribute to Fellini and continues the carnivalesque style of the film. The scene has been heavily criticized with Robert Kolker calling it perhaps "the most unfortunate thing Altman has ever done."[33] However, Kolker and others miss Altman's point of associating the sixties project of rebellion to a sideshow. If the film reflects the time, Altman says, that the youth rebellion and its backlash equate to one big circus. The only actor who does not parade is Bud Cort as Brewster who remains crashed on the floor dead. If Brewster is a contradictory representative of the counterculture, Altman implies that countercultural dreams will also collapse to defeat (or they already had by 1970) in the circus of American capitalism, that the rebellious lifestyle is bound to be absorbed into irrelevance.

Brewster's contrasts with the sixties counterculture are also revealing. He lives in Houston, Texas, far from the enclaves of hippiedom: San Francisco and New York among others. De Groot maintains, "As a cultural revolution, the Sixties was predominantly white middle-class, and urban. Miles from the epicenter, the great seismic shifts were felt as tiny tremors."[34] Brewster resides far from the epicenter and seems untouched by the changes in the decade; in fact, establishment values of respect for the status quo thrived in places such as Texas and the southwest in general. Brewster is a solitary figure pursuing his non-conformist goal with a single-mindedness that eluded those like Rubin and Hoffman who were as preoccupied with their own image as they were with changing the system. The counterculture chased excess in the form of sexual and chemical experimentation. However, Brewster lives an ascetic existence while building his wings and getting in shape.

Brewster ingenuously ignores sexual temptation, focusing on his goal of flight. He is presented as a young boy with a vague destiny as Louise tells him, arguing he must resist the temptation represented by Hope (Jennifer Salt), the woman who brings him food. Louise tells him that people like Hope, young people of the era, cannot be truly free, that sex is a consolation for their earthbound bondage, warning Brewster that he should not be trapped in this illusion. The mythical element becomes the clearest here as Brewster is portrayed as outside of human experience, bound for a superhuman adventure, to fly "away," which he tells Hope when she asks to where he is flying. Brewster's personal austerity indicates the limited freedom of the counterculture despite its lifestyle of dissent. Sexual expression was personally liberating for many in the sixties. However, it did not translate to social empowerment. Some tried to elevate it to a political level.

The Weather Underground, an urban revolutionary organization, conflated sex and politics. Peter Collier and David Horowitz assert that "Weather sex was like developing Weather politics — a search for the 'exemplary deed.'"[35] However, as the film indicates, such a fusion of sex and politics is illusionary, serving to even distract the self away from the type of focus that Brewster demonstrates.

Brewster eschews the search for the exemplary deed because he sees it as an unnecessary distraction from his pursuit of true freedom until he meets Suzanne (Shelley Duvall), a tour guide at the Astrodome. She appears to be a free spirited hippie woman. When they first meet, Brewster is attempting to steal her car, which does not bother her. She lets him drive her to where he needs to go. When he praises her car, she admits that it is not hers, that she stole it from a race car driver who promised to take her home, but tried to rape her instead. She says that she hit him over the head with a wrench and took his car. The social conflicts of the sixties are invoked by the character of Suzanne and her story. The race car driver, ironically named Billy Joe Goodwill, exemplifies the conservative rural working class depicted in Merle Haggard's popular song "Okie from Muskogee" which contrasts the decadent counterculture with the virtuous white rural residents of Oklahoma. His song exemplified a reaction against the counterculture by the white rural working class. Racing was and continues to be a favorite sport of the white rural class, so Billy Joe Goodwill exemplifies the farming class who was especially offended by the hippies.

In 1970 Theodore Roszak asserted that these cultural differences posed a significant challenge to the counterculture if it were to be a forceful political movement in American life. He pointed out that the white working class's culture differed significantly from the rebellious attitude of the counterculture.[36] Goodwill represents this difference though in his attempt to rape Suzanne he shows his class to have the same sexual desires as the counterculture. Once again, Altman constructs two opposing caricatures of the sixties: macho white male conservative and quirky white hippie woman. Billy Joe is portrayed as an angry fool who undermines the virtuous idea of the white rural class in Haggard's song. When he finds Brewster driving Suzanne's (Billy Joe's) car and tells Brewster that he will "scrum your head," he becomes one more of Brewster's victims whose body is comically discovered in the next scene. His violent sexual aggression is one more example of the hypocrisies of the age.

Although the Suzanne/Billy Joe opposition would imply that Altman favors the counterculture, Suzanne is not as free spirited as she seems. She tells Brewster about her former boyfriend, Bernard, who works for the opportunistic businessman Haskell Weeks. As Suzanne tells it, Bernard's is a standard story of a hippie artist whose wealthy parents make him forego his artistic endeavors, which consisted of etchings on cider bottles, in favor of a proper career working for Weeks. Suzanne proclaims him "a genius" who had long hair which he was forced to cut once he started working for Weeks. Suzanne takes Bernard's career path as a betrayal, a merchandising of Bernard's dreams. With Bernard's story, the film takes a jaundiced view of the sixties avant-garde art movement also hinting at Suzanne's superficiality given her attraction to a poser like Bernard whose artistic endeavors are a parodic version of the conceptual avant-garde art of the period. Suzanne's true character comes out after she and Brewster have slept together and he mistakenly feels that he can trust her. He confides in her about his project of flying and confesses his responsibility for the killings throughout Houston. When he tells her of his constructed wings, her reaction is to dismiss Brewster's desire to get away from Houston and all human society. Instead, she considers the way Brewster could profit from his invention, envisioning a wealthy upper middle class life in a tony Houston neighborhood of her choice. She intuitively becomes a savvy businesswoman who talks of lawyers and patents to protect the millions of dollars that Brewster could earn with his invention. She comes to imitate Bernard's material ambitions, revealing the true desires motivating the hippies.

Altman intercuts Suzanne and Brewster's post-coital interaction with Brewster telling Louise that he has slept with Suzanne. Brewster argues that Suzanne is not as duplicitous as Louise indicated, also stating that his sexual experience was not the self deluding experience Louise indicated. However, as Louise tells him, Brewster has succumbed to the delusion of freedom through sexual desire. Considering his invention, Suzanne already has a banal middle class life prepared for them, the type of life from which Brewster wants to escape. Brewster's capitulation to Suzanne's desires parallels the countercultural ethos of self indulgence which distracted many of the youth away from the practical project of building a more sustainable political program. Brewster never had such a project; however, his relationship with the materialist Suzanne leads (as Louise predicts) to his death. Suzanne's character presciently anticipates the criticism of the counterculture devolving into nothing more subversive than a new demographic for consumer goods. Brewster's childlike naivety is exposed in his relationship with Suzanne. The morning after they first sleep together he believes he loves her even after she is "talking crazy" (in his words) about turning his invention into one more consumer item. Both of Suzanne's boyfriends, Bernard and Brewster, are opposed in their ambitions. Bernard played the artist until he decided to go mainstream and work for Weeks. Many former hippies became entrepreneurs, embracing the materialist ethos that they initially fought, former Yippee Jerry Rubin being the most well known example. In contrast, Brewster is the more legitimate artist whose naiveté cannot comprehend Suzanne's orientation towards exploiting his invention and does not take it seriously. He thoughtlessly rejects Louise, in favor of Suzanne even after the latter rejects his dream of flight in favor of material wealth. Once he sleeps with Suzanne, his infatuation blinds him much as the hippies were consumed by the greatness of their own struggle unable to see their movement coupling with consumerism.

After Brewster leaves Suzanne in the throes of post-coital attraction, she immediately calls Bernard and tells him that Brewster is the mentally disturbed killer. Suzanne reunites with Bernard, telling him that she has "missed him so much," seeming to indicate her capricious personality, but in reality revealing her preference for a successful businessman and simultaneously indicating her desire for material wealth as opposed to joining Brewster's visionary future. Her quirkiness indicates superficiality. When Bernard makes sexual advances towards her, she refuses, protesting that it is not right because they are not married. Her erratic behavior continues a few minutes later when she then offers herself to Bernard who then uses her rhetoric, claiming that they should wait until they are married.

This scene shows the cartoonish element of Bernard's and Suzanne's characters. Altman establishes a frantic comic tone throughout the film, revealing the characters as slaves to their whims. While Bernard is a ridiculous sixties contradiction, Suzanne's betraying Brewster exemplifies the conservative element of the counterculture. Suzanne casually adjusts herself to the situation she is in. However, she is indicative of many members of the counterculture who pursued their own selfish desires as opposed to trying to create a new society. At heart they were consumers merely buying another product. Todd Gitlin disputes this idea when he argues that this criticism is more media driven hype than reality with the focus being more on Jerry Rubin's story than the experiences of those who were keeping the activist spirit alive in the nineteen eighties "as if a whole generation had moved en masse from 'J'accuse' to Jacuzzi; Jerry Rubin's move to Wall Street in the early Eighties garnered more publicity than all the union organizers ... among New Left graduates put together."[37]

Gitlin wants to believe that Rubin's story is unique and perhaps it is. However, the counterculture has been criticized for its materialist orientations for forty years. Theodore Roszak was already anticipating this orientation when he said that the counterculture might very well become a "consumer sideshow."[38] This concern is accurate despite Gitlin's attempts at explanations. Looking back in 2008, De Groot asserts that during the sixties "the most profound revolution that occurred was the emergence of a consumer society."[39] Even Alice Echols, who argues that the counterculture strongly challenged the status quo at the time, acknowledges that cultural and political rebellion was "appropriated by capitalists on the lookout for new markets to exploit new lifestyles to sell."[40] And the Jerry Rubins of the movement were more than willing to buy along with the generations coming after. Writing in 1997, Thomas Frank asserted that "rebel youth culture remains the cultural mode of the corporate moment, used to promote not only specific products but the general idea of life in the cyber-revolution."[41] All of these points indicate the historical prescience of *Brewster McCloud*. Bernard and Suzanne are comic caricatures that have a basis in the social and cultural developments of the time. Whether or not Jerry Rubin's story is a common one, Altman could already see the materialist bent of the era.

The film reinforces the rebellious spirit of the era both in its portrayal of authority figures and in its frenetic and chaotic style. Altman even slips some subtle racial politics into the narrative as the film begins with socialite Daphne Heap attempting to lead an African American band in a rendition of the national anthem. However, that attempt breaks down in Heap's heavy handed leadership and the musicians break out into "Lift Every Voice and Sing," the black national anthem, despite her attempts to reassert control. Altman also portrays Haskel Weeks' driver, Longwood's anger, giving subjectivity to a typically marginalized voice. After Weeks or Bernard leaves the car, the camera will stay on Longwood, making him the center of the screen as he exclaims about how stupid and lazy the wealthy are.

The portrayals of Wright, Weeks, Bernard along with the hyperbole surrounding supposed San Francisco super cop Frank Shaft typify the film's anti-establishment attitude which is deeply embedded in its cinematic innovation as well as indicative of a period in which art forms such as film, literature and popular music were undergoing much experimentation. *Brewster McCloud* participates in the aesthetic exploration of the period. Robin Wood asserts that the film possesses "a kind of reckless inventive-ness."[42] The film's stylistic irreverence is established with the disruption of the typical MGM beginning. Instead of roaring, the famed lion states with some helplessness that he forgot his lines, the famed corporate symbol is at a loss of how to proceed indicating that the standard rules for an MGM film are loosened much as the counterculture was revising social and cultural mores. Helene Keyssar echoes this view when she asserts "the MGM lion's announced inability to remember its line may be understood not as a threat but as an opportunity to improvise."[43]

The credits begin as Daphne Heap is leading the chorus in the national anthem. When she stops the band, the credits stop as well, halting the film and drawing attention to the medium of film. Stylistic revision is further communicated by the fact that Daphne Heap is played by Margaret Hamilton whom the audience would have recognized at the time as the Wicked Witch of the West from *The Wizard of Oz*. This revisionism is furthered with a shot of Heap's corpse wearing Dorothy's red shoes coveted by the wicked witch. Altman's audience at the time would have recognized the cultural reference along with a jokey audio reference to Shirley Temple Black and the parody of the action film *Bullitt*. These references reflect Altman's revisionist film history, which freely mocks the cinematic texts that have come before, paralleling the improvisation and questioning of the period. The film mocks the classical and popular cinematic texts that have come before, undermining their historical importance.

The apotheosis of the film's anti-establishment sensibility along with an indicator of its stylistic innovation is the lecturer (Rene Auberjonois) who anchors the film. The lecture serves no functional purpose in guiding the basic narrative forward and is thus a stylistic oddity. It is a framing device which, like the opening credits, brings attention to the fact that this is a film, breaking down the fourth wall of realism as the lecturer addresses the audience directly. This device parallels the type of metafiction being written by writers like John Barth and Donald Barthelme in the period that draws attention to the conventions of the novel. Helene Keyssar asserts that such self-consciousness exists throughout the film, asserting that Hope's fetishizing of Brewster's exercising body, as she masturbates, parallels "the deliberate confusion between rehearsals and performance that characterized much of the countercultural theater of the late sixties and early seventies."[44] The lecturer functions in a similarly meta performative way.

Like Barth's improvisation, the lecturer furthers a thematic purpose, asserting humanity's similarity to birds, enacting literally this similarity by transforming into a bird as the narrative progresses. Because he is a scientist, the lecturer possesses an expertise grounded in disinterested inquiry. However, his rationality is undermined by his becoming birdlike with the accompanying primal features of a bird. The lecturer debunks human reason, indicating that people are animal like and simultaneously unlike birds in their earthbound existence. Because Altman's parody involves creating characters who are blinded by their egos, the human/bird similarity serves to undermine human rationality and reinforce the point that humans are dominated by their primal instincts as the characters reinforce certain biologically driven behaviors. Haskell Weeks is a transparently ambitious businessman; Abraham Wright is old, greedy and lecherous; Frank Shaft mouths platitudes about "working stiff" cops while narcissistically tending to his turtleneck sweaters; Suzanne is blatantly materialistic; Brewster is a young naïf. All of these characters are unaware of their obsessions, making them comic targets. Although most of the targets are authority figures, the satire cuts against Suzanne and Brewster as well.

At the beginning, the lecturer refers to "the mortal damage man is doing to birds' environment" which may necessitate building "enormous environmental enclosures to protect both man and birds." As he speaks these lines, the camera focuses on the Astrodome, pride of humankind, at one time labeled "the eighth wonder of the world." The film debunks this sublime classification by indicating that the Astrodome functions as a type of prison, separating people from the environmental damage that they have done. The film comically anticipates the environmental movement that was just gathering steam at the time. The environmental movement, cinematic innovation, establishment backlash, youthful rebellion, hippie materialism, all of these can be found in *Brewster McCloud*. Even the patriarchal nature of the counterculture is invoked in the film. Many critics have echoed Alice Echols' take when she mentions that the sexual revolution reinforced "the deeply rooted sexual double standard" and hippie households were centers of the "traditional division of labor."[45] The Weatherman Underground was also an organization rooted in male privilege.[46] The three women in the film mirror these dynamics. Louise is a mother figure guardian; Hope desires and worships Brewster's body; and Suzanne is the free spirit who initiates Brewster into sexual experience. They all exist for him.

The film begins with bird defecation on a newspaper headline that reads "Agnew: Society Should Discard Some U.S. People," a direct reference to the politics of the era and a desire Brewster fulfills through his murder spree though probably not the people the vice-president had in mind. The politics of the film are complicated. Brewster could be read as exemplifying the tragic failure of the counterculture of the period, unable to realize his and the counterculture's lofty ambitions of soaring beyond social constraints while chased by the police. Gerard Plecki states that "Brewster's death ... accentuates the worthiness of his pursuit of freedom."[47] Similarly, Joan Tewkesbury, who wrote the screenplay for *Nashville*, said that Brewster's crash "is the saddest event in any of Bob's movies."[48] Neither of them connects Brewster to the loss of sixties dreams. However, the sadness can be compared to the elegy of a time and movement that did not succeed. Still, the film is not sentimental about sixties youth given that Suzanne and Brewster are also objects of satire. With the satire cutting both ways, the film inevitably undermines both the establishment and the counterculture, leaving a space in which rebellion and reaction are equally suspect heading into what was a new decade, revealing confusion and emptiness. The sixties continue to be a contentious decade with views ranging from Todd Gitlin's to Peter Collier's and David Horowitz's. *Brewster McCloud* stands as a necessary cultural artifact in making sense of the events of the period along with the differing perspectives on an era which is often viewed bitterly or nostalgically.

NOTES

1. Helene Keyssar, *Robert Altman's America* (Oxford: Oxford University Press, 1991), 17.

2. Robert B. Kolker, *A Cinema of Loneliness: Penn, Stone, Kubrick, Scorsese, Spielberg, Altman,* 2nd ed. (Oxford: Oxford University Press, 1988), 396.

3. Robert T. Self, *Robert Altman's Subliminal Reality* (Minnesota: University of Minnesota Press, 2002), ix.

4. Self, ix.

5. Self, x.

6. Self, x.

7. Kolker, 324.

8. Pauline Kael, *Deeper into Movies* (Boston: Little, Brown, 1973), 228.

9. Vincent Canby, "Innocence and Corruption; 'Brewster McCloud' Debuts at Coronet; Robert Altman Directs Slapstick Film," *The New York Times* 24 December 1970, 8.

10. John E. O'Connor and Martin A. Jackson, "Introduction," *Image as Artifact: The Historical Analysis of Film and Television*, eds. John E. O'Connor and Martin A. Jackson (Malabar, FL: R.E. Kreiger, 1990), xvii.

11. O'Connor and Jackson, xvii.

12. O'Connor and Jackson, xix.

13. Mitchell Zuckoff, *Robert Altman: The Oral Biography* (New York: Alfred A. Knopf, 2009), 205.

14. Robert Sklar, "Moving Image Media in Culture and Society: Paradigms for Historical Interpretation," *Image as Artifact: The Historical Analysis of Film and Television*, 119–135; here 120.

15. Sklar, 122.

16. Sklar, 125.

17. Sklar, 126.

18. Sklar, 126.

19. Robin Wood, *Hollywood from Vietnam to Reagan and Beyond,* rev. and expanded ed. (New York: Columbia University Press, 2003), 24.

20. Charles A. Reich, *The Greening of America* (New York: Random House, 1970), 225.

21. Theodore Roszak, *The Making of a Counter Culture* (Garden City, NY: Doubleday, 1969), 40.

22. Peter Collier, and David Horowitz, *The Destructive Generation: Second Thoughts about the Sixties* (New York: Summit, 1989), 15.

23. Reich, 234.

24. Alice Echols, *Shaky Ground: The '60s and Its Aftershocks* (New York: Columbia University Press, 2002), 20.

25. Zuckoff, 200.

26. Zuckoff, 198.

27. Charles Reich, 316.

28. Echols, 46.

29. Reich, 316.

30. Gerard De Groot, *The Sixties Unplugged* (Cambridge, MA: Harvard University Press, 2008), 263.

31. Echols, 47.

32. De Groot, 395.

33. Kolker, 349.

34. De Groot, 253.

35. Collier and Horowitz, 87.

36. Roszak, 72.

37. Todd Gitlin, *Years of Hope, Days of Rage*, rev. ed. (New York: Bantam, 1993), 433.

38. Roszak, 72.

39. De Groot, 395.

40. Echols, 48.

41. Thomas Frank, *The Conquest of Cool: Business Culture, Counterculture, and the Rise of Hip Consumerism* (Chicago: University of Chicago Press, 1997), 4.

42. Wood, 34.

43. Keyssar, 263.

44. Keyssar, 263.

45. Echols, 34.

46. Collier and Horowitz, 86.

47. Gerard Plecki, *Robert Altman* (Boston: Twayne, 1985), 25.

48. Zuckoff, 204.

7

Hard-Boiled Nebbish:
The Jewish Humphrey Bogart in
Robert Altman's *The Long Goodbye*
and Woody Allen's *Play It Again, Sam*

Jeremy Kaye

His estranged wife, Barbra Streisand, calls him "the American Jean-Paul Belmondo." ... His friend and partner in an 18-month-old production company, Jack Brodsky, calls him "the Jewish Richard Burton"; and Paul Mazursky, director of Bob & Carol [& Ted & Alice], says that he is "the Jewish Jimmy Stewart." But the man himself says simply: "I'm the Jewish Elliott Gould."
—"Elliott Gould: The Urban Don Quixote," *Time*, 1970.[1]

So long, Alvy Singer.... The neurotic nebbish is out; the swaggering ass-kicker is in.... Today's Jewish trendsetters are out and proud.
—"The New Super Jews," *Time Out New York*, 2003.[2]

"You got a banjo? I'll do my Al Jolson"

There is a remarkable scene midway through Robert Altman's *The Long Goodbye* (1973) in which Elliott Gould puts on blackface. After driving his friend Terry Lennox to Tijuana, Gould, playing Philip Marlowe, is hauled in by the police for questioning. Believing he had something to do with the brutal murder of Lennox's wife, the police take Gould/Marlowe's mug shot in a carnival photo booth and subsequently fingerprint him by dipping his entire hand in black ink. He is then thrown like a rag

120

doll into the interrogation room, his hand hitting the double-sided mirror on the way in, leaving a visible black handprint. This handprint is significant because it is our clue that Gould/Marlowe knows he is being watched by "the J. Edgar Hoover boys" on the other side of the mirror, and they become his theatrical audience for some of his signature repartee. In a sequence that is quintessential Altman, conversations run simultaneously in front of and behind the mirror. Behind it one police officer calls Gould a "cutie-pie" and the other calls him a "smart-ass." In front of it Gould looks directly into the mirror at the Hoover boys and begins to "put on my make up." "You got a banjo?" he asks his interrogator. "I'll do my Al Jolson." As he smears his hands over his face, the ink on them suddenly transforms into the burnt cork of blackface minstrelsy. Puzzled, his questioners ask, "What the hell are you doing? That's what I'd like to know." As he answers, Gould is no longer Philip Marlowe, but has become Al Jolson. "I'm getting ready to sing Swanee," he exclaims, before putting up his hands, swaying them back and forth, and launching into a well-known Jolson routine. "Swaaaa-neeeee," he sings. "How I love you...." Understanding who Gould has become, the cop sarcastically says, "Sure. I got Al Jolson singing." "He was *ooookaaaay*," Gould responds, his lilting emphasis on the final word offering his classic cadence of simultaneous approval and mystification.

What makes Gould's referencing of Jolson's blackface so intriguing, is that it can be read in two ways within the context of the film. First, it can be read as an aesthetic device, consciously drawing our attention to the fact that the Hollywood movie we are watching is indeed a "Hollywood movie." The film starts and ends with the song, "Hooray for Hollywood," and is filled with Altman's usual mélange of filmic allusions and Hollywood inside jokes. The film's vision of Los Angeles is not the modernist landscape of Raymond Chandler's noir, in which the hard-boiled detective is the only voice of truth and integrity among a sea of moral decay and corruption; rather, it is the postmodern landscape of parody, irony, and reflexivity — the hard-boiled hero lost in a marijuana haze of movie references, naked women offering him pot brownies, and a cat who, much to his dismay, will only eat Curry Brand cat food. This reading conforms to the spirit of Altman's oeuvre more generally, as one in which "[t]he richness of Altman's best films, as well as the meretriciousness of his worst, derives partly from his cultural schizophrenia."[3]

Whereas the first reading of this scene emphasizes the intentionality of postmodern play and pastiche, it nonetheless empties the historical field

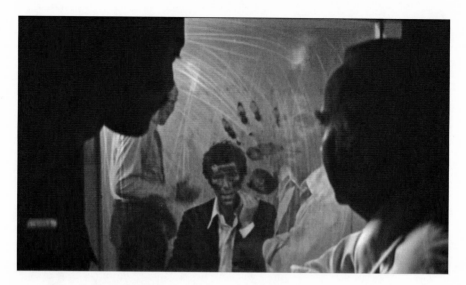

"You got a banjo? I'll do my Al Jolson." Elliot Gould dons blackface in *The Long Goodbye.*

of meaning and precludes a more nuanced analysis of the cultural and historical importance of Gould's blacking-up. A second reading of this scene, on the contrary, places the emphasis on the *effects* of the performance rather than the intentions; it shines a critical spotlight on what gets evaded when Altman's critics are too busy celebrating the "improvisatory games [he plays] with his actors."[4] Why, then, in the middle of their reinvention of the Humphrey Bogart persona — of their turning Bogie from hard-boiled hero to hard-boiled nebbish — do Altman and Gould invoke the specter of blackface minstrelsy?

Knowingly or not, when Gould puts on blackface, he and Altman are tapping into a vast historical archive of images connecting the Jewish male body to the mask of blackface. Al Jolson, of course, was the star of *The Jazz Singer* (1927), who famously dons the minstrel mask for his performance of "My Mammy" near the film's end. As Michael Rogin has argued about blackface minstrelsy in particular and racial masquerade more generally, Jolson's performance of blackface allows the racialized son of a Jewish cantor, Jakie Rabinowitz, to hide his Jewishness under the burnt cork and thus transform himself into Jack Robin, vaudeville performer and white American jazz singer.[5] Indeed, Rogin's argument about Jewish performers using blackface as a vehicle for Americanization is so convincing and has become so influential in Jewish studies and American studies that few scholars question how one-sided this assimilation narrative is — how the Jew got white. As Rogin himself states, "By painting himself black, he washes himself white."[6] For Jolson and other Jews of that time period, being Jewish and American was not a both/and decision, but was either/or. They were either Jewish immigrants or white Americans; they could not be both.[7]

If the Jew's Americanization via blackface required him to reject his Jewish past, according to Rogin, then Gould's 1973 performance of blackface does something slightly different. It uncannily rehearses Rogin's assimilation-via-blackface thesis while it simultaneously makes visible Gould's Jewishness by "outing" him within a genealogy of Jewish performers. This scene does not so much refute Rogin's thesis as it forces us to historicize it; what worked for Jewish performers in the 1920s may work differently for performers in the 1970s. Upon close examination, the early 1970s reveals itself to be a seminal moment in the history of changing representations of the Jew in popular film, when, as one scholar puts it, "ethnicity was becoming a box office 'plus' rather than a marginal minus."[8] In what follows, I discuss the Jewishness in that decade by comparing *The Long Goodbye* to a film released only a few months earlier, Woody Allen's *Play It Again, Sam* (1972). My readings of these films are mediated by an inkling that blackface, as a mode of racial masquerade assimilating Jews to the dominant whiteness, becomes reanimated by these two films as "Bogieface"— by which I mean to uncover how Humphrey Bogart becomes a racial mask to allow two "very" Jewish performers (Gould and Allen) to confront their relationship to whiteness. To be sure, these two films are obsessed with Bogart; but whereas Allen plays into a reified version of Bogart and in so doing keeps Jewishness separate from white Americanness, Gould "Jewifies" the Bogart character and thereby breaks down the binary between Jewishness and whiteness. A comparative reading of these films forces us to rethink the master narrative of Jewish assimilation that we have for too long taken for granted, while it may also offer insight as to how Jewishness has once again become all the rage in the first decade of the twenty-first century.

The Jewish 1970s: Bogie-Face in Woody Allen's *Play It Again, Sam*

"The early seventies was a weird time in American history," confirmed Elliott Gould recently. "Everything was cool."[9] The questions of history and context are crucial for understanding the way Gould's Jewishness functions within *The Long Goodbye*. This feeling of transition and ambiguity that permeated the era was especially acute for America's Jewish population.[10] In *How Jews Became White Folks* (1998), anthropologist Karen Brodkin locates the 1970s as a time in which the American Jew was so firmly ensconced in whiteness, that rather than alleviate racial anxiety, this radical assimilation prompted new sources of disquiet: "By the 1970s, the danger that Jews as a people might disappear because of their very success in becoming part of the white mainstream became a real possibility."[11] In response to this fear over "disappearance," many American Jews started to counter the assimilationist narrative by aggressively asserting their Jewishness in the public sphere.

To be sure, seventies films are so populated with self-consciously "Jewish" performers — Allen, Dustin Hoffman, Barbra Streisand, Gould, Mel Brooks, to name a few — that at least one film historian has speculated that the "era [was] so filled with Jewish characters that I am tempted to call it the Second Golden Age [of Jews in film] rivaled only by the 1920s."[12] It should be emphasized that the "reawakened ethnicity" that many Jews experienced in the 1970s was contingent upon their "virtual disappearance during three decades (1930–1960)."[13] According to Rogin, the exodus of Jews and Jewish themes from the screen was provoked by Hitler's rise to power in 1933. As Nazism in Europe brought the question of anti–Semitism to the fore of America's racial consciousness, "the Jewish moguls evaded anti–Semitism by simply eliminating Jews from the screen."[14] Studio heads orchestrated a genre shift from Jewish generational-conflict films (say, *The Jazz Singer* [1927]) to African American themed films (say, *Imitation of Life* [1934]), and thereby relegated Jewish performers to minor non–Jewish roles or left them off the screen altogether. In 1952, Henry Popkin wrote an essay for *Commentary* entitled "The Vanishing Jew of Our Popular Culture." Or, as Josh Kun recently notes in the case of television, "Though there were a number of Jews occupying central roles in primetime network television in the 1950s — Milton Berle, Sid Caesar, George Burns, Jack Benny — it was the performance of over and open Jewishness that had all but vanished from the screen."[15]

It seemed that in the Hollywood of the World War II era, Jews were ill equipped to fight fascism on the screen. Rather, Hollywood enlisted the hard-boiled masculinity of Humphrey Bogart in its ideological war against the Nazis. Bogart's signature role as Rick in *Casablanca* (1942), the disillusioned American ex-patriot who reluctantly joins the fight against the Nazis, launched him into superstardom in the early 1940s after years of "B" roles in gangster and noir pictures. Due to *Casablanca*'s enduring success, Bogart became arguably the most famous star of the post–World War II era, and just as important, as numerous film historians have documented, for the construction of everyday American manhood. Steven Cohan, for example, suggests that Bogart "structured the heterosexual masculinity of the average American man."[16] James L. Neibaur comments that Bogie's tough-guy persona "exude[s] the very qualities that still represent important aspects of American screen masculinity."[17]

Woody Allen's *Play It Again, Sam* (1972) offers us an excellent opportunity to measure the truly awesome affective power which Bogart elicits from his male audience. A hit play on Broadway in 1969, *Play It Again, Sam* became the biggest box office hit of Allen's career when it was made into a film three years later. Speaking in a 1993 interview, Allen describes the film's genesis in terms of the crippling nostalgia many Americans feel for the films of Hollywood's Golden Age, not coincidentally, also the era marked by the Jew's absence:

> I was always escaping into those films. You would leave your poor house behind and all your problems with school and family and all that and you would go into the cinema, and there they would have penthouses and white telephones and the women were lovely and the men always had an appropriate witticism to say and things were funny, but they always turned out well and the heroes were genuine heroes and it was just great. So, I think that had such a crushing influence, made such an impression on me. And I know many people my age who've never been able to shake it, who've had trouble in their lives because of it, because they still — in advanced stages of their lives, still in their fifties or sixties — can't understand why it doesn't work that way, why everything that they grew up believing and feeling and wishing for and thinking was reality was not true and that reality is much harsher and uglier than that.[18]

In *Play It Again, Sam* Woody Allen plays Allan Felix, the kind of man that Allen discusses in the above quotation, the kind of man who feels the "crushing influence" of the movies. Obsessive movie watching is presented in the film as both a character strength and a flaw, simultaneously allowing Allen/Allan to make his living as a film critic, but also costing him his marriage and any notion of masculine agency. "All we ever do is watch movies. You're one of life's great watchers," his wife tells him before leaving for another man. No one does Allen/Allan watch so intensely and neurotically as Humphrey Bogart. The film's opening shot contains not Allen/

Allan but Bogart in the famous last scene of *Casablanca*. The camera does a reverse shot, and then we see our hero, comatose, seated in a movie house, alone, his mouth open, transfixed by the image of "Bogie" on screen. His apartment is filled with Bogart paraphernalia and posters of *Casablanca* and *Key Largo* (1948) fill the walls. Allan Felix's reason for fetishizing Bogart is obvious: "Bogart is a perfect image," he says in a voiceover. "Who else am I going to identify with?" Allen/Allan defines his identity as one of life's great watchers against Bogart who is one of life's great doers. Indeed, Bogart is so real to both Allan Felix and Woody Allen that the former constructs a fantasy version of Bogie to play the angel on his shoulder telling him how to be a man, while the latter actually casts Bogart in his movie (or at least Jerry Lacy who does his best imitation with trenchcoat, hat, and lisp).

It is within the context of *Play It Again, Sam* that we can begin to gauge the ideological heft of Bogart's hard-boiled persona not only on men in the forties and fifties (when Bogart was making films), but also in the sixties and seventies when men like Allen/Allan idolized him. For some reason, Bogie keeps popping up in the sixties and seventies: on the pages of *Cahiers du Cinéma*, intensely theorized by such French New Wave notables as Bazin, Truffaut, and Godard[19]; in Susan Sontag's enormously influential 1964 "Notes on Camp" which used Bogart's performance as *The Maltese Falcon*'s Sam Spade to identify the new sensibility[20]; and in the growing number of "Bogart Festivals," starting at Harvard and spreading to college campuses across the U.S.[21] Steven Cohan traces the emergence of the "Bogie cult of the 1960s and 1970s":

> His tough-guy persona was celebrated even more in the "Bogie" cult that first became apparent with Jean-Luc Godard's reference to the star's value as an icon of masculinity in *Breathless* (1959), flourishing with a successful revival of Bogart's Warner Bros. films in art houses throughout the 1960s. *Play It Again Sam* (1972) then canonized the actor's standing as an icon of romantic masculinity when it invoked Bogart's ghost from *Casablanca* (1942) to personify for the meek, insecure hero (Woody Allen) the male fantasy of impeccable virility.[22]

Although Cohan fails to mention *The Long Goodbye*, we could certainly include Altman's film in the Bogie cult.

Here, it is worth noting that such a canonization of Bogart's image happens only in retrospect, decades after he was at the pinnacle of his stardom and even several years after he had died of cancer in 1957. According to Cohan, "As the Bogie cult of the 1960s and 1970s bears witness to, the

"**Bogart is the perfect image.**" Allan Felix (Woody Allen) in *Play It Again, Sam.*

Hollywood tough guy retained a supposed 'timeless' appeal as the touchstone of American virility, but only in retrospect."[23] James L. Neibaur likewise tells us that Bogart became the screen legend he is today only "after a strong cult following he garnered ... on college campuses during the 1970s."[24] Cohan and Neibaur help us to understand Bogie's revival in popularity as symptomatic of larger socio-historical shifts in conceptions of American masculinity. As David Savran and others have convincingly argued, white masculinity entered the 1970s in a state of crisis, suffering through a widely perceived loss of faith in traditional notions of manhood. To combat this crisis and to try and reconfigure their hegemonic status, Savran argues that the era's white men increasingly cultivated a sense of self-imposed "victimhood" at the hands of black power, feminism, and gay liberationist movements.[25] The Bogie cult can be seen simultaneously to exacerbate and to alleviate the crisis of white masculinity. White male subjects in droves identified with Bogart's hard-boiled masculinity, revealing their nostalgia for an "easier" time in which they had unquestioned agency over marginal social groups. "By encouraging them to identify with the hard-boiled detective," writes Robert J. Corber, "film noir allowed these men to recover temporarily their masculinity. A descendent of the gangster the hard-boiled detective embodied the form of male identity many men sought to recover as an antidote to their disaffection."[26] What we might thus call "Bogie-face" secured the masculinity of white men against the traumas they had suffered in the Vietnam era by offering white

Allan Felix (Woody Allen) and Bogart in *Play It Again, Sam*'s final image.

men a nostalgic image of the 1940s and its vision of America where white men could be tough-guys, unquestioned in their dominance.

The point, then, is to conceive how Bogie's persona worked as a racial mask for white men in the 1970s in much the same way that blackface worked as a racial mask for Jewish performers in the 1920s. While masquerading in blackface allowed Jews a way into whiteness, masquerading in Bogie-face offered white men a way to reconsolidate their whiteness. What happens, then, when a Jewish performer attempts to racially masquerade as Bogie? In the case of *Play It Again, Sam*, masquerading as Bogart does not make Allen/Allan any less of a Jew. In fact, whenever Allen/Allan affects Bogie's accents, mannerisms or actions, he is never more pathetically aware that he will never be Bogart. "Who'm I kidding?" he asks himself. "I'm not like that. I never will be. That's strictly the movies." Rather than aid his assimilation into whiteness, imitating Bogart accentuates Allen's/Allan's Jewish difference. When he looks in the mirror before a date, he sees not Bogie's whiteness but the visible excesses of his own Jewishness: bookworm glasses, long curly hair, hooked nose, hunched back. When he aggressively plants a kiss, Bogart-like, on his date, the woman does not swoon but is left cold, disgusted, and he is left muttering to himself, "I'm not Bogart. I'll never be Bogart. I'm a disgrace to my sex."

Of course, Allen/Allan is a disgrace to his sex not only because he fails to embody Bogie's tough guy masculinity, but also because his own Jewishness excludes him from the very identificatory chain that enabled the era's white men to symptomatically identify with Bogart in the first place. Allen/Allan's performance of the bumbling, hysterical, schlemiel figure is far from the "average American man" (Cohan's term) or "the white male as victim" (Savran's) who are able to secure their whiteness and heterosexuality through identifying with Bogart. At the end of the film, Allen/Allan makes one final effort to put on Bogie-face, the unrealizable romantic ideal of hegemonic white manhood that contains the text's (if not the Vietnam generation's) hope for remasculinization. After he consummates an affair with his best friend's wife (Diane Keaton), he chases them both to the San Francisco International Airport. He tracks down Linda (Keaton) on the tarmac, and gives her back to Dick (Tony Robert), sacrificing the woman he loves "for a pal" the way that Bogart would have done. Whereas the film's beginning finds him passively watching *Casablanca*'s final scene, here at the end he acts out that scene, playing Bogart to Keaton's Ingrid Bergman. At the moment of his greatest triumph, however, when he finally is able to don the Bogie-face, his Jewish schlemiel persona breaks through. "It's from *Casablanca*," he blurts out, unable to contain himself. "I waited my whole life to say it."

By giddily announcing to the audience that his lines are stolen from Bogart, Allen/Allan precludes his own assimilation into white Americanness and, more importantly, makes visible Bogie-face as a masquerade, as a performative technology and not an authentic identity position. Ironically, it is this failure to suture his identity with the Bogart-ideal — a failure iterated and reiterated for much of Allen's comic career — that ultimately made *Play It Again, Sam* a success. As film viewers, we do not want someone to imitate Bogart who commands the screen the way Bogart did. Instead, we want someone like Woody Allen who will forever fail to be like Bogart, because it is his failure that ultimately secures Bogart as an identificatory site for dominant, which is to say, non–Jewish, male subjects. On the one hand, this central paradox — Allen/Allan's desperate yearning to be like Bogie but inability to be like Bogie — is the main source of humor in the film, but it also reifies into a hierarchy the relationship the film sets up between Jew and Gentile, between Woody Allen and Humphrey Bogart. Indeed, the film's final image, of Bogie walking side-by-side with Allen/Allan, literalizes this hierarchy. Allen/Allan's Jewish persona is permanently positioned into a state of inferiority while Bogie's image becomes congealed as the unattainable fetish object needed to achieve ideal manhood. Woody Allen's inability to lay claim to that fetish keeps him Jewish — not a white American.

"The American Jean Paul Belmondo" /
"The Jewish Jimmy Stewart"

Arguably, there was no bigger American film star in late 1970 than Elliott Gould. Having skyrocketed to fame with Paul Mazursky's *Bob & Carol & Ted & Alice* (1969), Altman's *M*A*S*H* (1970) made him a cultural phenomenon. He was on the cover of *Time* in September, *Fortune* in October, and November saw him interviewed in *Playboy*. Taking his status as what *Playboy* called "the hottest actor in movies" seriously, Gould openly bragged, "I'm in a terrific position. Within reason, I can do whatever I want in TV or movies."[27] *Time*'s cover story was the crowning achievement in what it hailed as a "remarkable year." The magazine saw Gould as a new kind of star, a "Star for an Uptight Age," as the cover read. To accentuate his off-kilter status, the cover presents not a dignified photo of Gould at his most star-like, as is common practice in magazine profiles, but makes him into a cartoon: dark, curly hair, long sideburns, and a thick bushy mustache against a backdrop of bright rainbow colors. *Time* animates the cover drawing not only as a way to pay homage to Gould's place in the counterculture, but also, I think, as a way to turn Elliott Gould into a joke. It was as if the magazine was saying, "Gould is one of us. He understands the anxiety and absurdity of these times." To *Time*, Gould is not a star at all but is an anti-star: "It is not so much that he seems so ordinary as that he seems so little like a star. His clothes, whether custom made suits or crumpled fatigues, never quite fit; his hair could use a trim; and he can raise a heavy beard ... in a matter of days."[28] Gould is the star for an "uptight age" precisely because he represents the antithesis of an earlier era's glamorous stars such as Bogart or Brando. Where Bogie has elegance, Gould is a "klutz"; where Brando swaggers, Gould "stumbles."[29] As "the Urban Don Quixote," Gould is always a little bit off, yet not quite smart enough to figure out how.

Time attempts to make sense of a paradigm shift that enabled someone so unstar-like as Gould to ascend to prominence. Screenwriter Jules Feiffer suggests, "'There's been a shift in focus of movie heroes and movie stories.... Out of this shift came the possibility of careers for the likes of Gould, Alan Arkin and Dustin Hoffman. What really happened is that Hollywood is trying to update its mythology, and these are the stars of the new mythology.'"[30] While he is correct in identifying a "shift in focus" that has allowed different kinds of performers to become stars, Feiffer overlooks the central fact that the three actors who typify this "new mythology" are, in fact, Jews. The very shift in focus that enabled Gould's ascent to stardom is contingent upon the possibilities that Jews like Gould, Hoffman, and Arkin were able to hide their Jewishness enough to pass as mainstream (white) movie stars.

This is not to say that *Time* evades questions of Gould's Jewishness. On the contrary, it fetishizes it, texturing stories of his upbringing with details from commonly invoked Jewish stereotypes: for example, his family resembles a "comedy nightmare by Philip Roth," full with "overbearing mother" and "overshadowed father."[31] Even more so than Hoffman, whose Jewishness was much less commented upon in the era, Gould's hipness lies specifically in his successful ability to negotiate his Jewishness with whiteness, in his ability to be both other and one of us. In a sense, Elliott Gould (*née* Goldstein) is the fulfillment of Al Jolson's promise in *The Jazz Singer*. As Rogin tells us, "The movie [*The Jazz Singer*] was promising that the son could have it all: Jewish past and American future, Jewish mother and gentile wife."[32] The American dream of a melting pot, as we have seen, was far from the reality of the 1920s era. Rogin goes on: "That was not what happened in Hollywood. The moguls left their Jewish wives for gentile women in the 1930s and mostly eliminated Jewish life from the screen. They bade farewell to their Jewish pasts with *The Jazz Singer*."[33] Three decades after Jewishness had become invisible on screen, it is Gould who finally realizes the dream that both Jewishness and white Americanness could live within the same body. His persona could accommodate playing either Jewish (in 1969's *The Night They Raided Minsky's*) or American characters (in *M*A*S*H* and *The Long Goodbye*). As simultaneously "'the *American* Jean-Paul Belmondo'" and "'the *Jewish* Jimmy Stewart,'"[34] Gould fashions a third term — *both/and* rather than either/or. Where Allen is tied to stereotype, keeping Jewish and whiteness separate, Gould's fashions a Jewishness that Rogin's account cannot account for. He takes Mr. Smith to the synagogue as well as to Washington, and *that* is exactly where his utopian potential lies.

Gould's utopian fusion of Jewishness and Americanness permeates every aspect of *The Long Goodbye*. At first glance, his reinvention of Philip Marlowe seems to be a straight-forward lampooning of the Bogart persona, turning Bogie's most iconic character into a dim-witted *schlemiel*, revealing Gould's and Altman's contempt for traditional Hollywood storytelling and heroic archetypes. Yet, a closer examination reveals that the film uncomfortably straddles the boundary between being a send-up and a faithful adaptation of the noir genre. For every attempt to do away with the conventions of the hard-boiled detective (portraying Marlowe as mum-

"Nobody cares but me." Elliot Gould as authentic hard-boiled hero in *The Long Goodbye*.

bling, clueless, always a step behind; beginning the movie with a twenty minute diversionary anti-plot in which Marlowe impotently tries to find Curry-Brand cat food for his hungry cat), there are faithful touches that reestablish it within the noir tradition: he drives an old gumshoe's car through the streets of 1970s Los Angeles, a damsel in distress sets off the mystery by hiring Marlowe but of course is not to be trusted. Perhaps the most unsettling homage to the hard-boiled hero is at the film's end when Gould/Marlowe surprises the audience by embodying the Bogartian ideal of masculinity. After spending the entire movie a step behind every one else, falsely believing in his friend Terry Lennox's innocence, by the end of the film Gould/Marlowe has magically figured things out. He tracks Lennox down in Tijuana, realizing that he faked his own suicide to escape a murder charge. When Lennox tries to persuade Marlowe to let him go ("What the hell. Nobody cares"), Gould/Marlowe sighs, "Nobody cares but me," as he takes out a gun from his jacket that we never knew he had, righteously killing Lennox to avenge the latter's wife's murder. Unlike Allen, who at the end of *Play It Again, Sam* reveals his Jewishness by undercutting his identification with Bogart ("It's from *Casablanca*. I've waited my whole life to say it"), Gould/Marlowe fully embodies the master narrative of the hegemonic male hero. With the final scene providing the apex of Altman's and Gould's provocative mash-up of anti-noir and neo-noir, Gould's Marlowe is simultaneously a Jewish clown in Bogie-face (like Allen) and also an authentic hard-boiled hero (like Bogie).

Ultimately, it was Gould's both/and *Jewification* of Bogie — his making Marlowe a clown *and* a detective hero — that spelled critical and commercial doom for *The Long Goodbye*. We're okay with Jewish parody (Allen) or with Bogie's traditional heroism but not with Gould's awkward combination of the two. Critics bashed the film, singling out Gould's revisionist performance of Bogart as the target for pot shots. Gould's Marlowe "is an untidy, unshaven, semiliterate, dim-wit slob," wrote *Los Angeles Times'* critic Charles Champlin. "He is not Chandler's Marlowe, or mine, and I can't find him interesting, sympathetic or amusing, and I can't be sure who will."[35] Commenting thirty years after the film's theatrical release, Altman himself seems to understand why audiences rejected the film: Marlowe and Bogart had become bound together in the public imagination and by tampering with the iconoclastic Bogart, one risked disparaging Hollywood's entire golden age. "What the public was really saying [by rejecting the film]," Altman remarks, "was 'That's not Humphrey Bogart.'"[36] Even Pauline Kael, who celebrated the film in the *New Yorker*, saw its box-office failure as evidence not merely of Gould's waning popularity ("Audiences may have felt they'd already had it with Elliott Gould"), but more importantly with the fact that "Marlowe had already become Bogart and you could see him in it when you read the book."[37] She continues:

> I suspect that people are reluctant to say goodbye to the old sweet bull of the Bogart Marlowe because it satisfies a deep need. They've been accepting the I-look-out-for-No. 1 tough guys of recent films, but maybe they're scared to laugh at Gould's out-of-it Marlowe because that would lose them their Bogart icon.[38]

The "Jewish Jimmy Stewart" was as far as the public was willing to allow Gould. When he tried to become the *Jewish Humphrey Bogart*, audiences rebelled.[39] Bogart's image held too important a place for the era's ideology of masculinity to allow Gould to tamper with it. The 1970s didn't need Jimmy Stewart's "soft" masculinity the way it needed Bogart's hard-boiled masculinity. Whereas George Bailey would have simply prayed for better times, white men in the seventies knew better than to think that a guardian angel would come and save them. In Bogart, there was truth and reality in these hazy, relativistic times. Bogie became an incarnation of what Susan Jeffords so aptly dubbed "hard bodies," action stars of the post–Vietnam era who gave white men back their modernism in the face of a rampant postmodernism that threatened to make everything they had come to know meaningless.[40]

The Re-Judaization of America

"The crisis in ideological confidence of the 1970s," writes Robin Wood in *Hollywood From Vietnam to Reagan* (1986), "visible on all levels of American culture and variously enacted in Hollywood's 'incoherent texts' has not been resolved.... Instead it has been forgotten."[41] The fact that Woody Allen's homage to the Bogie cult, *Play It Again, Sam*, was a box office hit, whereas *The Long Goodbye* was such a failure that it relegated Elliott Gould into the doldrums of anonymity for years to come, seems like no coincidence in an era defined by a "crisis in ideological confidence." While appearing to alleviate this crisis, Allen's identification with Bogart actually foments it. By keeping the Jew separate from white Americanness, in a state of irreverent awe rather than equality, Allen's film resuscitates ideological values and adds to the hegemonic project of racial separation. Rather than being an incoherent text that Wood speaks of, *Play It Again, Sam* is utterly coherent. It uses the Jew as he so often has been used, as a tool to rehabilitate white manhood. In contrast, *The Long Goodbye* neither aggravates nor assuages the crisis; it makes the crisis visible. For Gould, Bogie is not a reified image to be bowed down to in idol worship, untethered to time or place, but is instead a live image to be parodied and reinvented. He deconstructs the fetishized image of Bogie, exposing the false nostalgia in the Bogie cult. By making Bogie a Jew, *The Long Goodbye* makes impossible the ideologically motivated identification of victimized white men with Bogie, and thereby challenges the racialist conventions of film noir.

The Long Goodbye toiled in relative obscurity for years, remaining a cult classic until its re-release on DVD in 2002. The main reason for its re-release may not have much to do with the film at all, but may have been a part of Hollywood's plan to make money on the reemergent Elliott Gould industry. A younger generation of fans who have come to know him on NBC's juggernaut *Friends* (1994–2004) or have seen him nominated for an MTV Movie Award in *Ocean's Eleven* (2001) might be curious to learn more about the Gould who was once a bonafied star. Always refusing to be stereotyped in his seventies heyday, Gould has become one of America's "New Super Jews" by performing a Jewish stereotype.[42] He plays schlemiel-cum-gangster Rueben Tishkoff in the recent *Ocean's* films, adorned with horn-rimmed glasses, gaudy red suit, and silk tie, a kinder, gentler version of *The Long Goodbye*'s Jewish hood, Marty Augustine.

Paradoxically, it is Woody Allen who has turned away from his Jewishness and has become, in a sense, "white." Allen's de-Judaization may be seen most conspicuously in the trend in his recent films to cast non–Jews to perform his hyper–Jewish character. The British actor Kenneth Branaugh awkwardly played the bumbling schlemiel character, no doubt a parody of "Woody" himself, to poor reviews in 1998's *Celebrity*. Also in that year, Allen's self-imposed exile from Jewishness took on a bizarre intonation when he played the disembodied voice of an anxiety-ridden ant with a stifling inferiority complex in the animated film, *Antz* (1998). As his relationship with Soon-Yi Previn has made him fodder for the tabloids, we have seen a much different image of Allen than the hysterical nebbish that defined most of his career. Rather than the scared-to-death, childlike, pathologically alive Allen wrestling with lobsters in *Annie Hall* (1977), we now see tabloid photos of an aging Allen, solemn, disembodied, a walking image of death that evokes Richard Dyer's famous analysis of zombies in his influential article, "White."[43] It is the chief irony of our story that Woody Allen has finally become Bogart, though not the one he so desperately wanted to be in *Play It Again, Sam*. Instead of the virile, fast-talking Bogie of John Huston's films, Allen has become the Bogie of "decomposition," of "death" that Truffaut and Bazin mourned on the pages of *Cahiers du Cinéma*.[44] Having come so late in his career, Allen's turn away from "Jewishness" may be interpreted as being done for personal reasons (his having become too old for traditional romantic leads, say, or the public having lost interest in his persona), but it also may be seen as endemic of a culture in which Jewishness has increasingly become a fetish. Jewishness was never something to be fetishized for Woody Allen; it was something to be disavowed, a tic that never seemed to go away. If the years of 1972–3 marked a temporary apogee in the reemergence of the Jewish question in Hollywood cinema after decades of systemic neglect, then the beginning years of the twenty-first century might mark the third Golden Age of the American Jew in cinema. That Woody Allen is unwilling to participate in this new golden age should be considered no insignificant coincidence.

NOTES

1. "Elliott Gould: The Urban Don Quixote," *Time*, 7 September 1970, 35–40, here 36.

2. Joanna Smith Rakoff, "The New Super Jews," *Time Out New York*, 4–11 December 2003, 13–18, here 13.

3. Robin Wood, *Hollywood from Vietnam to Reagan ... and Beyond* (New York: Columbia University Press, 1986; rev. and expanded ed., 2003), 29. Virtually all of the criticism on the film analyzes it in terms of its revisionary treatment of the film noir tradition, either as an "anti-genre movie" (see Helene Keyssar, *Robert Altman's America* [New York: Oxford University Press, 1991], 90), or as a "genre commentary" (see Norman Kagan, *American*

Skeptic: Robert Altman's Genre-Commentary Films [Ann Arbor, MI: Pierian, 1982]). See also Donald Lyons, "Flaws in the Iris," *Film Comment* XXIX.4 (July-August 1993), 44–53; B. Oliver, "*The Long Goodbye* and *Chinatown*: Debunking the Private Eye Tradition," *Literature/Film Quarterly* III.3 (Summer 1975), 240–48; G. Steward, "*The Long Goodbye* from *Chinatown*," *Film Quarterly* XXVIII.2 (Winter 1974–75), 25–32; William F. Van Wert, "Phillip Marlowe: Hardboiled to Softboiled to Poached," *Jump Cut* 3 (September-October 1974), 10–13; and Richard Ferncase, "Marlowe in the Me Decade," *Journal of Popular Culture* 25.2 (Fall 1991), 87–90.

4. Wood, *Hollywood*, 29. This scene goes curiously uncommented upon in the vast archive of critical work on Altman. Wood devotes an entire chapter to Altman's films, "Smart Ass and Cutie-Pie" (even naming it after the scene in question), but fails to bring up Gould's blackface. Similarly, Helene Keyssar analyzes this scene at length in *Robert Altman's America*, discussing Gould's blackface but neglecting the intertwined history of Jewish performers and blackface minstrelsy. Rather, Keyssar examines the film in terms of its self-reflexive, improvisatory performance techniques (e.g., "Marlowe displays his awareness that he is performing in front of a one-way mirror by blackening his face with fingerprint ink and singing 'Sewanee' [*sic*]," 93). On this point, see also Robert Kolker, *A Cinema of Loneliness: Penn, Stone, Kubrick, Scorsese, Spielberg, Altman* (New York: Oxford University Press, 1988, 3rd ed., 2000), 363; Virginia Wexman, "Rhetoric of Cinematic Improvisation," *Cinema Journal* 20.1 (Fall 1980), 29–41. On a documentary featurette accompanying the new DVD release, Elliott Gould describes how *Ocean's Eleven* director Steven Soderbergh was especially interested to know if the scene in question was unplanned. "Yes," Gould confirmed proudly. "Bob [Altman] gives me the right," "Rip van Marlowe," documentary featurette, *The Long Goodbye*, MGM DVD, 2002.

5. Michael Rogin, *Blackface, White Noise: Jewish Immigrants in the Hollywood Melting Pot* (Berkeley: University of California Press, 1996), 73–120. A note about terms: most cultural historians confirm that the Jew in America in the early twentieth century was not considered "white." Rather, the Jew was of an inferior race, bearing the mark of a racialized subject, looked upon as "oriental," "negro," or "off white." See Karen Brodkin, *How Jews Became White Folks and What That Says About Race in America* (New Brunswick, NJ: Rutgers University Press, 1998), 1–52.

6. Rogin, *Blackface*, 102.

7. Rogin writes: "[Blackface] allows the protagonist to exchange selves rather than fixing him in the one where he began. Blackface is the instrument that transfers identities from immigrant Jew to American," 95. Notice Rogin's use of either/or terms like "exchange" and "transfers." See also Neal Gabler, *An Empire of Their Own: How the Jews Invented Hollywood* (New York: Crown, 1989), who discusses how fiercely the Jewish heads of the Hollywood studios rejected their Jewish pasts in favor of American futures.

8. Sanford Pinsker, *The Schlemiel as Metaphor: Studies in the Yiddish and Jewish American Novel* (Carbondale: Southern Illinois Press, 1971, 1991), 168.

9. "Rip van Marlowe."

10. On the seventies as a transitional period in American cultural history, what he calls the "uncanny decade" or the "undecade," see Stephen Paul Miller, *The Seventies Now: Culture as Surveillance* (Durham, NC: Duke University Press, 1999).

11. Brodkin, 160.

12. Patricia Erens, "Between Two Worlds: Jewish Images in American Film," *The Kaleidoscopic Lens: How Hollywood Views Ethnic Groups*, ed. Randall M. Miller (Englewood, NJ: Ozer, 1980), 114–134, here 128. This linking of the 1970s and 1920s is literalized in *The Long Goodbye* itself, as we have seen, in Gould's reference to Jolson.

13. Ibid., 133.

14. Rogin, 209.

15. Josh Kun, *Audiotopia: Music, Race, and America* (Berkeley: University of California Press, 2005), 64.

16. Steven Cohan, *Masked Men: Masculinity and the Movies in the Fifties* (Bloomington: Indiana University Press, 1997), 80.

17. James L. Neibaur, *Tough Guy: The American Movie Macho* (Jefferson, NC: McFarland, 1989), 72.

18. Woody Allen, *Woody Allen on Woody Allen: In Conversation with Stig Bjorkman* (New York: Grove, 1993), 51.

19. Bazin called Bogart "the actor/myth of the war and post-war period," "The Death of Humphrey Bogart," *Cahiers du Cinema* 68 (February 1957), trans. Phillip Drummond, reprinted in *Cahiers du Cinema, The 1950s: Neo-Realism, Hollywood, New Wave*, ed. Jim Hillier (Cambridge, MA: Harvard University Press, 1985), 98–101, here 99. Similarly, Truffaut wrote in 1958 that "Humphrey Bogart was a modern hero," "A Portrait of Humphrey Bogart," *The Films in My Life*, trans. Leonard Mayhew (New York: Simon & Schuster, 1978), 295.

20. Susan Sontag, "Notes on Camp," *Against Interpretation and Other Essays* (New York: Farrar, Straus and Giroux, 1988), 275–292.

21. "Old Bogart Films Packing Them In," *New York Times*, 28 January 1965, 19.

22. Cohan, 80.

23. Ibid., 121.

24. Neibaur, 72.

25. David Savran, *Taking It Like a Man: White Masculinity, Masochism, and Contemporary American Culture* (Princeton: Princeton University Press, 1998), especially 1–38. For a similar argument, see Susan Jeffords, *The Remasculinization of America: Gender and the Vietnam War* (Bloomington: Indiana University Press, 1989).

26. Robert J. Corber, *Homosexuality in Cold War America: Resistance and the Crisis of Masculinity* (Durham, NC: Duke University Press, 1997), 14.

27. Richard Warren Lewis, "Playboy Interview: Elliott Gould," *Playboy*, November 1970, 77–94, 262–264, here 77, 262.

28. "Elliott Gould: The Urban Don Quixote," *Time,* 35–40, here 36.

29. Ibid., 38, 36.

30. Ibid., 35.

31. Ibid., 37.

32. Rogin, 86.

33. Ibid.

34. Quoted in "Elliott Gould," *Time*, 36, emphasis added.

35. Charles Champlin, "A Private Eye's Honor Blackened," *Los Angeles Times*, 8 March 1973, sec. G, 1 and 15, here 1.

36. "Rip van Marlowe."

37. Pauline Kael, "Movieland — The Bum's Paradise," reprinted in *Reeling* (Boston: Little, Brown, 1976), 182–190, here 184, 186.

38. Kael, 189.

39. Gould's performance as the Jewish Humphrey Bogart was not merely reviled by most critics but was completely illegible to others who were used to seeing Jewish performers only as stereotypes. One notable example of such illegibility was to Gould himself. Here's how J. Hoberman puts it in his highly readable recent profile of Gould: "Gould expresses (or feigns) puzzlement when it's pointed out that even in the role of Philip Marlowe, he comes across as Jewish: 'I just wanted to be American,' he insists. That's a pathos John Wayne and Humphrey Bogart never experienced," par. 30, *The Village Voice*, 10 April 2007, www.villagevoice.com/2007-04-10/film/the-goulden-age/1. A second, more expected, example is from some of the better known "Jews in Film" volumes, where analyses of *The Long Goodbye* are present but Gould is not included as a *Jew* in the film. Instead, these volumes focus on Marty Augustine, the film's Jewish gangster who represents, according to one volume, "the Jew as symbol of corruption," Lester D. Friedman, *Hollywood's Image of the Jew* (New York: Frederick Ungar, 1982), 231. A second volume similarly ignores Gould, stating,

"In *the Long Goodbye*, the Jewish character is again minor and negatively presented," Erens, "Between Two Worlds," 363. The hypervisibility of the Jewish gangster (Augustine prominently wears a Star of David around his neck and "acts like something of a clown" [Friedman, *Hollywood's Image* 233]) deflects the more ambiguous Jewishness of Gould.

40. See Susan Jeffords' *Hard Bodies: Hollywood Masculinity in the Reagan Years* (New Brunswick, NJ: Rutgers University Press, 1994).

41. Wood, *Hollywood*, 144.

42. Rakoff, "The New Super Jews." From Madonna's highly publicized conversion to the Jewish mystical tradition of Kabbalah to films like *The Hebrew Hammer* (2003) to the hip Jewishness espoused in *Heeb* magazine, "[y]oung people are embracing their identity as Jews in a way we haven't seen before," 16.

43. Richard Dyer, "White," *Screen* 29.4 (Autumn 1988), 44–64.

44. Bazin said that Bogart embodied the "immanence of death," "The Death of Humphrey Bogart," 98; Truffaut referred to Bogart's smile as the "smile of death," "A Portrait of Humphrey Bogart," 294.

8

A Cinema of Plenty:
Robert Altman and the
Multi-Protagonist Film

Maria del Mar Azcona

The end credit sequence of Robert Altman's last film, *A Prairie Home Companion* (2006), which was released shortly before the director's death, can be seen as a self-reflexive farewell and even a requiem for the type of filmic art that he embodied over more than four decades. In a film which is traversed by the presence of death and within a narrative context which is little more than a thin excuse for apparently spontaneous comic human interaction, the performance of the religious hymn "In the Sweet By and By" is filmed with the apparently haphazard style, improvisational acting, and piling of the frame with more or less well-known actors that are recurrent in the filmography of the U.S. director. Fictional and real-life performers, musicians, and crew members come onstage for this final sequence which is not just the ending of the last show that we see onscreen but also the very last in the director's career. Altman's penchant for big ensembles of characters is one of the most distinguishing features of his particular attitude towards films and filmmaking. This artificially spontaneous song captures not only a way of understanding cinema but a view of life that aficionados of Altman's movies have learned to interpret as the essence of his artistic discourse. In a film about endings and about the inevitability of death and oblivion, this sequence is a reminder of the legacy of its director. Though there is much more to Robert Altman's distinctive style than multiple characters and simultaneous narrative threads, in this essay I concentrate on this aspect of his work within the wider context of the multi-protagonist film, a generic form which has become widespread in the last two decades and one in whose emergence Robert Altman's movies played a crucial role. Among the director's varied approaches to multi-character casts, special attention will be given to *Short Cuts*, one of Altman's most paradigmatic experiments with this format and a referent for later examples of the genre.

Altman's career-long fascination with multi-character casts linked through incidental plot lines[1] was a key factor in the emergence and development of the multi-protagonist genre. Yet, Altman did not invent the pattern. The presence in a single film of a multiplicity of characters with various lines of action can be traced back to the beginning of the classical period and to Irving Thalberg's by then revolutionary idea of gathering a wide collection of the studio stars under the same roof in MGM's *Grand Hotel* (1932). The commercial strategy proved a success and was repeated in films like *Dinner at Eight* (1933), *Stage Door* (1937), and *The Women* (1939). Outside Hollywood, two of Jean Renoir's best-known films, *La grande illusion* (1937) and *La règle du jeu* (1939), also employed multi-protagonist patterns in order to weave intricate tapestries and represent the follies and decadence of a specific social group and the absurdity of war and frontiers. A similar interest in multi-character narrative structures could be found in some of Howard Hawks's films: the episodic and loose narrative lines of films like *Hatari!* (1962) and *Red Line 7000* (1965), for example, became a mere excuse for the exploration of complex group dynamics. Later on, the disaster film cycle of the 1970s combined some of these functions while adding a new one. Films like *Airport* (1970), *The Poseidon Adventure* (1972) and *Towering Inferno* (1974) packed their narratives with wide ensembles of well-known actors as a marketing strategy, and as a way of dwelling on gender and class conflicts, but also as a suspense-preserving mechanism since the proliferation of stars made it almost impossible to predict which one of them would survive the catastrophe.

Yet, no other film director used the multi-protagonist film so recurrently and consistently as to turn it into his auteur mark. *M*A*S*H* (1970) and *Nashville* (1975) were Altman's first two experiments with a narrative pattern that he would use, in varied forms, in fourteen films out of the thirty-four he directed for the big screen. When examples of the genre started to proliferate in the 1980s and 1990s, Altman's films became a familiar referent to classify a type of storytelling that could not be easily accommodated within any other generic category. Critical discourse started to activate webs of family resemblances and relationships that linked new multi-protagonist films to some of Altman's movies. Mike Higgins, for example, sees the shadow of *Short Cuts* looming large in *Playing by Heart* (1999) as does Roger Ebert in his review of *Lantana* (2002).[2] The adjective "Altmanesque" soon emerged as a shorthand term to refer to almost any kind of multi-stranded parallel storytelling and was applied to movies as varied as *Boogie Nights* (1997), *Magnolia* (1999), *Traffic* (2000), *Monsoon Wedding* (2001), *Cape of Good Hope* (2004), *Crash* (2005), and *Happy Endings* (2005), among many others.[3] The drastic increase in the number of films using this narrative pattern in the last twenty-five years and, especially, the recurrence of a set of visual and narrative conventions and thematic concerns have turned the structure into a proper genre. As shown by some of its latest entries such as *Crash*, *Syriana* (2005), *Babel* (2006), *Fast Food Nation* (2006) and *Crossing Over* (2009), the development of the multi-protagonist genre has run parallel to the cultural impact of a series of scientific and social discourses — such as chaos theory, the butterfly effect, the global village phenomenon and six degrees of separation theories — which have both challenged traditional notions of causality and emphasized the networked nature of human life and interaction in an increasingly shrinking and globalized world.

The thematic concerns of Altman's multi-protagonist films never gravitated towards the global aims of films like *Syriana* and *Babel*. Yet, their detailed explorations of the intricate nature of human interaction have become a central feature of the genre that other directors have expanded to wider scopes. Margrit Tröhler distinguishes between two categories of multi-protagonist films — ensemble and mosaic movies — depending on the existence or absence of a central meeting place in which all the characters come together at some point in the narrative.[4] Altman's stories tend to fluctuate between these two groups. His multi-protagonist casts are arranged in self-enclosed communities of professional performers in *Buffalo Bill and the Indians* (1976), *The Company* (2003) and *A Prairie Home Companion*, and in looser ad hoc groups of people that come together for a special occasion in *A Wedding* (1978) and *Gosford Park* (2001). In between these two tendencies, *M*A*S*H* explores the interactions between a very diverse group of soldiers brought together by the Korean War and *Cookie's Fortune* (1999) unearths long time secrets within a dysfunctional family and the small community that surrounds it. Films like *Nashville* and *Prêt-à-Porter* (1994) are more mosaic-like but use an overarching framing event — the Nashville music festival and the political rally in *Nashville* and the Paris Fashion Week in *Prêt-à-Porter*— to provide the temporal and spatial boundaries necessary for the mingling of characters and narrative lines. The temporal and spatial frames become more diffuse in *Short Cuts*, a movie which replaces the central meeting place by several narrative nodes where the paths of assorted inhabitants of L.A. intersect and crisscross at random.

Even films, like *The Player* (1992), *Kansas City* (1996) and *Dr. T and the Women* (2000), which appear to feature a single protagonist, use that central character not so much in the traditional way we have come to expect but as the hub around which the rest of the group revolves. Regardless of the actual degree of interaction between the characters — be it a tight group or a looser collection of individuals — Altman's multi-protagonist films usually develop into mural works which, with the director's peculiar comic touch, are rife with the tensions, conflicts, and anxieties that come from human relationships. Depending on the specific themes and concerns of each movie, these may be sexual, professional, racial, or class tensions, or a combination of them. They may not always come openly to the surface or at least not in the way we expect them to, but they are always sizzling underneath the narratives' otherwise incidental and sometimes almost irrelevant plot lines. Multi-protagonist patterns became the ideal narrative form for a director who, in his own words, wanted to make the audience find for themselves the drama in the situation rather than "serve it up to them."[5] In sum, the multi-protagonist template is a crucial component of Altman's stories and of his characteristic way of telling them.

The narrative arcs of Altman's films contradict most of the guidelines provided by some of the best-known scriptwriting manuals.[6] Apparently unimportant characters, who apparently do not contribute much to narrative development, and incidental details leading nowhere abound in his films. Rather than rushing forward towards crucial turning points and an inevitable conclusion, his stories move at a leisurely pace, if they move at all. Sometimes, the films flout linearity altogether and tend to expand "sideways" as a television producer lamented when he saw what Altman was doing to one of his scripts.[7] In *Prêt-à-Porter*, for example, a secret meeting between two men wearing identical Dior ties appears at first sight to be central in the development of the plot but is soon narratively buried under a succession of comparable encounters, conversations and interviews between different sorts of people — fashion designers, models, editors and reporters — all of whom have gathered for the Paris Fashion Week. Altman's particular way of telling stories overemphasizes and amplifies the retardation of narrative development which is almost intrinsic to most multi-protagonist narratives — since they have to shift between a multiplicity of characters and narrative lines — by introducing constant digressions and pauses in the narrative flow.

In *Prêt-à-Porter*, any interest raised by any of the narrative lines has to endure the interruptions brought about by both real-life and fictional fashion shows, likewise with the musical numbers in *Nashville*, *Kansas City* and *A Prairie Home Companion*. This does not mean that these moments are merely spectacle and are devoid of narrative content. They are not, or at least not completely, even if they may be hard to bear for spectators looking for non-stop and casually connected narrative events. Kiki (Tara Leon) and Dane's (Georgianna Robertson) rivalry over Jack Lowenthal (Rupert Everett) finally comes to the fore on the catwalk in *Prêt-à-Porter* and Yolanda's (Meryl Streep) resentment over her past affair with GK (Garrison Keillor) is fully verbalized in the course of a duct tape commercial in *A Prairie Home Companion*. Yet the continuous diversions and the concern with other apparently trifling moments of the characters' lives may even lead to a complete abandonment of the narrative in a more conventional sense.

The Company, Altman's one but last feature film, reduces the storyline to almost the bare minimum — some incidental moments in the lives of the members of a ballet company — while the rest of the film's running time is taken up by the mesmerizing and colorful ballet numbers. There are several story elements in *The Company*— a ballerina snaps her Achilles tendon; Ry (Neve Campbell) arrives too late from work on New Year's Eve and finds a romantic dinner for two on the table and her boyfriend fast asleep on the couch; a member of the company is made redundant almost right before the opening night — but, as the director himself remarked, these are just hints of stories which are never fully developed.[8] A similar effect is produced by the live songs and commercials which intersperse the backstage action and the performers' fond memories of their past in *A Prairie Home Companion*. These digressions, as well as other incidental and apparently unimportant moments in Altman's films, are neither merely cosmetic nor narrative padding but are actually what the movies are about. As Kolker argues, Altman's movies are about the periphery rather than the center of the action. "Events on the edges," he claims, "gain equal importance with events in the middle."[9] The high concept approach to filmmaking that was Griffin Mill's (Tim Robbins) motto and working basis in *The Player* could not be further from Altman's own view of the ideal film as one that manages to take the narrative completely out of it, and one in which the spectators "will sit and see the film and understand the movie's intention without being able to articulate it."[10]

Linear and straight-forward narrative development is usually replaced by an interest in simultaneous actions. To the constant shifting between different plot lines and characters that is intrinsic to multi-protagonist storytelling, Altman's movies add certain formal elements to create multi-dimensional spaces brimming over with actions and voices. One of his most characteristic ways of accomplishing this is to pack the frame with as many characters as possible. In "Les Boréades," his short segment in the collaborative film, *Aria* (1987), the frame is taken over by the inmates of an insane asylum attending a theatrical performance. They fill the screen in an even more excessive way than the performers in the scene from *A Prairie Home Companion* described at the beginning of this essay. As critics consistently argue, crowded frames are a favorite of the director.[11] The recurrent group scenes in *M*A*S*H*, the jazz performances in *Kansas City* and many of the scenes in *Nashville* are just a few of the many examples of populous frames that can be found in his filmography. Even when the number of characters is not enough to fill the frame, Altman may use elements of setting to artificially increase the amount of human figures on screen. In most of the backstage scenes in *A Prairie Home Companion*, the mirror-covered walls in the performers' dressing rooms multiply the bodies and faces, underlining the feeling of closeness and solidarity among the members of the radio show, a view of human relationships which is absent from other of Altman films. This visual density allows the director to develop more than one narrative thread simultaneously in two different parts of the frame, a strategy which forces spectators to be aware of the periphery as well as the center of the frame.

In *A Wedding*, the first visual evidence of the relationship between the butler and one of Nettie's (Lillian Gish) daughters recedes to the edges of the widescreen frame while the foreground is taken up by a snatch of an irrelevant conversation between the wedding photographer and one of the organizers. In *Short Cuts*, the camera that tracks along with Ann (Andie MacDowell) into Casey's (Zane Cassidy) hospital room as she is about to tell Howard (Bruce Davidson) that his father, whom he has not seen in years, is in the waiting room, suddenly leaves them offscreen and focuses on some passers-by precisely at the moment in which she is breaking the news to him. The after-dinner gatherings of the guests in *Gosford Park* arrange the characters on several spatial planes using the full width of the widescreen, forcing spectators to be constantly aware of the different levels along which the action is articulated, including the limits of the frame — according to Kolker, Altman's rule was to constantly impose peripheral action over the central focus.[12] While Ivor Novello (Jeremy Northam) is singing and playing the piano in the background — while Jennings (Alan Bates) to his left is enjoying the music in a less discreet way than the manor rules allow him to — Sylvia (Kristin Scott Thomas) and her sister, on the foreground left, engage in a private conversation about Sylvia's husband, Sir William (Michael Gambon). To their left, Mabel Nessbit (Claudie Blakley) is questioning her husband about his unjustified absence from the room. Just in case these three simultaneous actions were not enough, a game of bridge is also being played in the foreground right. Altman's films encourage and require audience participation and their visual density is such that, as has been mentioned before, the texts refuse to tell spectators where they should be looking and force them to increase their spectatorial activity. The flattening of the space with the telephoto lens that is usually mentioned in relation to Altman's visual style also produces a similar effect.

As Kolker argues, Altman's combination of the extreme width of the Panavision screen and the compressed depth created by the telephoto lens puts foreground and background on almost the same plane, cramming the screen space with people and objects.[13] Likewise with the aural density that Altman's films are famous for — what Helene Keyssar calls the director's "depth of focus in *sound*" (emphasis in original).[14] His penchant for overlapping dialogue goes back to the very start of his film-directing career — this being a technique which, as he repeatedly claimed, he did not invent and can be traced back to at least Howard Hawks.[15] In any case, some of his narrative experiments with sound have become landmarks of film sound technology.[16]

Multi-character casts, together with the aural and visual density of most of Altman films, result in a plethora of information which may pose some challenges to the spectators' recognition of the characters onscreen. Altman repeatedly argued that he always tried to cast famous actors in order to help spectators in this process.[17] Yet, probably for a similar reason, those films featuring the largest ensembles of characters — *A Wedding*, *Nashville*, and *Gosford Park* — usually include a "getting-to-know-each-other" scene in which both characters and spectators find out who is who in the filmic tapestry. The early scene at the canteen in *M*A*S*H* and the guest reception in *A Wedding* are not only a way of introducing characters to one another but also of introducing them to the spectators. A similar but related function is that of the "tour guide" — what Keyssar calls "the commentator"[18] — usually a newcomer or outsider to the group or the professional sector under scrutiny who shares the viewer's initial feeling of disorientation as is the case of Opal (Geraldine Chaplin), the inquisitive BBC reporter in *Nashville*, or Kitty (Kim Basinger), the inexpert fashion reporter in *Prêt-à-Porter*. The role of Mary (Kelly Macdonald) in *Gosford Park* is a similar one even if, unlike Opal and Kitty, who are ridiculed and laughed at through most of the narrative, Mary's lack of familiarity with the servants, the masters, and most of the protocols in Sir William's country house is used to foster spectatorial identification with her. Among the wide ensemble of characters onscreen, Mary becomes the spectators' major link with the filmic world. As she finds her way through the manor's labyrinthine corridors and class rules, she gradually discovers, as do we, the intricate links between the various characters. Subverting the conventions of the murder mystery genre and in accordance with Altman's approach to storytelling, these links end up proving more meaningful than the resolution of Sir William's murder.

Processes of identification also work differently in Altman's films. Although, as classical film theory argued, subject positions are generally multiple in traditional, even single-hero, film narratives, the protagonist inevitably attracts most of the spectators' engagement and becomes "the main object of audience identification."[19] Multi-protagonist films deny the spectators a privileged and straightforward access to the fictional world and force them to fluctuate among the wide ensemble of characters on screen, usually replacing close identification with a single character by multiple, transitory, and fragmentary engagement with a wider collection of figures and their viewpoints, attitudes, and ideological positions. Yet, identification patterns depend on other narrative strategies as well and do not work in the same way in all multi-protagonist films. Altman's films also show a considerable variety in this respect. The film's "tour guide" becomes the spectators' main access to the story world in *Gosford Park* but not in *Nashville* or *Prêt-à-Porter*, where identification with these characters is seriously compromised for various reasons. Although not without exceptions, this difficulty in identifying with the characters is a general feature of Altman's films, which tend to be extremely reluctant to give us access to psychological and emotional motivations and internal states. Neve Campbell's character in *The Company*, for example, becomes our main, even if rather weak, link with the fictional world not because her character is more psychologically rounded than the rest but because of her popularity as an actor — her fellow ballet dancers being actual members of the Joffrey Ballet of Chicago.

Identification processes become even more complex in *Short Cuts*, a film which resorts to parallel editing to narrate the storylines of twenty-odd characters who live in scattered areas of the city of Los Angeles — a fact that complicates the attainment of the type of spatial unity shown by *Nashville* and *Prêt-à-Porter*, for example. This spatial expansion is closely connected with the film's cultivation of a conscious detachment between characters and spectators — and as will be seen later on, also among the characters themselves — in order to put forward a specific view of interpersonal relationships. This particular attitude to human interaction is both representative of Altman's filmography as a whole and crucial to understanding later developments of the multi-protagonist film genre. Therefore, I would like to start my analysis of *Short Cuts* by exploring the ways identification works in the movie.

In a first viewing, any spectator watching *Short Cuts* will probably have difficulties to recognize who is who in the film's complex tapestry of different characters, thus compromising even, the process of recognition, the most basic of the three levels of engagement with film characters proposed by Murray Smith.[20] Yet, the protagonists acquire distinctive enough identities and personalities as the narrative moves on. Even if, as Robert T. Self maintains,[21] characters' names may be almost irrelevant, the family and friendship relationships between them gradually become clear as the film develops. Smith's second level of engagement, alignment — the process whereby, by means of a variety of formal and narrative devices, viewers gain direct access to what the characters know and feel — is at work but has serious limitations in *Short Cuts*. The use of parallel editing forces us to move continually from one set of characters to the next and makes our engagement with them brief and multiple — an illustration of the visual promiscuity that Keyssar has referred to in her analysis of Altman's visual style.[22] In addition, the extended use of external focalization hinders our access to the protagonists' subjective states. The film does not remain completely opaque about internal states — we can feel Jerry's (Chris Penn) sexual anxiety and frustration, Zoe's (Lori Singer) desperation at her mother's unwillingness or inability to be moved, and Claire's (Anne Archer) horror and repulsion at her husband's treatment of the corpse — but these moments are scarce in a film which tends to observe its protagonists' behavior from the outside and in which, significantly, aerial and overhead shots abound. Even in shorter distances the effect is more one of opacity than of transparency since many other formal elements — such as framing and sound — are enlisted to attain a similar purpose. A fight between Earl (Tom

Waits) and Doreen (Lily Tomlin) is shot exclusively from the outside of their trailer house, the characters doubly framed by glass doors and windows, a framing choice which also highlights their impossibility to break free from the living conditions they would like to leave behind.

As a cultural text, inevitably traversed by ideological discourses, *Short Cuts* is egregiously reluctant to offer clear-cut moral and ideological positions for the spectators. Instead, Altman adopts an entomological stance, observes his figures with some detachment and asks us to react in a similar way. For him, understanding the human being is no easy task, but this task would be further compromised if we were offered straightforward positions with which we were asked to sympathize. Smith's third category of engagement, allegiance, is therefore altogether curtailed in this film. Individual spectators will inevitably feel closer to one character or another, but the text is consistently reluctant to facilitate such approximations. When Claire finds out the way Stuart (Fred Ward) and his friends have dealt with the corpse they found in the river, she is horrified, but to the group of friends when the situation arises it seems the logical thing to do. The film is not asking us to support the fishermen's behavior but provides a context for their action. In its refusal to impose decisive judgment on its characters, it also warns about the dangers of jumping to conclusions all-too-hastily and without knowing more than one side of the story. The accidental swapping of two sets of pictures between Honey (Lili Taylor) and Gordon (Buck Henry), one of Stuart's friends, at the end of the movie further illustrates this point. While Honey and Lois (Jennifer Jason Leigh) leaf in disgust through the pictures of the corpse found in the river, Gordon is repelled by what he thinks are the photographs of a woman battered to death. Both parties are equally horrified at the other's fascination with the view of a female corpse, look at one another with gross suspicion and try to retain some way of identifying the other, just in case.

This proliferation of perspectives and the need to understand individual behavior in its particular context has become a recurrent convention of the multi-protagonist film. Although not all multi-protagonist movies engage with the spectators in the same way as *Short Cuts*— Smith's first level, recognition, is more compromised in *Syriana* than it is in *Short Cuts*, for instance, and films like *Crash* or *Babel* make it easier for the spectators to align with the characters — the genre has gravitated towards the inclusion of a wide panoply of viewpoints and voices, which in the complex and multi-sided worlds of films like *Crash*, *Syriana*, *Fast Food Nation*, and *Babel* are incompatible with easy generalizations and rushed ideological solutions.

Altman's ensembles have played a crucial role in gradually familiarizing spectators with polyphonic narratives. His filmic tapestries brim over with a cacophony of voices and discourses competing, if not for prominence, at least to be heard through the deafening noise of the privileged and taken-for-granted ideologies.

The proliferation of perspectives and sides to an issue is not the only feature of *Short Cuts* that has become a convention of the multi-protagonist film genre: its emphasis on chance and the interconnected nature of human life is a recurrent topic in later examples of the genre, such as *Magnolia*, *Thirteen Conversations about One Thing* (2001), and *Babel*. In *Short Cuts*, random chance is represented as intrinsic to life itself and it is this relentless and uncontrollable force, and not the characters' wills and wishes, that ultimately rules people's lives. Human beings are prisoners of life and helpless victims of its inscrutable and capricious designs — "Yesterday you own the world, the next day the world owns you," sings Tess (Annie Ross) in the sequence that opens the film. Serendipity, rather than causality, is the ruling agency in *Short Cuts*. The role of human individual agency that is so frequently championed in other texts becomes seriously compromised in a film in which individuals are constantly at the mercy of external circumstances, and where their determination and will plays second fiddle to other uncontrollable forces. Rather than the makers of their own destinies, human beings in *Short Cuts* are the puppets of chance, coping with the circumstances and reacting to what happens to them.

The earthquake with which the film ends is, apart from a way of stopping a narrative that otherwise could have continued infinitely, a graphic way of stating a similar idea: the characters struggle to stand on their own two feet while their whole world is crumbling around them. Yet, this pessimistic reading is not the only one that emerges from the film's surrender to the hegemony of chance. Serendipity in *Short Cuts* sometimes has fatal or very tragic consequences: it is random chance that causes Casey's accident and it was also that same force that caused Howard's own accident as a child and, as a consequence, Paul's (Jack Lemmon) estrangement from his family — "bad timing" is the way he puts it to his son when he sees him again more than three decades later. Yet, in accordance with the film's multiple perspectives, it is also that very unruly force that makes life worth living. As Tess sings at the beginning, "It's the unexpected that keeps us going." Having to accept the power of the uncontrollable in our lives is not tragic in itself. It is precisely that awareness that gives characters the hope that things may also turn out for the better, as in the case of Earl and Doreen's final happiness and their fantasy of getting out of Downey.

This same force also enhances the sense of the circuitry of human life and interaction that the film aims for. Apart from the many and manifold family, professional, and friendship ties between the characters, random chance thickens the social web by making characters' paths cross or collide in both consequential and inconsequential ways. The bakery, the hospital, the coffee-shop, and the night-club function as spatial nodes where the characters come together at different points in the narrative. While they remain unaware of each other's presence, we as spectators have the impression of being able to see everything. This creates in us a feeling of both insignificance and exhilaration, as we see the complexity and the wonders of the world in which we live. The movie celebrates the multiplicity of lives and stories that we cross in our daily lives, as well as its own unique power to convey that complexity of experience. A similar feeling emerges from the ways in which an event may branch off in unexpected directions: the characters may not know the direct and indirect consequences of their decisions but we do and are encouraged to see it all simultaneously. Casey being hit by Doreen's car affects a wide number of characters while Doreen remains unaware of it. It does not only affect his parents, but also the baker, since the elaborate birthday cake that Casey's mother ordered is never picked up, and Paul, who tries to regain contact with his long-estranged son. In a more indirect way, it is also the catalyst of Zoe's suicide and Tess's final despair — it is the latter's ice-cold reaction to the news of Casey's death that prompts Zoe's suicide in a desperate attempt to make her mother show a true emotional reaction again. Through these and other direct and indirect links, the film makes it impossible to draw clear-cut boundaries between the characters' storylines. They all become enmeshed in an intricate web, which not only reflects the networked nature of human life and interaction but also reveals the shortcomings and inadequacies of some of the tenets of an individualistic attitude towards life and shows that the characters' lives are ultimately inseparable from one another.

A similar impulse to join characters and lives is at work in the transitions between storylines. As Keyssar has noticed, editing in most Altman's films is not the hidden glue that links shots seamlessly to bring forward an illusion of continuity but rather an active way of creating meaning.[23] In *Short Cuts*, editing strategies combine with the film's overall narrative structure and themes to represent the intricacies of human interaction, linking apparently unconnected characters and storylines and calling attention to the similarities and parallelisms between their different situations. Visual and aural connections proliferate at the transitions between the storylines and emphasize undercurrents and deep links between the characters. Matches-on-action and graphic matches are extensively used to link the movement of characters from different storylines. A shot of Ralph (Matthew Modine) leaving through a door, for instance, cuts to one of Zoe entering the jazz club through another, and a shot of Betty (Frances McDormand) walking along a corridor matches one of Claire coming along a different one. The jar of Skippy peanut butter that graphically matches a shot of Sherri (Madeleine Stowe) and one of Marian (Julianne Moore) while they are talking on the phone may seem the only link between two sisters who seem to lead radically different lives. Yet, similar patterns emerge in their relationships with their husbands, a link that brings them together through different degrees of emotional numbness and a voluntary surrender to their domestic situations. Sherri's sardonic resignation to Gene's (Tim Robbins) constant lies and infidelities betrays her reluctance to actually confront the issue, an attitude which is not very different from Marian's quiet endurance of Ralph's sadistic jealousy and continuous humiliations. Yet, if Sherri's way of dealing with her problem comes through inane yelling, Marian conveys in her paintings the feelings that she has long forgotten how to express.

Visual continuity also emphasizes the links and undercurrents between some of these couples' domestic crises and intimate problems. As Claire returns home from the funeral of the unknown girl her husband and his fishing companions found in the river, unemployed Stuart asks her where she has been. Her husband's way of dealing with the corpse repels Claire even more than she can articulate and her only way of expressing her rage and disgust comes in the shape of bickering remarks. As she is about to leave the room and get changed for their dinner with Marian and Ralph, the film cuts to a shot of the latter at their wealthy house, editing together the movement of the two women across the room. The similar composition of the two shots highlights both the similarities and differences between the couples. Like Stuart, Ralph is sitting on the left of the frame asking questions which Marian keeps avoiding by moving around the frame. The huge emotional breach between both members of the couple is transferred from one shot to the next, and from one couple to another. Claire is appalled at her husband's lack of sensitivity towards the corpse of an anonymous female, while Stuart cannot even start to comprehend his wife's extreme concern. Ralph is similarly out of his wife's emotional reach and cannot even fathom what she is trying to convey by painting female nudes again and again.

Transitional aural cues are also used to anticipate a coming event. As Sherri shouts at her husband not to leave the dog outside because it might get run over, the film cuts to a shot of Casey running late for school and about to be hit by Doreen's car. A similar sense of foreboding emanates from the words heard over the graphic match that links the glass of milk that Ann leaves on Casey's night table with another glass of milk knocked accidentally on a televised recommendation on domestic accidents that Earl is watching: "accidents happen everyday, fortunately most are harmless, but some are very serious." They may also comment on a character or a relationship: the film cuts from Tess's description of her late husband as a "prick" to a shot of Stormy (Peter Gallagher) — voicing Betty's actual feelings towards her former husband — and Tess's singing "I don't know you" is heard during the transition to a shot of her daughter committing suicide. Again, even if it is Tess who is singing, the line seems more a reflection of Zoe's feelings towards her mother and her desperation at her mother's unwillingness or inability to express her emotions. In general, as with visual strategies, these aural links invite us to consider the web of connections that can be established between people and their emotional and moral predicaments at any given point of the narrative.

These editing strategies create invisible currents among characters and storylines and show them to be all enmeshed in an intricate social web in which similar situations, conflicts, and anxieties reverberate within each other and become magnified in the process. Yet, the visibility and abruptness of these editing devices is also a way of highlighting the characters' own estrangement and emotional isolation. In spite of the highly interconnected web in which they are all immersed, the film represents the emotional breaches between them as insurmountable, these abrupt cuts standing for the invisible walls that separate the characters, who are complete strangers even to those who are closest to them. These links and connections do not put forward the sense of a close community but rather a community of people living in isolation. Most of these rifts are a consequence of the problems of communication and of the emotional numbness that permeates the narrative and that affects all the relationships in it. Altman's films have never offered optimistic portrayals of either families or couples[24] and *Short Cuts* is no exception here. In this film, the crisis of love and the heterosexual couple, which permeates and traverses all social groups, has turned the family home into a prison which everybody tries to flee in a way or another, as shown by Gene's escapades and by Bill (Robert Downey Jr.) and Honey's surreptitious incursions into their neighbors' apartment. The scenes that take place inside the characters' apartments highlight the presence of lots of objects, walls, and corridors, which turn the house into a maze full of obstacles. The feeling of entrapment is enhanced by Altman's characteristic use of the telephoto lens and overlapping soundtracks — with the always-switched-on television sets contributing to shaping the cacophonous environment where communication is impossible. Within this view of domesticity, it is not surprising to find both the Kanes and the Wymans at the end of the film trying to continue their dinner party the morning after to postpone their return to the normalcy of their family homes, where their still unsolved conflicts will return to the foreground.

While the crises of the Kanes and the Wymans are left unresolved by the film's end, other couples — such as Sherri and Gene and Doreen and Earl — seem to have been able to overcome theirs. Yet, these final arrangements do not look any more definitive than the ones we saw during the previous three hours. The conflicts still persist and the film offers no evidence to believe that there will not be any more bitter quarrelling between Doreen and Earl or any more affairs in Gene's life; rather, the film offers more evidence to the contrary and Doreen's final comment on the earthquake — "this was not the big one" — encapsulates the nature of the characters' domestic crises. This sense of lives and stories going on beyond the film's boundaries is a consequence of an overall narrative structure which is ruled by random chance and is reinforced by the film's ending. *Short Cuts* falls into Richard Neupert's category of open story films: those films that acknowledge that while this stage of the story is finished the conflicts persist and there is no resolution to the conflicts onscreen.[25] After a shot of the Wymans and the Kanes toasting "to the lemonade" and ready to go back in the jacuzzi, the camera pans across the courtyard to offer first a panoramic view of LA and then a map of the city grid where separate homes and lives are linked by highways and the characters become imperceptible spots in a criss-cross pattern. The characters' toast posits itself not as a closed ending but as a stopping place, and the final movement of the camera contextualizes their conflicts within an even broader panorama. As in other multi-protagonist films, these final shots highlight the neverending nature of the conflicts onscreen while simultaneously calling attention to the insignificance and powerlessness of each of the characters, their stories, and predicaments in a large-scale social universe.

Robert Altman's attitude towards closure is as consistent as his overall attitude towards storytelling and the sense of closure missing in *Short Cuts* is also absent from most of his multi-protagonist movies. Even though all his films do eventually stop, they do not always end, and some actions, behavioral patterns, and motivations are left unexplained. His teeming tapestries and meandering narratives never seem to have been exhausted by the time we get to the final credits and always leave spectators with the feeling of lives continuing, an approach very much in tune with the philosophy of a director for whom death was the only possible ending: "the only ending I know about is death and the rest of it is stopping places."[26] This tendency towards open endings, which can also be found in most instances of the multi-protagonist film genre, is the more or less the logical consequence of this genre's interest in the interactions between characters to the detriment of plot, its emphasis on serendipity and the unplanned over more predictable cause-and-effect links, and its potential for the inclusion of a panoply of viewpoints and voices.

The wider the perspective, the more difficult it becomes to describe in a coherent and unified way a set of events or their narrative resolutions or to ascribe to them an absolute meaning. Altman's films, like multi-protagonist movies in general, challenge closure and neat and tidy resolutions. Instead of providing answers, they prefer to keep asking questions and suggest connections, similarities, and parallelisms between apparently unrelated individuals and situations. Yet, the precarious sense of teleology they offer and their emphasis on the intricate nature of human interaction have come to represent in a very suggestive and direct way the complexities of our contemporary shrinking and globalized world. Robert Altman's crucial role in bringing these larger processes to film cannot be underestimated. For almost four decades, the U.S. filmmaker taught us not to listen through the noise but to listen *to* the noise — to the deafening and wonderful noise of lived lives and to the constant humdrum of the intricacies of human nature in an increasingly interconnected world.

NOTES

1. David Thompson, ed., *Altman on Altman* (London: Faber and Faber, 2006), 164.

2. Mike Higgins, "*Playing by Heart*," *Sight and Sound*, 9.9 (1999): 52–53; here 53; Roger Ebert, "*Lantana*," http://rogerebert.suntimes.com/apps/pbcs.dll/article?AID=/20020118/REVIEWS/201180303/1023 (2002) (accessed January 26, 2005).

3. Richard Sharp, "Robert Altman: A Season with the Company," http://chicagofilm.com/features/altman.default.asp (2003) (accessed November 11, 2005); Ed González, "*Cape of Good Hope*," http://www.slantmagazine.com/film/film_review.asp?ID=1701 (2005)

(accessed November 16, 2005); Jonathan Romney "Edinburgh Cringe," *Sight and Sound*, 15.8 (2005): 1, 26–29.

4. Margrit Tröhler, "Les film à protagonistas multiples et la logique des posibles," *Iris* 29 (Spring 2000): 85–102; here 85–86.

5. Robert Altman in David Thompson, ed., *Altman on Altman*, 197.

6. Syd Field, *Screenplay: The Foundations of Screewriting* (1979; New York: Dell, 1994).

7. Patrick McGilligan, *Robert Altman: Jumping Off the Cliff. A Biography of the Great American Director* (New York: St. Martin's, 1989), 170.

8. In Thompson, 207.

9. Robert Kolker, *A Cinema of Loneliness: Penn, Kubrick, Scorsese, Spielberg, Altman* (Oxford: Oxford University Press, 1988), 320.

10. Robert Altman in Aljean Harmetz, "The 15th Man Who Was Asked to Direct *M*A*S*H* (and Did) Makes a Peculiar Western," *Robert Altman: Interviews*, ed. David Sterrit (Jackson: University Press of Mississipi, 2000), 3–10; here 8.

11. Kolker, 35.

12. Kolker, 311.

13. Kolker, 312.

14. Helene Keyssar, *Robert Altman's America* (New York and Oxford: Oxford University Press), 37.

15. Bruce Williamson, "Robert Altman," *Robert Altman: Interviews*, ed. David Sterrit, 32–64, here 56; Michael Wilmington, "Robert Altman and *The Long Goodbye*," *Robert Altman: Interviews*, ed. David Sterrit, 134–162, here 140.

16. Rick Altman, "24-Track Narrative? Robert Altman's *Nashville*," *Cinémas: Journal of Film Studies*, 1.3 (Spring 1991), http://www.revue-cinemas.umontreal.ca/vol001 no03/08-altman.htm (accessed July 22, 2009)

17. In Thomson, 165, 171, 195.

18. In Keyssar, 44.

19. David Bordwell, *Narration in the Fiction Film* (Madison: University of Wisconsin Press, 1985), 157.

20. Murray Smith, *Engaging Characters: Fiction, Emotion and the Cinema* (Oxford: Clarendon, 1995).

21. Robert T. Self, *Robert Altman's Subliminal Reality* (Minneapolis: University of Minnesota Press, 2002), 257.

22. Keyssar, 35–36.

23. Keyssar, 23.

24. Glen Mann, "*Short Cuts* to *Gosford Park*: The Family in Robert Altman," *A Family Affair: Cinema Calls Home*, ed. Murray Pomerance (London and New York: Wallflower, 2008), 160–173.

25. Richard Neupert, *The End: Narration and Closure in the Cinema* (Detroit: Wayne State University Press, 1995), 102.

26. Robert Altman in Paul Fischer. "Upstairs-downstairs with Altman" http://www.io film.co.uk/feats/interviews/r/robert_altman.shtml (2001) (accessed July 1, 2009).

9

Art and Performance:
Consolation at the End of Days

Robert T. Self

As a major figure for thirty years in the delineation of an American art cinema, Robert Altman made films that foreground structure rather than story and form instead of representation. They usually characterize limited individuals living in constrained circumstances of powerlessness and subservience. They reveal a cynical attitude toward the commercially motivated values of contemporary culture. They reflexively identify the entertainment industry as complicit in the troubles of modern American society. The multiple strands and fragments of narration in Altman's films regularly depict contradictory, powerless, isolated and fragmented individuals.

When they construe social personality within a larger community — as in *M*A*S*H* (1970), in *Nashville* (1975), in *Secret Honor* (1984), in *The Player* (1992*),* and many others—the individual appears as dependent on group need or subservient to the authority of others. Generally these representations of the self emerge as functions of socially constructed gender roles. Altman's films describe a masculine subjectivity of guilt, insecurity, and defensiveness, in conflict with both the authority and the stress of the phallocentric culture. Conversely, his films about women, the most formally complex and psychologically confusing of Altman's films, represent women as marginal, dependent, and handicapped by the coercions of patriarchal authority.

Although they occasionally call attention to themselves self-consciously as films, Altman's movies since *M*A*S*H* have repeatedly reflected the world of mass media and the negative effects of "the show business." *The Player* is his most overt satire and cynical critique of the entertainment business. The film not only chronicles the greed of the film industry; it more pointedly and self-consciously locates the impetus of classical Hollywood cinema in the anxiety of a patriarchy that seeks satisfaction in the objectification and control of the desirable female. Its reflexive analysis of these issues reiterates masculine insecurities and feminine dependency.

With the exception of *Come Back to the 5 & Dime, Jimmy Dean, Jimmy Dean* (1982), these films about show business all contain significant sequences of artistic performances. In these moments, they delight in the enthralling spectacle of entertainment, even as they obliquely construct art-cinema narratives to challenge the unspoken desires, anxieties, and estrangements that motivate the values of the contemporary entertainment world. They also reflexively indict show business as an accessory in the violence and alienation of modern life. Country music's mix of desire and debilitation focuses *Nashville*. Racist nationalism shapes the Wild West show of *Buffalo Bill and the Indians* (1976). Gendered and psychotic addiction to movie stars drives *Come Back to the 5 and Dime*. *Vincent and Theo* (1990) chronicles the tensions among artistic integrity, financial necessity, and public taste. Jazz approximates and expresses the chaotic weave of narrative fragments in *Short Cuts* (1993*)*. The fashion world dazzles the eye and coerces the body in *Prêt-à-Porter* (1994). *Kansas City* (1996) contrasts the innovation of black Kansas City jazz with the white authority of 1930s machine politics. Their fictions critique the entertainment-making business, the system of mass-media storytelling, and their constructions of reality, and display the negative effects of those constructions on social subjectivity.

In 2001 I published a book entitled *Robert Altman's Subliminal Reality* that summed up Altman's art-cinema practice.[1] A key feature of that work involves its simultaneous appreciation for and criticism of the entertainment world. The subjects of the last four films of his career then bring this fascination to a crescendo: Hollywood movies and pop music in *Gosford Park* (2001) independent filmmaking in *Tanner on Tanner* (2004), ballet in *The Company* (2003) and radio variety shows in *Prairie Home Companion* (2006). *Gosford Park* indeed not only sums up the "subliminal reality" of Altman's complex narratives but stands as one of the best films of his career. *Tanner on Tanner* similarly continues a line of satirical films about American presidential politics begun with *HEALTH* (1979) thirty years earlier.

Two of these last films, however, represent remarkable departures from the characteristic form, style, and theme of the earlier films. In previous films the fascination with performance parallels examination of the cultural debilitations that accompany entertainment. *The Company*, however, conveys an acceptance of that cultural surround even as it elevates everything in the film structurally, stylistically, and thematically to the level of performance. Then his last film, *Prairie Home Companion*, looks one last time at the entertainment business, now through radio, but rather than a critique of the broadcast system, Altman's last film finds consolation in the medium as the show faces death. Social identity revolves around a confrontation with death and a celebration of craft in these last movies.

A cue for understanding these last films may be found thirty years earlier in *Nashville*. That film revealed a bleaker vision but nevertheless contained illuminating perspectives on perseverance and artistry in Altman's films that are especially striking in these last two works. The country music star Haven Hamilton sings his hit "Keep A-Goin'." The other central music star in *Nashville*, the tragic figure Barbara Jean, also sings about her music that "Writin' it down kinda makes me feel better." The sense of performance and art as consolation emerges dramatically here. In Altman's last films, the art of radio and ballet say again, "Making these movies kinda makes me feel better." They are indeed ways to "Keep A-Goin'!"

In these last films negative critique of show business and authority loses weight and moment. *The Company* performs a ballet of what may be Altman's most consistently developed art film. Here his interest in the cinema as a lyric art, like poetry, like painting, like music consumes dramatic narrative and creates an expressive celebration of the labor, the finances, the craft, the risks, and the beauty of visual and performing art. *Prairie Home Companion* performs the last radio show, and his last film, with lively humor and quiet grace. It turns the end into fiction, and it confronts death with performance.

The Company

The Company in particular is an art film about an art form. His other films about entertainment are about popular art. Ballet, however, is a classical art, and here Altman makes one of his most personal, contemplative, and lyrical films, indifferent to popular genre, box office success, or narrative discourse. *The Company* traces a year in the life of the Joffrey Ballet in Chicago. Like the generic tension of the classical backstage musical, it once again contrasts behind-the-scene work required to produce the show with the performance glory of ballet, mingling the making of the show with numerous dance performances in the most painterly work of Altman's career. The film is a poetic exploration of the physical and emotional stresses of producing this strenuous art. Here Altman is the quintessential director of the art cinema, serenely in touch with his craft, painting a picture about performance and production in which politics and personal relationships and moviemaking are all part of the dance.

The Company emphatically lays bare a perception of himself as a filmmaker that Altman asserted throughout his career, that he was more of a painter than a storyteller. A survey of his films from 1967 to 2004 reveals his famous experimentation with visual variations on the traditional Hollywood genres. He depends upon audience familiarity with generic narratives — the western in *McCabe & Mrs. Miller* (1971), the thriller in *Gingerbread Man* (1998). the gangster narrative in *Thieves Like Us (1974)*, science fiction in *Quintet* (1979*)* — in order not to retell any traditional story but to use its very familiarity to explore things that interest him more. He liked to claim that starting with well-known stories and characters allowed him to poke around in the corners of already familiar canvases to develop minute details about people and places. Character motive, personal relationships, and causal behavior become ambiguous, diffuse, implicit. Individual personality, bits and pieces of action, plot trajectories interact within the spaces and across the times of these films like tonal signatures or pigments of paint.

A central characteristic of the art cinema is its liberation of the visual and spatial systems of film from the logical system of narrative. Altman's large casts and divergent stories actively assist in this process when he wants the story to be read in *3 Women* (1977) like a dream, in *Kansas City* like jazz, in *Gosford Park* like a tapestry. The multiple fragments in *Short Cuts* coalesce ultimately not just as the threads of disrupted stories but as the musical accompaniment to the classical, new age, and jazz compositions that shape the whole film. Consequently, part of the difficulty in following the complex play of stories in Altman's films is their modernist assumption that meaning emerges from the simultaneous perception of connections among images and phrases in space that have no consecutive relationship to each other in time.

Altman's films strikingly illustrate that the art cinema is a lyrical as well as a narrative art. The somber palette of gold and green in *Images* (1972); the restless, sensuous, and ambiguous zoom and pan shots in

Nashville and *3 Women*; the pointillistic final sequence in the blizzard in *McCabe & Mrs. Miller*; the exhilarating color and music of fashion in *Prêt-à-Porter;* the compulsive repetition of red and black throughout *The Gingerbread Man*; the stunning contrast of primary colors during the ballet performances with the honey-brown spaces of rehearsal and life in *The Company*—these qualities reflect the eye of a painter. Altman consistently asserted that the goal of his films was an emotional rather than an intellectual effect:

> I look at film as closer to a painting or a piece of music; it's an impression ... an impression of character and total atmosphere.... The attempt is to enlist an audience emotionally, not intellectually.[2]

On one hand, then, *The Company* as a kind of musical employs a central narrative concern of that genre, the dual story that links making the show, staging the performance, with the completion of an off-stage romance between lovers in the cast or production company. On the other hand, it cares little about finishing the behind-the-scenes romance that links Ry (Neve Campbell) and Josh (James Franco) or the tensions among Mr. A. (Malcolm McDowell), the artistic director of the company, and the various performers and dance masters of the ballet. Altman uses his craft to transform traditional romance into music: "I just didn't want to do this obligatory story so I did it the way as if it was a pas de deux, as if it were a dance."[3]

From another perspective the film is also a documentary that contains three central narrative situations: the story of the actual dancers, the choreographers, the ballet masters and mistresses, and the artistic director of the Joffrey Ballet; the story of fictional lovers Ry and Josh; and the story of the ballet performances themselves. Altman employs only a handful of actors for a small number of fictional roles — all of whom he admonished not to act — to complement the "real" people in the dance company. All these stories are minimal. Indeed the first viewing of the film leaves significant confusion about what happens in them. A second viewing reveals that what happens is actually very slight. The dancer Ry breaks up with her boyfriend in the company, gets promoted into a lead dancing position on several pieces because of an injury to another dancer, meets a young chef in a local bistro, starts a new romance, injures her arm in the final dance and in turn yields her place in the performance to an understudy. In another major story, we watch the more complicated process of dance production in the life of a season with the company: the repetition required to prefect small dance moves and large sequences; planning sessions among the artistic staff; dance masters' critique of dancers' work; tensions among dancers and directors; dress rehearsals; interactions among dancers in dressing rooms, restaurants, apartments; and receptions after performances. Altman asserts:

> As for plot, all the stories have been told. There're only about six or seven of them, which we've seen a billion times. In this film, I chose to start the stories — the new kid in the company, the kid with the mentor — and not finish them. Viewers can recognize the stories and finish them by themselves.[4]

The film cues a number of elliptical stories, subliminally hinting at larger personal relationships whose connections disappear below the horizon line of the film's attention — the artistic director of the dance company, the art designer, the leading dancers, the understudies, the walk-ons all have stories finished, passing, developing; all of them are evoked, but none are explicated. Romance — its failure, its beginnings, its development and possibility — is part of a myriad, behind-the-scenes dance. These events are represented in minimal and disconnected ways; they are in fact, in Altman's words, "just vignettes" that "don't take us anywhere."[5]

In the fall of 2002 during the shooting of *The Company*, I visited Altman's set at Chicago's Auditorium Theater, the ornate Adler and Sullivan 1889 architectural landmark that is the home of the Joffrey Ballet. Practically the entirety of the film was shot in the auditorium, the offices, and the studios of the ballet company. Four separate camera setups covered the stage, and each camera fed its own monitor in a bank of monitors arrayed behind the stage-left curtain. Altman watched the action while seated in front of these monitors; after each shot he instantly reviewed the footage from each camera with his cinematographer from *Gosford Park*, Andrew Dunn, and made adjustments for subsequent takes. Altman's "office" was a dressing room just off this stage location, where he and I met during the break in his shooting of scenes of the ballerina's career-ending leg injury. This space was busy for a while with visits from Neve Campbell, Gerald Arpino, and a reporter from the *New York Times*. When he and I had a chance to discuss the film, he spoke enthusiastically about the quality and the flexibility of the high definition digital cameras he was using for the first time. He was particularly interested in his ability to replay production shots from a large collection of small disks, separate digital magazines of each shot in the production. He called in a visual imaging assistant who placed several boxes of these magazines on the floor in front of a specially masked monitor and then one by one played individual shots at Altman's

direction. We watched some dozen shots from earlier moments in the production, each of them ordered by Altman's sense of the purpose he envi-
sioned for them in the film. Shots from the Christmas "roast party," for
instance, would not make sense he asserted without an experience of earlier
scenes which the scene was designed to "recapitulate." He intended in the
film to go behind the scenes as he had in other films to capture the demanding life of the ballet dancers, but ultimately his concern in the film was
with the dance.

He screened for me a variety of shots of the personal lives of characters
in the film and described them in terms "what you can't see in these single
shots." He had in mind the other shots with which they would finally be
edited to construct, not sequences in the narrative, but part of the ballet
of the film. Altman described his interest in the minimal romance of Josh
and Ry as deriving not from its narrative potential but from the dance of
their relationship: "the little love story that we did do in it between Franco
and Neve, we did it as a ballet. We took all the words out of it, we just
made it a dance."[5] In our meeting he was particularly fascinated with the
shots from one camera showing the Neve Campbell character playing pool
in a bar. Another camera he explained had shot the Josh character in the
bar making a phone call, drinking a beer, watching the pool player. Altman
anticipated that they would finally come together in the editing that would
make of the love story a *pas de deux*, the classical dance of a couple in
ballet. Moreover, as Altman described with excitement this as yet only
imagined sequence in the final film, the cinematic dance would be edited
to the Rodgers and Hart "My Funny Valentine" playing on the soundtrack.
The romance, its moods, the music and the editing of these would constitute the film's romantic *pas de deux*. As Altman described the film:

> The [initial] dance to "My Funny Valentine" was one of the very
> first things we did — we actually shot it during pre-production.... It
> seemed to set up a nice theme for Neve's character when she met James
> Franco. I wanted to play that because we took all of the words out of
> that relationship — all the plot — and basically made it a pas de deux....
> The whole point of all of that stuff was that I wanted to do those scenes
> with Franco and Neve like they were doing a pas de deux. So I kept
> using the same music in different renditions. If you shove all those
> pieces together, you would have something like a ballet.[6]

Altman was interested to show me different shots from the production
that were intrinsically interesting, but none of which were yet meaningful
without the other shots and music to be added in the editing. He was

describing ultimately the aesthetic form that organized all these materials in the imagination of the director. Much like *Nashville*, where each of its twenty-four character roles is an image, a pigment, a shape in the revolving wheel that constitutes the visual figure of that modernist cinematic poem, the aesthetic design of this film is less narrative than musical. Altman conceives of *The Company* both as about ballet and as a ballet.

While the film works like *Nashville* and *Prêt-à-Porter* with the same kind of alternation between performance and behind-the-scene dramatizations of performers and production, that structure is shaped here by Altman's intricate choreography of these lives. Each major element of the film dances in a pair with others. Thus the Ry-Josh dance moves in tandem with the representations of the dancers' social life (the birthday party, the roast, the bowling party, and perhaps most significantly the wedding of one dancer to another). This mix of social community in turn dances in telling tension with other moments of loneliness, the most dramatic occurring in another subtle dance between Ry and Alec (Davis Robertson). The single male dancer practices alone in the studio to the strenuous melodic lines of Bach's "Suite for Unaccompanied Cello, No. 1 in G Major," from the dancer's own ballet *Strange Prisoners*. His dance is broken by editorial cutting away to Ry arriving in her apartment by the elevated train tracks, starting a bath, messaging her blistered feet, breaking into tears. The tough cello music continues on the soundtrack across both scenes. Here the film orchestrates an ensemble of social scenes that pirouette around solitude and the slim possibility of togetherness.

This social component of personal relationships in the film further dances in partnership with scenes of the company at work. In its mix of the real and the fictional, Altman dramatizes production meetings and rehearsals that depict the actual life of the creative process of the Joffrey Ballet. The rehearsals in particular depict the actual choreographers, ballet masters and mistresses working with the dancers singly, in small groups, in full company as they conceptualize, learn, and repeat dance moves. In one scene the principle dancers for the "Funny Valentine" number are replaced by their understudies because of an injury to the ballerina. In another scene, the dance master and two dancers repeat a lifting move to perfect the angle of their arms. In another two dancers argue about the counting of a particular rhythm. Elsewhere, a dancer disagrees with the artistic director's conceptualization of a dance sequence. In one of the most poignant moments in the film, during the dress rehearsal on the day of a performance, the principle ballerina snaps her Achilles tendon. The breaking of the tendon and the ending of the dancer's career sound simul-taneously across the practice stage, where nevertheless the rehearsal must continue with a replacement dancer. Production is a dance between these various dancers as they perform in concert and the diverse concerns of management over budgets, artistic egos, performance evaluations, and negotiations over new shows.

Even as it glances at the pain, debilitation, and liberation that accom-pany production. *The Company* depicts a world where craft ultimately con-sumes life, where loneliness and personal pain and meager resources disappear into the dedication and struggles of performing, and where finally the dance consumes the dancers. The film performs the personal lives of these dancers in concert with their professional lives. It performs the work of their craft in tandem with the business of dance.

All these pressures converge at the Christmas party sequence when the company stages a roast to parody the dances from the season and their various dance masters. Like the film its little vignettes reflexively recapit-ulate the work, the stress, and the creativity of their lives. This sequence too works only in the context of the scenes that have gone before in the film. As Altman explained during shooting, this scene cannot be under-stood without knowing earlier sections in the film and earlier parts of the company's season. Parts of previous performances, earlier rehearsals, earlier artistic conceptualizations, earlier exhibitions of personality and tempera-ment and ego emerge again here in a dance that cathartically mirrors and deflates the tensions under which the dancers work.

The principle of duality contained in the concept of the *pas de deux* indicates the aesthetic power of the film. It represents the romance between Ry and Josh. It organizes the relationships among the dancers and their dances; its set design distinguishes lived space from performed space. The dual design choreographs the interaction of music and movement in both spaces, as well as the figural and rhythmic representations of bodies in the dances. Most apparently it emerges in the play of cinematography and editing in the stylistic system of the film. Ultimately it characterizes the ballet structure of the film itself. The private and the personal dance together in a *pas de deux* with the professional and consume significant time in the film. But these personal and professional dimensions of the film also circle in tandem with the film's documentary representation of ten ballet performances by the Joffrey, representing fully a third of the film's screen time. The dances convey both the richness of ballet and the power of the cinema to shape as well as reflect that richness.

The film notably distinguishes the personal and professional worlds of the company from the danced world by the color scheme of the mise-en-scène. In Ry's apartment, in the dance studio, on the rehearsal stages, the dominant lighting code varies along monotonal axes of gray or brown. In the studio, a cold gray natural light from the developing Chicago autumn outside fills the space through large windows and expands through the floor-to-ceiling mirrors on the opposite walls. In the Auditorium Theater, home of the Joffrey in Chicago, Altman's crew set up a single huge light bulb in one corner that lit the whole space with a yellow-brown haze — a visual code that dominates the other visual spaces of the personal and professional lives of the company. On the other hand, from the opening performance of the ballet "Tensile Involvement" during the credit sequence to the bows of the company at the curtain of "Blue Snake" and the film's final credit sequence, ten different performance sequences emerge in a vibrant, dramatic mix of primary and complementary colors. Not just in the costuming but in the stage lighting as well, the danced world is remarkable in its display of strikingly colorful contrasts to the brown tones of the lived world.

"Tensile Involvement" presents a kaleidoscopic array of red, blue, and yellow lighting, as the dancers wear costumes of yellow with red markings. The flesh-colored costumes of "Light Rain" dresses the dancers in shining gold. "Trinity" mixes a brilliant array of colors in the costumes of each dancer, one male wearing maroon tights and a blue tunic, another male in blue tights and orange tunic, another in red tights and green tunic, another in green tights and orange tunic, yet another in pink and maroon, while the women dancers in contrast wear a mix of six different pastel colors — light blue, pink, yellow and green, all of whom dance under a mottled screen of lighting that splashes the dancers and costumes in a scintillating array of changing gold light against a blue floor. In "Creative Force" the dance company all wear vibrant red costumes and dance rapidly against a deep blue background and floor.

The final ballet "Blue Snake" presents an amazing palette of color: Initial white clad costumes give way to zebra-colored costumes and makeup, replaced by dancers dressed in scarlet, followed by a yellow-costumed male and blue-costumed female whose dancing yields to green amoebas attacked by yellow and white balls, the finale then featuring a purple-clad ballerina with a purple balloon on her head. Even in the dances that engage minimal colors in costume and lighting, the intensity of light and camera perspective sharply distinguishes it from the monotonal world of production and personal lives. What Altman calls his "show off piece,"[7] "The White Widow," features a solo ballerina dancing hypnotically in a rope, wearing a solid white gown and swaying against a black background and blue floor all speckled dramatically by the abstract patterns of the gobo lighting.

This energetic rainbow of dances, dancers, costumes, and lighting in the ten featured ballets of the film contrasts sharply with the representations of personal and production spaces in *The Company*. That contrast reiterates the dance Altman has created between these two elements, his *pas de deux* between performance and creation. This dance structure further shapes the tension between the actual dances as performed on the stage by the Joffrey and Altman's capturing and conveying those performances cinematically. The entire Joffrey Ballet company worked with Altman's crew to perform for his cameras the various dances screened in the film. Because of the problems of warming up and the physical dangers of performance, most of the ballets seen in the film were shot only once. For these shoots, Altman typically used a four-camera set-up — with one camera on a track moving left to right behind the front section of spectators (usually extras hired for the occasion), a second camera situated in the upper wings stage right, a third camera situated one-third of the way back from the stage in the right orchestra, and a fourth camera set stage left on a stationary boom, the range of which extended over the entire space from the front to the back of the stage and from chest height to directly over any space on the stage.

Thus while the number of takes was severely limited to protect the bodies of the dancers from injury, Altman had numerous shots and angles of all these performances. None of the ballet performances runs the dance's entire length, so every dance appears for a length of time edited to fit the film design. They range in length from fifty seconds to over eleven minutes. Every dance is characterized by a dynamic array of camera angles and distances and editorial rhythms that strikingly augment the motion and rhythms of the dancers themselves. What results then on screen is never a straight, objective presentation of any of the dances, but another *pas de deux* between the company's dancing and Altman's style. The craft of the cinema dances with the craft of ballet.

The ballet "Creative Force" is illustrative. It runs for two minutes and forty-two seconds with forty cuts. The dance puts eight couples into a swirling mix of solo, duet, and ensemble movements to a percussive Latin beat. Most of the shots from the four cameras work to catch bits and pieces of the dancers in motion. For a moment the cameras cut between what seems to be just two couples, the cameras moving with their whirling dance and seeming now to shoot one couple and then the other. Close-ups move to catch the movement of many feet; a medium close-up fills the screen with the motion of many bodies and slowly zooms out to reveal a half dozen couples. As the dance comes to its climax, the dancers whirl into a large circle facing each other and a cut to one slightly longer medium shot for the first time reveals, as music and editing and dancing come to the end, that sixteen dancers have been filling the stage. Only the last two shots of the sequence show the entire ensemble.

The film employs not just cinematic style but organizational structure as well to develop a formal drama, a "grand pas de deux" with a traditional five-part ballet structure. The movement of the dances among individuals, couples and ensemble; the play of modernist percussion, Latin rhythms, classical orchestration, new age laments, and jazz both reflect the eclectic reach of the Joffrey and the aesthetic order of the film. They dance around five separate renditions of the ironic and bittersweet love song "My Funny Valentine": The versions by Elvis Costello, Lee Wiley, and Chet Baker are jazz variations that play throughout the developing romance of the couple. In its classical variation at the beginning of the film, dancers, piano, and cello perform against the wind, rain, and thunder of a dramatic summer storm to announce the ballet's central theme. The last rendition is the somber orchestrated performance of the song over the closing credits. The "entre" and the "coda" of Altman's ballet celebrate the contradictions of romance contained in the lyrics.

The film concludes in a *Grand Pas d'Action* which serves to bring the ballet to a climactic conclusion. "The Blue Snake" represents not a climax in union, but a conclusion in tension. This dance of film and ballet constitutes the figure the film makes. This long sequence that has been prepared throughout the film epitomizes the structural *pas de deux* that mixes dancers and choreography, rehearsal and performance, the costumes and bodies and music of the dance and the movement of camera and editing in the cinema. Altman choreographs the fluid tracking, zooming, changing perspectives of his cameras into a ballet called *The Company* which dances in concert with the dances it captures.

The structural movements of the ten performances within the film take what Altman calls the "obligatory" elements of dance and romance and converts them in turn to variations on the concept of duality, the underlying principle of the *pas de deux*: "the sense of duality, of complementing, of pairing ... the formation of simple structures organized by culture as symmetry through reflection":

> In the association of identities, the pair could be understood as complementing identities which generate a newer sense emerging from the peculiarities of each one rather than as two antagonistic poles of opposing signs, each denying the existence of the other.... Between the dance partners a dialectic game is born. This is not only the addition of their individual movements but also the creation of something new.... In most expressions related to dancing we find strong components of symmetry both in the choreography and in the dancers' steps. What is interesting about this subject is that symmetry is more obviously present in the relations and in the abstract structure of the composition than in the equivalent attributes of the participants.... Such surfaces are always more than two ... and the resulting shape often connects itself to the sense of "the pair."[8]

The film achieves an aesthetic statement resonant with Eisenstein's theoretical sense of cinematic montage at the headwaters of modernist cinema. In *The Company* the distrust of narrative order, the knowledge of broken subjectivity, the hostility to mercenary systems of creativity in other Altman films merge into the poetic order of the art cinema. I don't tell stories, says Altman; I paint. And his cinema dances. The creative tensions among opposing forces in production, in self-realization, in narrative discourse coalesce in *The Company* to produce an aesthetic unity that echoes Yeats' famous meditation upon the integrity of art and nature:

> Labour is blossoming or dancing where
> The body is not bruised to pleasure soul.
> Nor beauty born out of its own despair,
> Nor blear-eyed wisdom out of midnight oil.
> O chestnut-tree, great-rooted blossomer,
> Are you the leaf, the blossom or the bole?
> O body swayed to music, O brightening glance,
> How can we know the dancer from the dance?

Prairie Home Companion

The Company finds organic wholeness in the process of aesthetic production, artistic order against the chaos of love and work. *Prairie Home Companion* poses the community of production against the dissolutions of life. Altman's last movie conveys the whirl of performances and backstage interactions during the fictionally last broadcast of a popular radio show, which happens of course to be the popular, and continuing, radio program, Garrison Keillor's *Prairie Home Companion*. Throughout his career this same dramatic entertainment milieu afforded Altman occasions to explore splintered relationships, broken communication, inexplicable behavior, and marginal lives in the service of the entertainment industry. The venues of popular entertainment offered glimpses of a world where death more likely waited at the end of the film than any rosy conclusion of conflict. In *Prairie Home Companion* these same narrative situations, minor characters, and cynical perspectives yield a different effect. Here they perform the consolation of art. Here the past provides positive motives for the present, the production community affords comfort and support, performance offers solace, and death comes gently, in beauty and grace.

In the second sequence of *Prairie Home Companion* we watch the relaxed interactions of a dozen characters in, around, behind and below the stage just as this last radio show is set to begin. The sequence introduces central characters in the narrative and several ongoing story lines — the early days of the Johnson Sisters' musical act, Lola's poetry writing, the early days of Dusty and Lefty on TV, the first days of Garrison Keillor in radio, Molly's pregnancy, old acts on the show, the tensions of live production. Cutting amid all these lines and the activity of these and other characters, the cameras pan and zoom into a mise-en-scène full of mirrors that magnifies the actors' images and their presence. Over the action recurs with increasing urgency the voice of the stage manager warning of the impending show time. Amidst this cacophony of action, sound, and gaze, the scene climaxes in a long uncut shot of the host of the show. In a two-minute shot the camera tracks Keillor as he leaves his dressing room below stage, chats nonchalantly and constantly with other characters, and seems oblivious to the impending, and final, curtain call. The camera cranes up through a trapdoor to catch him as he walks at last across the stage and approaches the curtain, the production assistant pointing him to his spot, urging him to check his zipper, removing makeup napkins from his neck. It's show time, and as the curtain rises, Keillor turns smoothly from these several minutes of chaotic activity to face the applauding theatre audience and calmly swings into the theme song of the radio show.

This scene sets the stage literally and figuratively for the narrative of the film: crisscrossing stories of nostalgia, chaotic behind-the-scenes energy, and assured professional performances constitute the last night in the life of a popular, thirty-year old radio program. Part of the film's attraction for audiences derived less from its status as a fiction than from its status as a documentary of the real life Garrison Keillor and his extremely popular radio show. Since the mid–1970s the show, its performers, and its acts have been a staple of National Public Radio. To attend the film was not to see a story but to watch a performance.

To capture the complex array of characters and musicians who routinely populate the show was of course impossible in this two-hour film, but one absence in particular puzzled and frequently irritated these fans looking for a documentary of their favorite program. Nearly every performance of the show contains one of Keillor's popular stories about his fictional home town Lake Wobegon, "the little town that time forgot and the decades cannot improve ... where all the women are strong, all the men are good-looking, and all the children are above average." Except for one song, however, that Keillor says he wants to send out to the folks in his hometown, the film contains no reference to the famous make-believe place. Many clues like this indicate that the movie is not meant to be seen as a documentary of a very popular radio show that indeed continues today, but to be read as a fiction about the end of a show with the same name.

Altman and Keillor together craft the facts of the show into meditation on the end of things. The film enjoys a teleological force, an end-directed goal unlike other Altman films. Even as narrative attention is splinted like the audience's gaze by all the mirrors in Rhonda and Yolanda's dressing room, the film is organized finally by the chronology of the two-hour long show. In the larger context, an apparent plot chronology involves the long history of the show, the sale of the theatre by its owners and its closure to make way for a new parking lot, and the ultimate end of the show. The major plot tension then centers around the somber figure of the "Axman" as a representative of the destructive new owners and the ominous "Dangerous Woman" dressed in white both of whom point forebodingly to the inevitable end.

The film begins as an aesthetic fiction. In a shot self-consciously modeled after Edward Hopper's painting "Nighthawks," the camera slowly zooms in as the sound track carries the voice of actor Kevin Kline intoning, "A dark night in a city that knows how to keep its secrets." Here are the famous opening lines of Keillor's regular satiric send-up of film noir and radio detective series, "Guy Noir, Private Eye." This fictional figure in the radio show now becomes a real character in a fiction film with a painted backdrop. The film, then, like *Nashville*, *The Player*, and *Prêt-à-Porter* earlier in Altman's career and in *The Company* and *Tanner on Tanner* here at the end, blends the documentary and the fiction in complicated ways, the one confused with the other and each commenting on the other. The continuing presence of real stars are marshaled here against the imaged story of death. Keillor and his band and several of his regular ensemble play themselves, but actors Meryl Streep, Lily Tomlin, Tommy Lee Jones, and Virginia Madsen play fictional performers. At the same time, actual but fictional regulars on the show like Guy Noir, Lefty and Dusty, normally voiced by the radio cast, are played by actors Kevin Kline, Woody Harrelson, and John C. Reilly. Just as the play of multiple mirrors in several of the film's sets disrupts the gaze and splinter the representation of the imagined death of a real show, this play of real, fictional, and imaginary characters confuses the plain of narration and disrupts the power of the ending as inevitability.

Instead of this divergent play of perspectives reflecting Altman's usual technique of "subliminal" narration, however, this multiplicity constitutes part of the humor of the film, like Altman's joke of having the line of tap dancers perform on a radio show. He happily asserts in the DVD commentary on the film, "I believe that everybody sees things differently. Nobody sees the same anything."[9] Where this aesthetic shapes the multiple perspectives and ambiguities of more pessimistic films like *Nashville*, *The Player*, and *Short Cuts*, here this narrative divergence reflects what he playfully calls the "Hindenburg Principle." He puns on the famous Heisenberg Uncertainty Principle from physics that undergirds much multiplicity of representation in modernist art. His intention here organizes multiplicity as a variety of playful misdirections. The film organizes the narrative from the point of view of Guy Noir. Opening and closing on Noir in a local diner with his voice over, the film comically and ironically poses the detective in the position of knowledge. Noir's confused and comic sense of awareness represents a joking resistance to death. For him, the "Dangerous Lady" (Virginia Madsen) is at once some "crazy lady" who, with show's imminent demise, may just be the person "who can save our bacon," and the mysterious and inexplicable harbinger of death — but is also an object of Guy's typical sexual interest in beautiful women: "She was wearing a Mount Rushmore t-shirt and I never saw those guys look so good. Especially Jefferson and Lincoln." In Altman's film Guy Noir hits on Death.

Altman specifically asserts that "obviously this film is about death."[10] As the film tracts the trajectory of the show's last performance, its narrative beginning, middle, and end also constitute various representations of the performers, their performances, and their conversations backstage as they face this end. The tension between backstage behavior and performance behavior works to suggest the characters' resistance to this inevitability. Except for Lola, the youngest, the characters in this film all reflect a quiet, confident, assured sense of identity that is almost serene in the face of death. Altman's typical disinterest in a coherent continuity of plot yields to an exploration of the meanings, values, personalities, and actions that stand in opposition to death. The film's end brings no narrative conclusion but rather a metaphoric comment on the thematic concerns with death and loss that course throughout the story. The angel of death enters the diner to confront Noir, Keillor, and the Johnson sisters who sit and stare at her apprehensively.

Across Altman's work such conclusions convey visually abstract images that signal the broader, more ambivalent, and ambiguous meanings that his films always enclose. *M*A*S*H* concludes with the image of a poker game bisected by the zoom of a telephoto lens to a close-up of an enshrouded body on a jeep leaving the hospital complex. *The Long Goodbye* concludes with Marlow's walk down a lane like the ending of *The Third Man*. *Cookie's Fortune* concludes with Emma and Mississippi police officers fishing from the end of a dock at a local lake. *Dr. T* concludes on a very long helicopter shot of the desert locale across the border where Dr. T has been exiled by a mighty wind. *Gosford Park* ends with the departure of the guests. These endings are "formal" because each of these films, like most of his movies, end with an image that is itself complex and resonant with subliminal narrative threads of the story. The Dangerous Woman is one of the most symbolic representations in Altman's films, but most important in *Prairie Home Companion* she condenses the preoccupation with death as the most persistent aspect of social reality in the film. And death is everywhere.

In some ways it emerges in the constant telling of stories from the past, albeit stories about beginnings. "How long you been doing radio, GK?" The text reveals an obsession with that question, answered in a myriad of tales from Keillor — about a pontoon boat on the Mississippi during Mark Twain days, a man kite surfing with his swimming trucks around his ankles, an ore boat in distress on Lake Superior during a violent storm — about the beginning of a career that will end with the curtain on tonight's show. Lefty warns Lola about Dusty with a tale about how he learned gospel music while serving a prison sentence in San Quentin. Rhonda and Yolanda reminisce about their family, their start in show business, and the reduction of their sister act from four to two. Stories about their mother abound because "she was our inspiration, you know."

Tragedies of the past lead to discoveries of hope, even for the aged Chuck. GK recalls former acts on the show, remembers old jokes, and reminisces with Lola about her daddy "who ran off with my mother's best friend after singing a hymn at Grandma's funeral." The impending death of the show motivates all these representations of a past that has inexorably brought them to this moment. Yolanda observes philosophically, almost confrontationally in contrast to Altman's past assertions about narrative order that way leads on to way by chance:

> I think you've got to be grateful for everything that happens to you because that's what got you here, and if you hadn't gone through whatever you went through, you wouldn't have wound up where you are right now. So disappointment doesn't get you anywhere.

Death stalks the set of the Fitzgerald theatre literally as well as metaphorically. Yolanda recounts her daddy's climbing into a hospital bed where momma was having her tubes tied, pulling the sheet over his face, and dying in mortification after hearing that his daughter Wanda had been arrested for stealing a doughnut. The angel tells Keillor how as Lois Peterson in life she had killed her marriage by cheating on her husband and then had died running off the road on her way to meet her lover. The corporate Axman, come to watch the end of the last show, recounts the death of his former self and his Christian rebirth. Rhonda and Yolanda sing about "an old brown dog named Rusty/He just laid down and died." Lola sings the folk classic "Frankie and Johnny" at the end of the film: "the gun went rooty-toot-toot/Shot the bastard in the heart." Yolanda explicitly confronts GK about the death of their romance. The angel of death has purposely come to take the old performer Chuck, who dies in his dressing room during intermission. She also dispatches the Axman to his death on a dark winding road on his way back to the airport.

And the show of course is dying throughout the film. In many Altman movies the central narrative progresses across the dying of one of the film's characters — off-screen, beneath the surface of the story, in the background, or occasionally as a major event: in *McCabe and Mrs. Miller, Brewster McCloud* (1970), *Thieves Like Us* (1974), *Nashville, Buffalo Bill, Quintet* (1979), *A Perfect Couple, Come Back to the 5 and Dime, Vincent and Theo, The Player, Short Cuts, Prêt-à-Porter, The Gingerbread Man, Gosford Park.* Death comes slowly, or suddenly, or finally — sometimes inexplicably, often violently. Altman early in his film career said about the inconclusive ending of his films that "Death is the only ending I know."[11] In this last movie, the radio show is a ghost long past its prime, "a live radio variety show, the kind that died fifty years ago, but somebody forgot to tell them." As the film begins, a series of old radio shows echo on the sound track as a radio tower looms against a rural sunset: the live stock report, a recipe, a sermon, a baseball game, a soap opera, a traffic report — ghosts of dominant forms from the popular medium of the mid-twentieth century, about to be joined by this popular variety show whose very essence is a nostalgic look at the past. The angel of death stands looking at the major characters of the film in the diner in the last scene of the film, and on the commentary track, in his last movie, Altman drolly asserts, "She's coming for the rest of you."[12]

Twelve of Altman's films from *Nashville* to *The Company* and *Prairie Home Companion* examine cultural systems of entertainment, of art, of show business. The films clearly indicate the range of Altman's interests — in the origins of production, the politics of creation, the economics of distribution, the individual costs of imagination, the circulation of aesthetic meaning, the value of artistic experience. Two dimensions in particular characterize Altman's fascination with the energies and business of art: the alluring spectacles of the show business, and the negative effects of those representations on social identity. Yet as these films reveal that the popular culture is motivated by the greed and exploitation of media producers, they further reveal a need for the audience to escape. If death is a commodity of show business in *Nashville,* the power of music is also restorative: Barbara Jean sings in that film, "Writing it down kinda makes me feel better / Keeps me away from them blues." Josie and Niecy in *Cookie's Fortune,* assert in their rollicking blues bar music "wild women don't get the blues." Dressed confidently in haut couture, Anne Eisenhower performs the power of the fashion industry in *Prêt-à-Porter.* Yolanda in *Prairie Home Companion* spontaneously asserts at one point, "Singing is the only thing that puts me right." On stage she tells the audience that music was "the only way we knew to make Mama happy."

Altman is everywhere aware of one of the oldest values of art and entertainment in a broken world — as a defense, as a bulwark, as a light, and a consolation against death's dark descent. If death is everywhere in *Prairie Home Companion,* so are the shields against its power. Like the women and the warmth of Mrs. Miller's brothel in *McCabe & Mrs. Miller,* these texts offer places of solace. The director who said he would make movies "till they throw dirt in my face," the movie maker who even as he had heart replacement surgery in the early 1990s made eight movies in that decade fully understood the consolation of art. Keillor in one of his patented humorous descriptions of the Scandinavian personality articulates a revealing aesthetic vision of humanity:

> We're not a sunshiny people; we're not a paradise people, a beach people. We're a dark people, people who believe it could be worse, and we're waiting for it to become worse. We come from people who brought us up to believe that life is a struggle, and if you should ever feel really happy, be patient, this will pass. So we could all use a little sunshine in our lives.

Prairie Home Companion contains an impressive repertoire of defenses against this kind of darkness, the end symbolized both by the Angel of Death and the end of the radio show. Poetry, jokes, religion, music, commercials, and radio itself are all part of the kaleidoscopic array of resistance to that inevitability and bring "a little sunshine." Like Powdermilk Biscuits, "they're good for you and pure mostly."

Yolanda's daughter is Lola, the "suicidal teenager" who writes a poetic contemplation of "suicide," "equity," and "Fair Trade" that she calls "Soliloquy 4 a Blue Guitar."

> Death is easy, like jumping into the big
> air & waving hello to god
> god is love, but he doesn't necessarily
> drop everything to catch you.
> Does he?
> So when you hook the hose up to your tailpipe.
> Don't expect to wake up & get toast 4
> breakfast.
> The toast is you....

The amalgam of longing and candor and humor in the poem typifies much of the creative work in the lyrics and music that confront death in the film. Thus Guy Noir sits at the piano on the stage amidst the workmen's destruction of the Prairie Home set at the end and sings the "carpe diem" lyrics from renaissance poet Robert Herrick's famous "To the Virgins, to Make Much of Time":

> So gather ye rosebuds while ye may,
> Old time is still a-flying,
> This same flower that smiles today,
> Tomorrow will be dying.

Dusty and Lefty sing choruses of bad jokes because "it's mighty lonesome out there on the Prairie" where you can't talk to your horse about philosophy ("Because you can't put Descartes before the horse"). This blend of humor and pathos occurs throughout Keillor's script and his show.[13] When he finishes his lament on the unfulfilled longing for love, he breaks into the advertising jingle for Prince of Pizza (sung to the tune of "La Donna E Mobile"): "One Prince of Pizza slice/Puts me in paradise." His extended pitch for duct tape becomes a comic meditation on entropy, the fact that "things fall apart. It's the way of the world.... Life is short and all repairs are temporary and it's almost just about the only thing that really works sometimes, duct tape"—and comedy and singing and poetry and religion.

Certainly one of the most traditional and ubiquitous consolations about death is religion. Altman's films across his career hardly celebrate any positive religious belief. If anything, the dominant mood of these films is ironic, holding opposing values in suspension against each other. Christian beliefs are satirized throughout his films—for instance, the Lord's Supper sequence early in *M*A*S*H* and later the church production of Wilde's *Salome* in *Cookie's Fortune*. In *Nashville* the central sequence of religious services serves as an ironic focal point for much of the musical energy of the country-western culture. Barbara Jean's moving rendition of the hymn "In the Garden" in that film describes a sincerely felt space of emotional solace for the tragic country singer and stands almost like a counterpoint to the rest of Altman's depiction of religious value and belief.

In *Prairie Home Companion* then the active presence of a religious sensibility is all the more surprising because of its omnipresence. The "Dangerous Lady" in particular conveys a peaceful acceptance of death. When she consoles Chuck's old girlfriend, she says soothingly, "The death of an old man is not a tragedy.... Forgive him for his shortcomings and thank him for his love and care." In the middle of the film, she tells Guy Noir to "listen very carefully and don't be afraid. I am the angel Asphodel. I come to do my work and bring mercy into the world and to carry out the Lord's will and honor His holy name. With every breath of my being may I proclaim the glory of the Lord." Then when she talks to Keillor, she describes her work: "I comfort people who are desperately sad. And I take people up to God."

There is perhaps irony and humor in this bald attribution of religious significance to the angel figure, but her name is important in its association with the Greek mythological Elysian Fields where heroes experience new life after death. Moreover, Virginia Madsen brings loveliness, a gentle demeanor, and a quiet grace to the role that conveys an angelic peacefulness to her scenes and dispels any sense of irony. Her words to Noir feel sincere when she stands under a lamp that casts a halo around her head early in the film:

> Do you believe in the fullness of time and the spirit? Most people don't, you know. But it would be good, Mr. Noir, if you opened your heart to the fullness of time — and to the spirit which upholds and sustains us all through this world. Amen.

The energy is further matched by the philosophical assertions throughout the film that equally find solace in the continuation of life beyond any present death. Yolanda believes that "one door closes and another opens." The angel comforts Chuck's mourning girl friend, "Tell him he will be remembered, and turn away and live your life." When she laments, "It's the last show. I'm never going to see these people again," the angel quietly observes, "You'll see them again.... Every sparrow is remembered." Even the Axman quotes scripture to point out that "you've got to lose your life before you find it."

Much of this religious consolation is carried in the music of the film. When reminiscing with Lola about their parents, Yolanda and Rhonda break spontaneously and quietly into singing, "Softly and tenderly Jesus is calling / Calling for you and for me... /Come home come home, / ye who are weary come home." Later on stage they perform "Sewanee River" as though it were a hymn:

> We knelt in prayer with our aunts and uncles.
> Who loved us where we were young
> In the valley of darkness, they are the shepherds
> Who lead me to the pastures green
> And I'll sit with mama by the still waters
> And goodness and mercy follow me.

Later Keillor and his musical regulars sing, "Let the light from the light house shine on me" with the lyrics, "My lord does just what he says, / He heals the sick and he raises the dead." Keillor exults about the music and praises the Johnson Sisters because "they've kept alive all these wonderful old songs that have been around for ever." At the very end of the show, and for its final curtain call, the ensemble cast sings "In the sweet bye and bye, / We shall meet on that beautiful shore."

Even the secular music works as a defense against loss. Lefty assures Lola that there are "a lots of good songs about death." Before his death Chuck sings about the value of friends who have helped him along life's highway. In the face of their broken romance, Keillor and Yolanda sing, too. And as the end of the show approaches, the whole cast sings the sadly elegiac "Red River Valley": "But remember the Red River Valley / And the one who has loved you so true."

The final bulwark against the end may be the radio show itself, the medium against its very death. Keillor asserts, "Every show's the last show. That's my philosophy." Members of the show ask him if he's planning any final words, and he insists, "I don't do eulogies." "We don't look back.... That's the beauty of radio: it vanishes the moment you do it. There is no past; we never get old, never die. We just ... keep on going." Moreover he responds to the insistence that Chuck's death needs to be recognized, "The way to pay attention ... is to do your job." GK's final admonition to his listeners could well be the philosophy informing the show and the film: "Remember to keep your feet on the ground, your hopes up high, pray for rain, keep the humor dry."

T.S. Eliot captures the strategy of his famous modernist poem "The Waste Land" in the lines, "These fragments I have shored against my ruins." The ruins of romance, of marriage, of beginnings and youth, of the radio show, of life itself emerge here amid the organizing and shaping fragments of song and joke, of religious symbol and hymn, of performance, of commercial advertising, and indeed of entertainment media. Even as the film ends, it can't resist one last joke of resistance: It's too bad the theater's owner Old Man Soderberg couldn't have heard the great eulogy pronounced at his funeral — "And to have missed it by just a few days." In his final film, Altman and these performers on the stage of the Prairie Home Companion, overlooked by the name and the bust of F. Scott Fitzgerald, beat on in aesthetic boats against the currents of death. As the angel of death approaches the diner, Yolanda exclaims: "I loved that last show. I want to do one last show after another until I'm in a wheelchair and then keep doing them. As long as I can still remember the words."

The curtain falls then on both performances, on the radio program and the opera company, and also on the career of this experimental and prolific filmmaker. In these conclusions critique of the show business world becomes consolation in the face of death. Performance that has always been circumscribed by the crassness of the show business now transcends production. In his last films, artists, performances, structures all reach a kind of fullness that diminishes the limitations of body and story and system. The play and experimentation with genre, narrative form, and social value is as sharp as any other Altman film in *Gosford Park*. The self-conscious representation of art and politics in *Tanner on Tanner* conveys a wit and irony fully consonant with the political satire and social criticism of

Altman's maverick career. But *The Company* and at last *Prairie Home Companion* achieve a rich quiescence. Life's drama falls into silence before the beauty and grace of dance. At the final moment, performance in the face of death becomes a celebration. Here then at the last curtain in the final show, Altman's last film echoes William Butler Yeats' resistance of art to death:

> Yet they, should the last scene be there,
> The great stage curtain about to drop,
> If worthy their prominent part in the play,
> Do not break up their lines to weep.

NOTES

1. Robert T. Self, *Robert Altman's Subliminal Reality* (Minneapolis: University of Minnesota Press, 2002).

2. Robert Altman, quoted in Judith M. Kass, *Robert Altman: American Innovator* (New York: Popular Library, 1978), 21.

3. Chris Neumer, "Robert Altman Interview," *Stumped Magazine* (http://stumped-magazine.com/interviews/robert-altman-company.html, June 2002).

4. Robert Altman, "The Total Film Interview — Robert Altman" (http://www.total film.com/features/the-total-film-interview-robert-altman, June 1, 2004).

5. Robert Altman, Director's Scene Commentary, Behind-the-Scene Documentary. *The Company*, 2003. DVD: Columbia Tristar Home Entertainment, 2004.

6. Peter Sobczynski, "An Interview with Robert Altman and Malcolm McDowell" (http://www.criticdoctor.com/petersobczynski/interview/altmanandmcdowell, January 2, 2004).

7. Robert Altman, Director's Scene Commentary, *The Company*.

8. Guillermo Olquin, Lucia Castellano, Elena Andrade, Moriana Abraham, Federico Fuente, "Pas de Deux," Mathematical Institute of Serbia, Program in Industrial Design Morphology (http://www.mi.sanu.ac.rs/vismath/castellano/index.html).

9. Robert Altman, Director's Scene Commentary, *A Prairie Home Companion,* DVD: New Line Home Video, 2006.

10. Robert Altman, "Radio and *A Prairie Home Companion*," New York: Paley Center for Media, 2006.

11. Paul Monticone, "Robert Altman in the 1970s," *Brattle Street Film Notes* (http://brattleblog.brattlefilm.org/?tag=death&paged=2, January 26, 2007).

12. Robert Altman, Director's Scene Commentary, *A Prairie Home Companion.*

13. Robert Altman, "Forward," in Garrison Keillor, *A Prairie Home Companion: The Screenplay of the Major Motion Picture* (New York: Penguin, 2006).

Combined Bibliography

Allen, Woody. *Woody Allen on Woody Allen: In Conversation with Stig Bjorkman.* New York: Grove, 1993.

Altman, Robert. Director's Scene Commentary. *A Prairie Home Companion,* 2006. DVD: New Line Home Video, 2006.

_____. Director's Scene Commentary, Behind-the-Scene Documentary. *The Company,* 2003. DVD: Columbia Tristar Home Entertainment, 2004.

_____. "Forward," in Garrison Keillor, *A Prairie Home Companion: The Screenplay of the Major Motion Picture.* New York: Penguin, 2006.

_____. "'It's OK with Me': Interview with Robert Altman." *Stop Smiling,* November 21, 2006. http://www.stopsmilingon line.com/story_detail.php?id=705.

_____. "The Total Film Interview — Robert Altman." *Total Film,* June 1, 2004. http://www.totalfilm.com/features/the-total-film-interview-robert-altman.

_____. "24-Track Narrative? Robert Altman's *Nashville.*" *Cinémas: Journal of Film Studies,* 1.3 (Spring 1991). Accessed July 22, 2009, http://www.revue-cine mas.umontreal.ca/vol001 no03/08-altman.htm.

_____, and Garrison Keillor, "Radio and *A Prairie Home Companion.*" New York: Paley Center for Media, 2006. Audible Audio Edition, 2009.

Arendt, Hannah. *Eichmann in Jerusalem: A Report on the Banality of Evil.* New York: Viking, 1963.

Bailey, Blake. *A Tragic Honesty: The Life and Work of Richard Yates.* New York: Picador, 2003.

Barthes, Roland. *The Pleasures of the Text.* Trans. Richard Miller. New York: Hill and Wang, 1975.

Bazelon, Irwin. *Knowing the Score: Notes on Film Music.* New York: Van Norstrand Reinhold, 1975.

Bazin, Andre. "The Death of Humphrey Bogart." *Cahiers du Cinema* 68 (February 1957). Trans. Phillip Drummond. Reprinted in *Cahiers du Cinema, The 1950s: Neo-Realism, Hollywood, New Wave.* Ed. Jim Hillier. Cambridge, MA: Harvard University Press, 1985. 98–101.

Bettelheim, Bruno. *The Informed Heart: Autonomy in a Mass Age.* Glencoe, IL: Free, 1960.

Biskind, Peter. *Down and Dirty Pictures: Miramax, Sundance, and the Rise of Independent Film.* New York: Simon & Schuster, 2004.

_____. *Easy Riders, Raging Bulls.* New York: Touchstone, 2003.

_____. *Easy Riders, Raging Bulls: How the Sex, Drugs and Rock 'n' Roll Generation Saved Hollywood.* New York: Simon & Schuster, 1998.

Boddy, Kasia. "*Short Cuts* and Long Shots: Raymond Carver's Stories and Robert Altman's Films." *Journal of American Studies* 34.1 (2000): 1–22.

Bordwell, David. *Making Meaning: Inference and Rhetoric in the Interpretation of Cinema.* Cambridge, MA: Harvard University Press, 1991.

_____. *Narration in the Fiction Film.* Madison: University of Wisconsin Press, 1985.

Bourne, Michael. "Goin' to Kansas City and Robert Altman Takes You There!" *Down Beat* March 1996: 22–27.

Brauer, Ralph. "Who Are Those Guys? The Movie Western During the TV Era." *Journal of Popular Film* 2 (Fall 1973): 118–128.

Braverman, Harry. *Labor and Monopoly Capital.* New York: Monthly Review, 1988.

Brodkin, Karen. *How Jews Became White Folks and What That Says About Race in America.* New Brunswick, NJ: Rutgers University Press, 1998.

Brown, Royal S. "Film Music: The Good, the Bad, and the Ugly." *Cineaste* 21 (1–2).

_____. *Overtones and Undertones.* Berkeley: Univeristy of California Press, 1990.

Burt, George. *The Art of Film Music.* Boston: Northeastern University Press, 1994.

Callahan, Dan. "Death Becomes Him, Robert Altman's *Prairie Home Companion.*" *Bright Lights Film Journal* 53 (August 2006). http://www.brightlightsfilm.com/53/prairie2.php.

Canby, Vincent. "Innocence and Corruption; 'Brewster McCloud' Debuts at Coronet; Robert Altman Directs Slapstick Film." *The New York Times,* 24 December 1970.

Carver, Raymond. *Short Cuts: Selected Stories.* New York: Random, 1993.

Champlin, Charles. "A Private Eye's Honor Blackened." *Los Angeles Times,* March 8, 1973, G1+.

Cohan, Steven. *Masked Men: Masculinity and the Movies in the Fifties.* Bloomington: Indiana University Press, 1997.

Cole, Alyson M. *The Cult of True Victimhood: From the War on Welfare to the War on Terror.* Stanford, CA: Stanford University Press, 2007.

Collier, Peter, and David Horowitz. *The Destructive Generation: Second Thoughts about the Sixties.* New York: Summit, 1989.

Cook, David. *Lost Illusions: American Cinema in the Shadow of Watergate and Vietnam, 1970–1979.* New York: Scribner, 2000.

Cooper, Reg. "The Art of Annie Ross." *Jazz Journal International* 32. 7 (1970): 9–10.

Corber, Robert J. *Homosexuality in Cold War America: Resistance and the Crisis of Masculinity.* Durham, NC: Duke University Press, 1997.

Davis, Mike. *Prisoners of the American Dream: Politics and Economy in the History of the U.S. Working Class.* New York and London: Verso, 1999.

Debord, Guy. *La Société du Spectacle.* Paris: Gallimard, 1972.

De Groot, Gerard. *The Sixties Unplugged.* Cambridge, MA: Harvard University Press, 2008.

Des Pres, Terrence. *The Survivor: An Anatomy of Life in the Death Camps.* New York: Oxford University Press, 1976.

Dyer, Richard. "White." *Screen* 29.4. (Autumn 1988): 44–64.

Ebert, Roger. "The Company." *Chicago Sun–Times,* December 24, 2003, http://rogerebert.suntimes.com/apps/pbcs.dll/article?AID=/20031224/REVIEWS/312240304/1023.

_____. "*Lantana,*" 2002. Accessed January 26, 2005, http://rogerebert.suntimes.com/apps/pbcs.dll/article?AID=/20020118/REVIEWS/201180303/1023.

_____. "A Prairie Home Companion." *Chicago Sun–Times,* June 9, 2006, http://rogerebert.suntimes.com/apps/pbcs.dll/article?AID=/20060608/REVIEWS/60606001.

Echols, Alice. *Shaky Ground: The '60s and Its Aftershocks.* New York: Columbia University Press, 2002.

Edelstein, David. "Good Company: Robert Altman's Miraculous Ballet Drama." *Slate,* January 21, 2004. http://www.slate.com/id/2094148/.

_____. "Radio End-of-Days, The Sweet, Sweet Sadness of Robert Altman's *Prairie Home Companion.*" *New York Magazine,* June 4, 2006. http://nymag.com/movies/reviews/17181.

Elkins, Stanley M. *Slavery: A Problem in American Institutional and Intellectual Life.* Chicago: University of Chicago Press, 1959.

"Elliott Gould: The Urban Don Quixote." *Time,* September 7, 1970, 35–40.

Ellison, Ralph. *The Collected Essays of Ralph*

Ellison. New York: Modern Library, 1995.

Emerson, Jim. "Ebert's Altman Home Companion." *Chicago Sun–Times*, November 21, 2006. http://rogerebert.sun times.com/apps/pbcs.dll/article?AID=/ 20061121/ PEOPLE/ 60424007.

Erens, Patricia. "Between Two Worlds: Jewish Images in American Film." *The Kaleidoscopic Lens: How Hollywood Views Ethnic Groups.* Ed. Randall M. Miller. Englewood, NJ: Ozer, 1980. 114–134.

Fermaglich, Kirsten. *American Dreams and Nazi Nightmares: Early Holocaust Consciousness and Liberal America, 1957– 1965.* Waltham, MA: Brandeis University Press, 2006.

Ferncase, Richard K. "Robert Altman's *The Long Goodbye*: Marlowe in the Me Decade." *Journal of Popular Culture* 25.2 (Fall 1991): 87–90.

Field, Syd. *Screenplay: The Foundations of Screenwriting.* New York: Dell, 1994 (1979).

Fischer, Paul. "Upstairs-downstairs with Altman," 2001. Accessed July 1, 2009, http://www.iofilm.co.uk/feats/interv iews/r/robert_altman.shtml.

Frank, Thomas. *The Conquest of Cool: Business Culture, Counterculture, and the Rise of Hip Consumerism.* Chicago: University of Chicago Press, 1997.

Friedan, Betty. *The Feminine Mystique.* New York: W.W. Norton, 1963.

Friedman, Lester D. *Hollywood's Image of the Jew.* New York: Frederick Ungar, 1982.

Gabbard, Krin. *Jammin' at the Margins: Jazz and the American Cinema.* Chicago: University of Chicago Press, 1996.

_____. "Robert Altman's Jazz History Lesson." In *Black Magic: White Hollywood and African American Culture.* New Brunswick, NJ: Rutgers University Press, 2004.

Gabler, Neal. *An Empire of Their Own: How the Jews Invented Hollywood.* New York: Crown, 1989.

Gallagher, Tess. *Under Stars.* St. Paul, MN: Graywolf, 1978.

Gee, Maggie. "*A Prairie Home Companion*: Altman's Last Ride." *OpenDemocracy*, February 2, 2007. http://www.open democracy.net/arts-Film/prairie_alt man_4312.jsp.

Gerard, Lillian. "Belles, Sirens, Sisters." *Film Library Quarterly* 5 (Winter 1971– 72): 14–21.

Gilbey, Ryan. *It Don't Worry Me: Nashville, Jaws, Star Wars and Beyond.* London: Faber and Faber, 2003.

Giles, Paul. "Ritual and Burlesque: John Ford and Robert Altman." In *American Catholic Arts and Fictions: Culture, Ideology, Aesthetics.* New York: Cambridge University Press, 1992. 296–323.

Gitlin, Todd. *Years of Hope, Days of Rage.* Rev. ed. New York: Bantam, 1993.

Goffman, Erving. *Asylums: Essays on the Social Situation of Mental Patients and Other Inmates.* Garden City, NY: Anchor, 1961.

Goldman, Michael. "Altman and Lachman Push for Digital Performance." *Millimeter*, August 26, 2006. http://digitalcon tentproducer.com/mil/features/video_ filmic_hd/.

Gonzalez, Ed. "*Cape of Good Hope*," 2005. Accessed November 16, 2005, http:// www.slantmagazine.com/film/film_re view.asp?ID=1701.

Gourse, Leslie. *Louis' Children: American Jazz Singers.* New York: Quill, 1984.

Grant, Barry Keith. "Purple Passages or Fiestas in Blue? Notes Toward an Aesthetic of Vocalese." *Representing Jazz*, ed. Krin Gabbard. Durham, NC: Duke University Press, 1995. 285–303.

Harmetz, Aljean. "The 15th Man Who Was Asked to Direct *M*A*S*H* (and Did) Makes a Peculiar Western," 1971. In David Sterrit, ed., 3–18.

Harris, Mark. *Pictures at a Revolution: Five Movies and the Birth of the New Hollywood.* New York: Penguin, 2008.

Hartwig, Codie Leonsch. "*A Prairie Home Companion*; A Hit for Garrison Keillor, Robert Altman and Company." *Associated Content*, June 26, 2006. http:// www.associatedcontent.com/article/ 39502/a_prairie_home_companion_a_ hit_for.html?cat=38.

Haskell, Molly. "*Nashville*." *The Village Voice.* June 11, 1975.

Hegel, G. *Phänomenologie des Geites.* Berlin: Nabu, 2010.

Heidegger, Martin. *Introduction to Metaphysics*. New Haven: Yale University Press, 2000.

Heylin, Clinton. *Despite the System: Orson Welles and the Hollywood Studios*. Chicago: Chicago Review Press, 2005.

Higgins, Mike. "*Playing by Heart.*" *Sight and Sound*, 9.9 (September 1999): 52–53.

Hoberman, J. "The Goulden Age." *The Village Voice*, April 10, 2007. www.village voice.com/2007-04-10/filim/the-goulden-age/1.

Hoggart, Richard. *The Uses of Literacy*. New York: Pelican, 1981.

Hunt, Mary Ellen. "*The Company*: Altman's Take on the Joffrey is Artsy not Artistic." *Ballet-Dance Magazine*. January 2004. http://www.criticaldance.com/maga zine/200402/articles/companymovie. html.

Jacobs, Diane. *Hollywood Renaissance*. Cranbury, NJ: A. S. Barnes, 1977.

Jameson, Fredric. *The Ideologies of Theory*. London and New York: Verso, 2008.

_____. *Signatures of the Visible*. New York: Routledge, 1990.

Jeffords, Susan. *Hard Bodies: Hollywood Masculinity in the Reagan Years*. New Brunswick, NJ: Rutgers University Press, 1994.

_____. *The Remasculinization of America: Gender and the Vietnam War*. Bloomington: Indiana University Press, 1989.

"Joffrey Ballet." http://www.joffrey.com/ company.

Kael, Pauline. *Deeper into Movies*. Boston: Little Brown, 1973.

_____. "Movieland — The Bum's Paradise."

_____. *Reeling*. Boston: Little Brown, 1976.

Kagan, Norman. *American Skeptic: Robert Altman's Genre-Commentary Films*. Ann Arbor, MI: Pierian, 1982.

Karlin, Fred, and Rayburn Wright. *On the Track: A Guide to Contemporary Film Scoring*. New York: Schirmer, 1990.

Karp, Alan. *The Films of Robert Altman*. Metuchen, NJ: Scarecrow, 1981.

Kass, Judith M. *Robert Altman: American Innovator*. New York: Popular Library, 1978.

Keyssar, Helene. *Robert Altman's America*. New York and Oxford: Oxford University Press, 1991.

King, Geoff. *New Hollywood Cinema: An Introduction*. New York: Columbia University Press, 2002.

Kolker, Robert. *A Cinema of Loneliness: Penn, Kubrick, Scorsese, Spielberg, Altman*, 2nd ed. Oxford: Oxford University Press, 1988.

_____. *A Cinema of Loneliness: Penn, Stone, Kubrick, Scorsese, Spielberg, Altman*, 3rd ed. Oxford: Oxford University Press, 2000.

_____. "Screening Raymond Carver: Robert Altman's *Short Cuts.*" In *Twentieth-Century American Fiction on Screen*, ed. R. Barton Palmer. Cambridge: Cambridge University Press, 2007. 179–190.

Kun, Josh. *Audiotopia: Music, Race, and America*. Berkeley: University of California Press, 2005.

Lambert, Hendricks, and Ross. *Sing a Song of Basie*. Audio CD. Columbia.

Lewis, Richard Warren. "Playboy Interview: Elliott Gould." *Playboy Magazine*. November 1970.

The Long Goodbye. Dir. Robert Altman. Perf. Elliott Gould. United Artists, 1973.

Lyons, Donald. "Flaws in the Iris." *Film Comment* XXIX.4 (July-August 1993): 44–53.

Man, Glenn. "*Short Cuts* to *Gosford Park*: The Family in Robert Altman." In *A Family Affair: Cinema Calls Home, ed. Murray Pomerance*. London and New York: Wallflower, 2008. 160–174.

Mandel, Howard. "Cutting It." *Sight and Sound* 4.3 (March 1994): 11.

Marmorstein, Gary. *Hollywood Rhapsody: Movie Music and Its Makers 1900 to 1975*. New York: Schirmer, 1997.

Mast, Gerald, Marshall Cohen and Leo Braudy, eds. *Film Theory and Criticism*. New York and Oxford: Oxford University Press, 1992.

McCabe and Mrs. Miller Collection. Academy of Motion Picture Arts and Sciences. Margaret Herrick Library. Los Angeles.

McCabe and Mrs. Miller Script—Dialogue Transcript." http://www.script-o-rama. com/movie_scripts/m/mccabe-and-mrs-miller-script.html.

McCabe and Mrs. Miller. VHS Soundtrack,

1971. Burbank, CA: Warner Home Video, 1990.

McClelland, C. Kirk. *On Making a Movie: Brewster McCloud*. New York: New American Library, 1971.

McGilligan, Patrick. *Robert Altman: Jumping Off the Cliff. A Biography of the Great American Director*. New York: St. Martin's Press, 1989.

McKay, Brian, and Robert Altman. "The Presbyterian Church Wager." David Foster Productions, July 27, 1970. Script online at www.awesomefilm.com.

Merrill, Robert. "Altman's *McCabe and Mrs. Miller* as a Classic Western." *New Orleans Review* (Summer 1990): 79–82.

Miller, Stephen Paul. *The Seventies Now: Culture as Surveillance*. Durham, NC: Duke University Press, 1999.

Miller, Toby, et al. *Global Hollywood 2*. London: British Film Institute, 2005.

Montgomery, John Warwick. *The "Is God Dead?" Controversy: A Philosophical-Theological Critique of the Death of God Movement*. Grand Rapids, MI: Zondervan, 1966.

Monticone, Paul. "Robert Altman in the 1970s," *Brattle Street Film Notes*, January 26, 2007. http://brattleblog.brattlefilm.org/?tag=death&paged=2.

Nachbar, Jack. "Riding Shotgun: The Scattered Formula in Contemporary Western Movies." In *Focus on the* Western. Ed. Jack Nachbar. Englewood Cliffs, NJ: Prentice Hall, 1974.

Naughton, Edmund. *McCabe*. New York: Berkley Medallion, 1960.

Neibaur, James L. *Tough Guy: The American Movie Macho*. Jefferson, NC: McFarland, 1989.

Neumer, Chris. "Robert Altman Interview." *Stumped Magazine*, June 2002. http://stumpedmagazine.com/interviews/robert-altman-company.html.

Neupert, Richard. *The End: Narration and Closure in the Cinema*. Detroit: Wayne State University Press, 1995.

O'Connor, John E., and Martin A. Jackson eds. *Image as Artifact: The Historical Analysis of Film and Television*. Malabar, FL: R.E. Kreiger, 1990.

O'Connor, Rory. "Sound Track: Strike Up the Band." *American Film* 4 (4): 64–65.

Ogletree, Thomas W. *The Death of God Controversy*. New York: Abingdon, 1966.

"Old Bogart Films Packing Them In." *New York Times*, January 28, 1965, 19+.

Oliver, B. "*The Long Goodbye* and *Chinatown*: Debunking the Private Eye Tradition." *Literature/Film Quarterly* III.3 (Summer 1975): 240–48.

Orwell, George. *Essays*. New York: Everyman's Library, 2002.

Perlstein, Rick. *Nixonland*. New York: Scribner, 2008.

Pinkerton, Nick. "Radio Days: Robert Altman, an Interview." *Reverse Shot*. http://www.reverseshot.com/article/robert_altman.

Pinsker, Sanford. *The Schlemiel as Metaphor: Studies in the Yiddish and Jewish American Novel*. Revised and Enlarged Edition. Carbondale: Southern Illinois University Press, 1991.

Plecki, Gerard. *Robert Altman*. Boston: Twayne, 1985.

Rakoff, Joanna Smith. "The New Super Jews." *Time Out New York*, 4–11 December 2003, 13–18.

Reich, Charles A. *The Greening of America*. New York: Random House, 1970.

"The Religious Affiliation of Robert Altman, Acclaimed American Director." *Adherents,* July 5, 2005. http://www.adherents.com/people/pa/Robert_Altman.html.

"Rip van Marlowe." Perf. Robert Altman and Elliott Gould. Documentary featurette, *The Long Goodbye*, MGM DVD, 2002.

Rogin, Michael. *Blackface, White Noise: Jewish Immigrants in the Hollywood Melting Pot*. Berkeley: University of California Press, 1996.

Romney, Jonathan. "Edinburgh Cringe." *Sight and Sound* 15.8 (August 2005), 1, 26–9.

Roszak, Theodore. *The Making of a Counter Culture*. Garden City, NY: Doubleday, 1969.

Rowin, Michael Joshua. "Robert Altman: Dancer in the Light." *Reverse Shot*. http://www.reverseshot.com/article/robert_altman_0.

Ryan, William. *Blaming the Victim*. 1971. New York: Vintage, 1972.

Sarris, Andrew. "Liberal Midwesterners Unite: The Altman/Keillor Show." *New York Observer*, June 18, 2006. http://www.observer.com/node/39012.

Savran, David. *Taking It Like a Man: White Masculinity, Masochism, and Contemporary American Culture*. Princeton, NJ: Princeton University Press, 1998.

Schwarz, Roberto. *O Pai de Família*. Sao Paulo: Paz e Terra, 1978.

Scofield, Martin. "Closer to Home: Carver versus Altman." *Studies in Short Fiction* 33.3 (1996): 387–399.

Scott, A.O.. "Altman's Casual Chaos Meets Keillor's Rhubarb-Tinged Nostalgia in *A Prairie Home Companion*." *New York Times*, June 9, 2006.

Self, Robert T. "Robert Altman." *Senses of Cinema*, December 2004.

_____. *Robert Altman's McCabe & Mrs. Miller: Reframing the American West*. Lawrence: University Press of Kansas, 2007.

_____. *Robert Altman's Subliminal Reality*. Minneapolis: University of Minnesota Press, 2002.

Sharp, Richard. "Robert Altman: A Season with the Company," 2003. Accessed November 11, 2005, http://chicagofilm.com/features/altman.default.asp.

Short Cuts. Soundtrack CD. Imago 72787-21014. 1993.

Silberman, Marc, ed. *Bertolt Brecht on Film and Radio*. London: Methuen, 2000.

Sinclair, Upton. *The Jungle*. New York: Doubleday, Page, 1906.

Skinner, B.F. *Beyond Freedom and Dignity*. New York: Alfred A. Knopf, 1971.

Sobczynski, Peter. "An Interview with Robert Altman and Malcoln McDowell." *Critic Doctor*, January 2, 2004, http://www.criticdoctor.com/peter sobczynski/interview/ altmanandmc dowell.

Sontag, Susan. "Notes on Camp." In *Against Interpretation and Other Essays*. New York: Farrar, Straus and Giroux, 1988. 275–292.

Smith, Murray. *Engaging Characters: Fiction, Emotion and the Cinema*. Oxford: Clarendon, 1995.

Steinbergs, Alan. "*A Prairie Home Companion*: Radio Show-turned-film Finds Alt-man at His Best." *Associated Content*, June 21, 2006.

Sterrit, David, ed. *Robert Altman: Interviews*. Jackson: University Press of Mississippi, 2000.

Steward, G. "*The Long Goodbye* from *Chinatown*." *Film Quarterly* XXVIII.2 (Winter 1974–75): 25–32.

Stewart, Robert. "Reimagining Raymond Carver on Film: A Talk with Robert Altman and Tess Gallagher." *New York Times Book Review*, September 12, 1993: 3, 41–42.

Szondi, Peter. *Theory of the Modern Drama*. Chicago: University of Minnesota, 1987.

Thompson, David, ed. *Altman on Altman*. London: Faber and Faber, 2006.

Thoret, Jean-Baptiste. *Le Cinema Américain des Années 70*. Paris: Editions Cahiers du Cinema, 2009.

Tröhler, Margrit. "Les films à protagonistes multiples et la logique des possibles." *Iris* 29 (Spring 2000): 85–102.

Truffaut, Francois. "A Portrait of Humphrey Bogart." *The Films In My Life*. Trans. Leonard Mayhew. New York: De Capo Press, 1978.

Tuska, Jon, ed. *Close-Up: The Contemporary Director*. Metuchen, NJ: Scarecrow, 1981.

Van Wert, William F. "Phillip Marlowe: hardboiled to softboiled to poached." *Jump Cut* 3 (Sept-Oct 1974): 10–13.

Wexman, Virginia W. "Rhetoric of cinematic improvisation." *Cinema Journal* 20.1 (Fall 1980): 29–41.

Whyte, William H., Jr. *The Organization Man*. Garden City, NY: Doubleday Anchor, 1957.

Williams, Raymond. *The Politics of Modernism*. London and New York: Verso, 1994.

_____. *Television and Cultural Form*. London: Wesleyan University Press, 1992.

Williamson, Bruce. "Robert Altman," 1976. In Sterrit, ed.: 34–62.

Wilmington, Michael. "Robert Altman and *The Long Goodbye*," 1991. In Sterrit, ed.: 131–151.

_____. "The Company." *Metromix Chicago*, December 22, 2003. http://chicago.metromix.com/movies/review/movie-review-the-company/1 content 8734/.

Windreich, Leland. "*The Company*, Fleeting Events in a Dancer's World. *Ballet-Dance Magazine*, February 2004. http://www.ballet-dance.com/200402/ articles/ companymovie2.html.

Wood, Robin. *Hollywood from Vietnam to Reagan and Beyond*. Rev. and expanded ed. New York: Columbia University Press, 2003.

Yates, Richard. *Revolutionary Road*. 1961. New York: Vintage, 2008.

Zacherek, Stephanie. "A Prairie Home Companion." *Salon*, June 9, 2006. http://www.salon.com/entertainment/ movies/review/2006/06/09/prairie.

Zuckoff, Mitchell. *Robert Altman: The Oral Biography*. New York: Alfred A. Knopf, 2009.

About the Contributors

Rick Armstrong is an assistant professor of English at Kingsborough Community College of the City University of New York. He has presented papers at the Modern Language Association and the Midwest Modern Language Association. He contributed "First Principles of Morals: Evolutionary Morality and American Naturalist Writers" to *The Oxford Handbook of American Literary Naturalism* (2011).

Michael Murphy has appeared in more than forty films including Altman's *M*A*S*H*, *Brewster McCloud*, *McCabe and Mrs. Miller*, *Nashville*, and *Tanner '88*.

Krin Gabbard is a professor of comparative literature and English at the State University of New York Stony Brook. He has published many articles and books on film and media including *Black Magic: White Hollywood and African American Culture* (Rutgers University Press, 2004), *Jamming at the Margins: Jazz and the American Cinema* (University of Chicago Press, 1996), and *Hotter Than That: The Trumpet, Jazz, and American Culture* (Faber and Faber, 2008).

Richard R. Ness is an associate professor of film and media studies at Western Illinois University. He is the author of *Alan Rudolph: Romance and a Crazed World* (Twayne/Macmillan, 1996).

William Graebner is a professor of history emeritus at the State University of New York Fredonia. He has published many books and articles including *The Age of Doubt: American Thought and Culture in the 1940's* (Twayne, 1991). He has also published in *Literature/Film Quarterly* and sits on the board of *American Studies*.

Marcos Soares is a professor of English at the University of São Paulo. He has published in the *Utopia, Dystopia, and Science Fiction Journal* out of Melbourne and in the *Anpoll Journal* out of São Paulo.

Jeremy Kaye is a lecturer in the University Writing Program at the University of California Riverside where he completed his Ph.D. He has been the recipient of a Mellon Grant; has published in *The Hemingway Review*; and presented at the Modern Language Association conference.

Maria del Mar Azcona teaches film studies at the University of Zaragoza in Spain. She is the author of *The Multi-Protagonist Film* (Blackwell, 2010), and the co-author (with Celestino Deleyto) of *Alejandro González Iñárritu* (University of Illinois Press, 2010).

Robert T. Self is a professor of English and acting associate dean of the College of Liberal Arts and Sciences at Northern Illinois University. He has published numerous articles and books on Altman, including *Robert Altman's* McCabe and Mrs. Miller: *Reframing the American West* (University Press of Kansas, 2007) and *Robert Altman's Subliminal Reality* (University of Minnesota Press, 2002).

Index